$23-

The African American Encounter
with Japan and China

The African American

Encounter with Japan and China

Black Internationalism in Asia, 1895–1945

Marc Gallicchio

The University of North Carolina Press   Chapel Hill and London

Designed by Jackie Johnson
Set in Bodoni Antiqua
by Tseng Information Systems, Inc.

The paper in this book meets the guidelines for permanence and
durability of the Committee on Production Guidelines for Book
Longevity of the Council on Library Resources.

Library of Congress Cataloging-in-Publication Data
Gallicchio, Marc S., 1954–
The African American encounter with Japan and China :
Black internationalism in Asia, 1895–1945 / Marc Gallicchio.
p. cm.
Includes bibliographical references and index.
ISBN 0-8078-2559-x (alk. paper) —
ISBN 0-8078-4867-0 (pbk. : alk. paper)
1. Afro-Americans—Relations with Japanese.   2. Afro-Americans—
Relations with Chinese.   3. Afro-Americans—Politics and government—
20th century.   4. Racism—Political aspects—United States—History—
20th century.   5. United States—Relations—Japan.   6. Japan—
Relations—United States.   7. United States—Relations—China.
8. China—Relations—United States.   9. United States—
Foreign relations—Citizen participation.   I. Title.
E185.61.G166   2000
327.1'7'08996073—dc21   99-086390

Publication of this work was aided by a generous grant from the
Z. Smith Reynolds Foundation.

Portions of Chapters 8 and 9 have appeared previously in somewhat
different form in Marc Gallicchio, "Colouring the Nationalists:
The African-American Construction of China in the Second World War,"
International History Review 20 (September 1998): 571–96;
reprinted with permission.

04 03 02 01 00   5 4 3 2 1

Contents

Illustrations

Acknowledgments

Many people helped me complete this study. Waldo Heinrichs has generously aided me through every step of my career. This time I waited until I thought all was said and done before asking him to read the manuscript. He kindly showed me that there was a little more to do and better ways to say it. For that help and much more I am very grateful. Many friends at Villanova University also took time away from their work to help me with mine. In particular I am indebted to Lawrence Little, who read the entire first draft and gave me the benefit of his expert knowledge of African American history and his impressive editorial skills. Adele Lindenmeyr read the whole draft at an important stage of this process and provided me with valuable suggestions for improvement. I would also like to thank the two anonymous readers at the University of North Carolina Press for their careful reading of the manuscript and their helpful comments and criticisms. I hope they will see that I have endeavored to incorporate most of their suggestions into the final work.

Villanova University supported me in many ways, most importantly with a sabbatical in the fall of 1995 and a Faculty Summer Research Grant. In the course of researching this project I relied heavily on the resourcefulness of the staff at Villanova's Falvey Library. I am especially thankful to Therese Dougherty and the staff of the Interlibrary Loan Office for their efficient handling of my many requests and to Instructional Media Services for the loan of a microfilm reader. Two graduate students at Villanova, Linda Thomas and Nigel Furlonge, provided invaluable assistance by tracking down material and checking sources for me. Finally, many of the themes in this book were developed while I was teaching Villanova's world history course with Fred Carrier, Maghan Keita, and Lawrence Little.

At the risk of omitting some people, I also want to thank the many historians who shared their work with me, commented on mine, wrote recommendations for me, and otherwise helped me to develop the ideas presented in this book. In particular, Marc Jackson provided me with important material on Kokuryūkai and shared his historical insights and matchless sense of humor. I also wish to thank Cemil Ayden, Bill Brands,

Jay Clarke, Warren Cohen, Sally Griffith, Seth Koven, Kenneth Kusmer, Jonathan Rosenberg, Nancy Tucker, Katie Sibley, and Nona Smith. I am grateful to Professor Edward Ingram for his helpful suggestions and for permission to reprint material that originally appeared in the *International History Review* as "Colouring the Nationalists." Professor Robert A. Hill deserves special mention for having greatly facilitated the study of twentieth-century African American history through his numerous editorial projects, many of which are cited in this work.

During the academic year 1998–99 I had the good fortune to live in Tokyo while teaching as a Fulbright Visiting Lecturer in American Studies. There Professor Kumei Teruko generously guided me through the archives of the Japanese Foreign Ministry and translated the files cited in the bibliography. Nakashima Tomoko, a graduate student at the University of Tokyo, kindly provided me with a translation of Yuko Takemoto's article, "W. E. B. Du Bois and Japan." Many other friends and colleagues in Japan shared their insights with me and gave me the opportunity to present my findings to interested scholars and students. I especially thank Terachi Koji and Yanaka Hisako at Kyoritsu Women's University and Endo Yasuo, Yaguchi Yujin, and Yui Daizaburo at the University of Tokyo.

Finally, at the University of North Carolina Press I wish to express my appreciation to Paula Wald, who served as project editor; to Stevie Champion, who copyedited the manuscript; and to Lewis Bateman, executive editor, who supported this project throughout the editorial process.

Abbreviations

The following abbreviations are used in the text.
For abbreviations used in the notes, see pp. 213–14.

AME: African Methodist Episcopal
CIG: Counter Intelligence Group, MID
CIO: Congress of Industrial Organizations
Comintern: Communist International
CPUSA: Communist Party, United States of America
FBI: Federal Bureau of Investigation
MID: Military Intelligence Division, U.S. Army
NAACP: National Association for the Advancement of Colored People
ONI: Office of Naval Intelligence
UNIA: Universal Negro Improvement Association

The African American Encounter with Japan and China

Introduction: Black Internationalism

In late 1959 Harold Isaacs wrote his friend Rayford Logan, "Dear Ray, A quick question: Is there such a thing as any Negro reaction to Japan's victory over Russia in 1905?"[1] Isaacs, who was researching a book on black Americans after World War II, had been concerned with the role of race in international affairs ever since his service as a war correspondent for *Newsweek* magazine in the China-Burma-India theater. His first book published after the war, *No Peace for Asia*, opened with a vivid description of the racial prejudices held by most Americans who served in the theater. Later, in the mid-1950s, he organized a study at the Massachusetts Institute of Technology (MIT) to explore American images of China and India.[2] One of the participants in that study was Rayford Logan, a Howard University historian.[3]

Logan, who in the 1930s had been dubbed "a bad Negro with a Ph.D." by an admiring black newspaper, was an ardent civil rights leader who had helped pressure President Franklin D. Roosevelt into launching the Fair Employment Practices Commission in 1941 and had tirelessly worked to make World War II a war against racism at home and abroad.[4] Logan, as it turned out, was well placed to answer Isaacs's query.

In a different context Isaacs's question might easily have been considered provocative. In the prewar era black American admiration for Japan would have created suspicion about African American loyalty. By the late 1950s, however, the intense feeling surrounding the issue had faded. Nevertheless, the subject of black sympathy for Japan could still stir unpleasant memories for all Americans genuinely concerned with race relations.

In recent years scholars of African American history have taken a renewed interest in how black Americans viewed and sought to influence international events. In particular, these historians have chronicled African American leaders' interest in the plight of Ethiopia, Haiti, India, and other colonial areas.[5] But little has been written about African American interest in Japan and China.[6]

This study attempts to contribute to the growing body of scholarship on African American internationalism by restoring Japan to the prominent place it occupied in the minds of black Americans in the decades before World War II. In enlarging the area of inquiry to include East Asia, I have also reconstructed black American thinking about China, a topic almost completely neglected by scholars. To understand the origins of African American thought about both countries I have extended the period under consideration backward beyond the 1930s, where most recent studies have begun, to the late nineteenth century.

This inquiry into black American interaction with Japan and China builds on the substantial scholarship in the field of diplomatic history that has analyzed the ways nongovernmental groups approach foreign affairs. In reconstructing how African Americans approached Japan and China, this study takes the reader onto the borders of the great power system to provide an important new perspective on American foreign policy in the early twentieth century.[7] Black Americans constantly observed and commented on international events in black-owned newspapers and journals. African American protest organizations devoted considerable attention to foreign affairs, sending representatives abroad and hosting prominent figures from Japan and China and colonial areas in Asia and Africa. Out of this experience African Americans developed a new form of internationalism that guided their thinking about world politics for much of the twentieth century.

African American interest in world affairs can be traced as far back as the abolitionist movement of the pre–Civil War era. That interest and the resulting desire to shape international events took on a new life when the United States obtained its overseas empire and Europe partitioned Africa. During the years when much of the world came under the sway of Europe or the descendants of Europeans in the United States, black Americans developed a view of world affairs that drew a connection between the discrimination they faced at home and the expansion of empire abroad. Black internationalism, as this worldview will be called in this study, was an ideology that stressed the role of race and racism in world affairs. The term as it is used here is not meant to imply that all African Americans shared this view. Indeed, it will be shown that many did not. Nevertheless, the expression "black internationalism" seems appropriate because it conveys the extent to which many African Americans believed that color (or race) determined world politics. This belief in the existence of a color scheme to international affairs served as the guiding principle of black internationalism. As a corollary to that main principle, black internationalists believed that, as victims of racism and imperialism, the world's darker races, a term they employed to describe the non-European world, shared a common interest in overthrowing white supremacy and creating an international order based on racial equality.

Black internationalism provided African Americans with a comprehensive explanation for world affairs that placed their own experience during one of the darkest moments of their history, what Rayford Logan called "the nadir," into a global context. It reminded them that they were not alone in the world and that others, indeed the majority of the world's inhabitants, suffered a similar fate. As black internationalism took shape and gained adherents among African Americans, Japan's triumph over Russia in 1905 encouraged black Americans to believe that the long era of white dominance was ending. Suddenly, the white world appeared vulnerable. Japan's victory punctured the myth of white supremacy and provided colonial peoples the world over with a model for achieving independence.

For the next four decades Japan occupied a prominent position in black internationalism. Black intellectuals, journalists and editors, leaders of radical mass movements, and mainstream civil rights organizations wrote and spoke admiringly of Japan. They frequently viewed international events from a Japanese perspective, convinced that what benefited that nation would improve the condition of the world's darker races. The rise of the Japanese empire did not create black internationalism, nor did black internationalism depend on the existence of a powerful Japan to serve as a symbol of the latent power of the world's nonwhite peoples. Nevertheless, if historians wish to understand how African Americans viewed international events in the first half of this century, they need to consider the relationship between black internationalism and the rise of the Japanese empire. As this study will show, Japan was never far from the thoughts of most black internationalists.

Japan's repeated professions on behalf of racial equality also convinced colonial peoples and many black Americans that Japan might serve as a champion of the darker races. As early as the Paris Peace Conference, African Americans sought contacts with Japanese diplomats to confer on issues of mutual interest. By the 1920s Japan had gained a prominent place in the ideology of black internationalism. In an era when white writers warned of a rising tide of color and the U.S. Congress acted to exclude Japanese and Chinese immigrants, black internationalism's emphasis on the role of race in world affairs provided black Americans of differing political views with a radical alternative to the prevailing discourse on international events. It was in this period that black internationalists also formed an explanation for Japanese imperialism in China that would persist until 1941.

Japanese aggression in China posed an ongoing problem for black internationalists because it refuted the widely held belief in the solidarity of nonwhite peoples against racism and imperialism. Black internationalists eventually resolved the Chinese contradiction in a way that left their positive assessment of Japan intact. The ease with which black internationalists dismissed Chinese aspirations and accepted Japanese benevolence revealed the problems inherent in perceiving race and racism as the dominate forces in world affairs. To see Japan as an imperialist nation like the other industrialized countries, as "the Prussia of the East," in labor leader A. Philip Randolph's words, would have required black internationalists to shed their admiration for Japan and drastically alter their views on the role of race in world affairs. Apart from black Socialists and Communists, few African Americans were prepared to take this step in the 1920s and early 1930s.

The depression and the rise of fascism proved a defining moment for black internationalists. The events of the mid-1930s, most notably the invasion of Ethiopia and the reemergence of a left-liberal domestic coalition, inspired the formation of an antiracist, anticolonial alliance that drew black supporters from across the political spectrum. This movement grew rapidly primarily because it found a way to reconcile class and race analyses of world affairs by concentrating its attention on events in India and the regions of the African diaspora. But for many black internationalists, Japan remained a separate matter.

Japan's invasion of China below the Great Wall further complicated the problem of reconciling Tokyo's imperialism with a color-coded view of world affairs. By this time, however, black internationalists had mastered a panoply of excuses to explain away Japan's actions. Despite the enlistment of many black activists into the growing left-liberal coalition against racism and colonialism, there was no shortage of black internationalists willing to apologize for Japan. Most black Americans who expressed support for Japan limited their enthusiasm to the realm of debate and commentary, but some, primarily from the most hard-pressed economic class, sought membership in what they thought was a Japanese-led alliance against white supremacy.

When war between Japan and the United States commenced, black internationalists faced a dilemma. Black leaders found themselves in a situation where expressions of empathy or support for Japan were no longer tenable. The government's intelligence and internal security agencies were well acquainted with African American interest in Japan. In the crisis brought on by the war officials in these agencies intensified their search for subversives among black Americans. In such an atmosphere dissent could easily be treated as disloyalty. Nonetheless, as the stream of letters into black newspapers and street corner debates revealed, many African Americans perceived the Pacific war as a race war. Black leaders kept in step with their constituents by retaining a racial analysis of the war's causes while avoiding allusions to Japan as the champion of the darker races. This shift in emphasis enabled black internationalists to retain the main part of their message and gain white adherents in the process. Black internationalists and their liberal allies warned that racism imperiled the nation by wasting its human resources and alienating its allies. The elimination of racism, they argued, was a matter of national security.

Black internationalists hoped that the moment of maximum danger would force government officials to see racism and discrimination in a new light. In promoting an anticolonial and antiracist agenda, black leaders looked to other countries for assistance and leadership. As the only nonwhite country among the Big Four allies, China assumed a new importance for black American leaders. The rediscovery of China by black internationalists enabled them to continue to emphasize the importance of race in world politics while insulating them from charges of sedition that their earlier attachment to Japan had provoked. This sudden and awkward elevation of Nationalist China as a potential champion of the world's subject peoples raised additional questions about the utility of black internationalism as a means of understanding world politics or as a strategy for reform at home. By the war's end black internationalists reached a new consensus about China, but they were less certain about what lessons, if any, could be gained from their long affair with Japan.

[1]

The Champion of the Darker Races

Japanese torpedo boats struck the Russian naval base at Port Arthur on the evening of 8 February 1904, inflicting heavy damage and closing the entrance to the harbor. The Russians were caught by surprise. The entire battle lasted less than an hour. Although the Japanese attack came without a declaration of war, both countries had previously taken bold steps to protect their rival claims in Korea and Manchuria, including the issuance of an ultimatum from Tokyo. Japanese nationals were evacuated from Port Arthur several days before the attack and diplomatic relations were severed on 6 February. As the struggle for mastery in northeastern Asia shifted to land warfare, the Russians anticipated an easy victory over the Japanese, whom they derided as "monkeys." Once again Japanese military prowess surprised the Russians, but neither side found victory as easily as they hoped. Port Arthur did not fall to the Japanese until January 1905. The Japanese took Mukden, in central Manchuria, later that winter. They suffered heavy casualties in both campaigns and seemed ready to negotiate an end to the war rather than face a large Russian army still intact in northern Manchuria. The fighting continued, however, as both sides hoped that gains on the battlefield would improve their position at the peace table. The Russians placed their hopes on a climatic naval battle that would destroy Japan's recently won naval supremacy and break its line of communications with the mainland. Instead, the tsar's Baltic Fleet sailed halfway around the world and directly into the Japanese line of fire in the Straits of Tsushima on 27 May. Within hours the Russian armada was devastated. The next day the Russians surrendered the remnants of their fleet.[1]

The significance of Japan's victory was immediately grasped in distant

Japanese soldiers holding the line in Manchuria after firing
the shots heard around the nonwhite world, ca. 1905–6.
(Photograph by Standard Scenic Company; Library of Congress)

places. When Alfred Zimmern, a lecturer at Oxford University, learned of
Japan's victory, he promptly shelved his talk on Greek history and spoke
to his students about the "most important event which has happened, or is
likely to happen, in our lifetime; the victory of a non-white people over a
white people."[2] In Capetown, South Africa, not far from where thousands
of Chinese workers labored in the gold fields, a European lecturer warned
his audience that Japan's success had awakened in China a movement of
"China for the Chinese." He hoped that it would not also be "South Africa
for the Chinese."[3]

Many black Americans saw the outcome of the war as a matter of great
significance to their own lives. According to eminent African American
scholar W. E. B. Du Bois, Japan's stirring victories broke the "foolish modern magic of the word 'white'" and raised the specter of a "colored revolt

against white exploitation."[4] The news of Japan's victory reached a black American public that was already attentive to world affairs and attuned to viewing events from the perspective of the world's subject peoples. In the decade before the Japanese navy stunned the white world by destroying the tsar's Pacific and Baltic fleets, African Americans had begun to display a renewed interest in world events. During that time the resurgence of European and American imperialism in Africa, the Middle East, and Asia elicited the attention of educated black citizens. As Lawrence Little has shown, members of the African Methodist Episcopal (AME) Church carefully studied and debated the major international events of their day through the church's main publications, the *Christian Recorder* and *Church Review.* An important national institution in the life of African Americans, the AME Church drew its leadership from the middle and professional classes of black America. In this respect the emergence of an elite group of African Americans interested in foreign policy closely paralleled the rise of a "foreign policy public" among white Americans.[5] Other black-owned publications, including the Washington, D.C., *Colored American,* which was subsidized by Booker T. Washington and edited by Republican loyalist Edward E. Cooper, the more independent-minded *Colored American Magazine* (Boston), the *New York Age,* published by militant reformer Thomas T. Fortune, as well as journals in Kansas City, Indianapolis, Baltimore, and Cleveland, regularly covered events abroad.[6]

Advocates of commercial expansion and boosters of business opportunity among the black business community and the growing network of black-owned newspapers frequently used the same language as their white counterparts to promote economic expansion. African Americans who burned with a zeal to spread the gospel also sounded like their missionary brethren in the white community. But although African Americans trumpeted many of the traditional themes Americans regularly invoked to expand the empire of liberty, they often added their own variations to the old standards. By virtue of their common ancestry, African American missionaries, according to the *Church Review,* were also best equipped to carry the word to their unenlightened brothers and sisters in Africa and the Caribbean. Some missionaries saw themselves as fulfilling the biblical prophecy in which the displaced children of Ethiopia (Africa) returned to redeem their homeland for Christ. Others saw themselves as a civilizing vanguard in a secularized form of Ethiopianism. Various editors insisted that African Americans were ideally suited to develop the wealth of Africa and the South Pacific. Black promoters assumed that race offered African American migrants greater protection against the harsh climate and disease of the tropics while the advantages of American civilization would enable these pioneers to develop the land to its fullest potential. African Americans who sought opportunity in an expanding American empire also hoped that by exercising the same entrepreneurial spirit that their white compatriots prized so highly, they might finally be recognized as full citizens of the republic.[7]

If some believed that their race made them especially equipped to conduct America's civilizing mission in the tropics, others recognized that American color prejudice forced them to cast their gaze outward in the first place. For these African Americans, their own battle against race prejudice at home led them to sympathize with the nonwhite subjects of empire around the globe. Discerning a color scheme in the pattern of Western imperialism, these budding internationalists rejected the idea that empire held benefits for anyone of color. How, they asked, could one prevent the spread of American racism within an expanding American empire? In 1898 the Spanish-American War and the seizure of the Philippines by the United States forced African Americans to confront this very question.

By the end of that year, what began as a war to liberate Cuba from a decadent Spanish empire verged on becoming a war to acquire Spain's former empire in the Caribbean and Pacific. Like most Americans, African Americans supported the war against Spain as a war of liberation. Black volunteers rallied to the colors and fought gallantly in Cuba and Puerto Rico. The virtual unanimity within the black community soon fractured, however, when it became clear that President William McKinley would claim the Philippine Islands as a prize of war. When war broke out between American soldiers and Philippine nationalists, Henry M. Turner, a prominent AME bishop, castigated any black soldier who contemplated fighting in a war to deny another man his freedom and announced that "having once been proud of the flag . . . as a Negro we now regard it as a worthless rag."[8]

A vocal but disorganized anti-imperialist movement also sprang up among white Americans, but many of these white opponents of empire were motivated by a racism even more virulent than that espoused by the paternalistic McKinley. Southern and western Democrats warned of a "mongrelization" of the white race and a tidal wave of unfit immigrants sweeping over the nation if the United States acquired the Philippines with its millions of dark-skinned natives. Like the northern genteel reformers who launched the Anti-Imperialist League, the predominantly Republican African Americans faced the painful choice of disavowing the party of Abraham Lincoln and making common cause with segregationist but anti-imperialist southern Democrats. When McKinley ran for reelection in 1900 against Democratic nominee William Jennings Bryan, the black press lamented that African Americans faced "a cruel choice of dilemmas, the racist imperialist or the racist anti-imperialist." Some African Americans chose the "racist anti-imperialist." The AME's publication *Voice of Missions* grudgingly supported Bryan. But of those black Americans who were still able to exercise the franchise, most voted for McKinley. Party loyalty and the fear that racism at home might actually worsen under a Democratic president led many to support the Ohio Republican. Fear of a loss of party patronage also held black Americans fast.[9]

The discomfort that most black Americans felt in supporting McKinley was evident in the justifications they gave for their position. As disturbing as the acquisition of overseas empire was, they argued, it might yet benefit the cause of freedom at home and abroad. In endorsing McKinley in October 1900, the AME's *Review* gave two cheers for Western imperialism. "The fact remains," declared the *Review*, "that the rape of Africa, Asia and the islands will open them up to Western progressiveness, invention, comfort, personal liberty, and the Christian religion."[10] Others, including Bishop Benjamin Tanner and Theophilus Steward, an AME leader serving as an army chaplain in the Philippines, voiced the hope that the forced inclusion of millions of nonwhite subjects within the American empire might ultimately unite Americans of color in the cause of equality.

Whether one saw the Philippines as "Indian country" opened for home-steaders or the Filipinos as a people waiting in darkness for the benefits of Christian civilization, the response was one in which the American part of the African American identity held sway. Even Bishop Tanner's dream, that nonwhite subjects within the new empire might struggle together for equality under the same flag, was in many respects a nationalist solution to the problem of American racism. But the fierce struggle in the Philippines also produced a more internationalist response to the problem of imperialism. As early as 1899, a columnist in the AME's *Review* declared: "if we further consider that almost all other movements involving the existence and integrity of weaker governments are against the dark races in Africa and Asia, and add to that the domestic problems of the American Negro, we are faced with a startling world movement." Ending on an optimistic note, the writer predicted that events would one day unite the "dark skinned races" of the world. In the same magazine a year later, and only months after his famous pronouncement that "The problem of the twentieth century is the problem of the color line," W. E. B. Du Bois also referred to a future global alliance of nonwhite peoples.[11] One can readily see in these predictions of nonwhite solidarity some of the earliest stirrings of an idea that would come to have such a strong hold on black and white Americans for the next four decades.

In one sense, this belief in a global alliance of the oppressed was a response to the era's pervasive racial theories that justified the subjugation of nonwhite peoples. Distorting the evolutionary concepts of Charles Darwin, academics and pseudoscientists worked hand-in-hand to promote the idea of white supremacy. Identifying themselves as members of a superior Anglo-Saxon race, American imperialists became self-described lawgivers who increased freedom by extending American rule. Although racial theorists spoke in terms of a racial hierarchy, ordering and reordering the place of such supposed races as Poles and Italians, all agreed that a vast chasm separated the alleged lesser breeds from the dominant whites. American leaders frequently justified the acquisition of overseas territory by asserting that this new imperialism was really not new at all. Americans had traditionally kept nonwhite peoples in a position of subordination for their own good, the advocates of empire argued; now they were just extending that system to the Philippines, Puerto Rico, and Hawaii. American soldiers in the Philippines made the point more bluntly by dehumanizing their Filipino adversaries with the same racial epithets they used to belittle blacks and Native Americans at home.[12]

It stood to reason, therefore, that the nonwhite peoples of the world would link arms in what one author has called "a fellowship of humiliation."[13] But there was more to the idea of nonwhite solidarity than this tart description would imply. The belief in the possibility of a global league of nonwhite peoples was a daring and idealistic vision in an era of intense nationalism. American history was replete with examples of different peoples maintaining strong ties to their native lands. The idea of a global alliance of nonwhite peoples was different, however, in that it required black Americans to do more than simply stress the African side of their identify in looking at the world. A sense of kinship linking the lands touched by the African diaspora was an important part of African American thinking about foreign affairs, but what might be called "black internationalism" was unusual in that it reached beyond the world's Black Belt to embrace nonwhite peoples everywhere as allies in the cause of liberation.

Although the spread of U.S. imperialism to Cuba, Puerto Rico, and the Philippines did the most to crystallize the thinking of black commentators about their relationship to subject peoples elsewhere, events in China between the mid-1880s and 1900 contributed to their growing sense of identification with the world's darker races. During the 1880s writers in the AME publications regularly expressed sympathy for the Chinese who were victimized by French and British gunboat diplomacy. In 1884 the *Review* opposed Republican candidate James G. Blaine for his support of Chinese exclusion legislation. Nevertheless, when Japan fought China in 1895, the views of some African Americans were barely indistinguishable from those of white citizens. The *Review* greeted Japan's swift defeat of China in 1895 as a victory for the nation that had more readily accepted Christianity. In humbling China, Japan had opened that haughty nation to the gospel.[14]

When Chinese patriots attacked American and European missionaries during the Boxer Rebellion, however, the *Review* prayed that the multinational relief expedition would show "Christ-like" sympathy for the "unenlightened natives."[15] The thought of U.S. involvement in the suppression of another nationalist movement clearly troubled many black Americans. Despite his support for William McKinley in an election year, Edward Cooper "did not blame the Chinese for resenting the interference of foreigners." Other black opponents of U.S. expansion voiced harsher criticisms when it appeared that black soldiers would participate in the China expedition. Rather than send armed troops to China, McKinley's critics advised the president to dispatch the troops into the South instead. The AME's Bishop Turner minced few words in condemning black soldiers who would fight the Chinese. "This is not our war," Turner told readers of the *New York Age*, "and the black man who puts a gun upon his shoulder to go and fight China should find the bottom of the ocean before he gets there."[16]

Slowly, but noticeably, leading black clergymen, journalists, and educators were devising their own perspective on international events. Given black support for McKinley in 1900 and the grudging acknowledgment by many that in the event of a war with China black soldiers would have to do their part, it might have been easy to overlook the changing attitudes of black leaders. After all, the African American response to the Sino-Japanese War matched that of most Americans who believed, as Theodore Roosevelt explained, that only a "good thrashing" could wake China from its slumbers. One could even see similarities in the views of black and white Americans toward their government's response to the Boxer Rebellion. By 1900, with the war in the Philippines under way and the death toll mounting, black and white Americans had reached similar conclusions about the undesirability of obtaining additional territory. In the midst of the Boxer Rebellion the McKinley administration acknowledged the widespread opposition to further expansion by issuing its second Open Door

Note disavowing any designs on Chinese territory. In other words, white and black Americans were in agreement about U.S. aims in China. They had arrived at that point, however, by somewhat different routes. White Americans were likely to point to the cost of empire to the United States, whereas black Americans more readily sympathized with the Chinese. As shown in the next chapter, black Americans shared many of the commonly held prejudices about the Chinese in America. But they also knew that federally sanctioned discrimination against African Americans and Chinese had developed out of the same bigoted impulses.[17] Consequently, the prospect of seeing China partitioned like Africa by "The Anglo-Saxon race," which had "gotten the idea that the earth belongs to it," created a sense of a common predicament that white opponents of empire were unlikely to share.[18]

African American responses to the Russo-Japanese War also bore a superficial resemblance to those of other Americans, but here, too, important differences lay just beneath the surface. U.S. officials in Washington and in embassy and consular posts throughout northeastern Asia welcomed Japan's initial victories over the tsar's forces on land and sea. American relations with Russia had reached a high point during the Civil War but had steadily deteriorated after that. Reports in the press of tsarist brutality and Jewish persecution had erased most of the good feeling Americans once had for Russia. Harmonious governmental relations also began to give way to economic friction as the tsarist regime extended its control into northeastern Asia.[19] Conversely, during the previous three decades a modernizing Japan had shown itself to be receptive to U.S. guidance. For a time, the image of Japan as America's Asian pupil pervaded the American popular press and most officials in Washington began to regard Japan as a potential counterweight to Russian expansion in Manchuria. The view from Korea, part of Japan's burgeoning empire, was somewhat different. Willard Straight, the vice consul in Seoul during the war, became a confirmed opponent of Japanese expansion as a result of the "constant strain of having to be polite and seek favors from a yellow people."[20] Beneath Straight's discomfort lay an even more profound anxiety that Japan had emerged as the leader of the East's multitudes against the West.

Although he shared many of the racial assumptions of his era, Theodore Roosevelt did not succumb to fears of a "yellow peril" rising in the East. Instead, the president believed that if Japan carved out a sphere of influence in Korea and southern Manchuria, an area of minor economic interest to the United States, it would redirect Japanese expansion away from the western Pacific and thus reduce the chances for a collision between the two countries. Roosevelt obtained formal Japanese approval of this arrangement, with each party respecting the special interests of the other, in 1905.[21]

African Americans cheered Japan's victories as well, but they cheered louder and from pride that America had such an able student as Japan. Black Americans readily identified with Russian Jews as an oppressed minority and likened the Russian knout (a whiplike tool of torture) to the overseer's lash.[22] Given their antipathy toward Russia, most black Americans welcomed Japan's victory as a twofold blessing. The hated Russians, "the white men of Southern Europe," had been overwhelmed by a non-white nation.[23] Reginald Kearney has observed: "As a result of this war American blacks began to look at the Japanese differently. Where previously they had been contented to see the Japanese much like other Americans did, blacks began to view the people of Japan more from a racial perspective and embraced them as colored people."[24]

Black American journalists celebrated Japanese exploits and evaluated Japan's achievements for lessons that might be applicable to the conditions blacks found in the United States. "A very valuable result of the battle of Mukden," the *Voice of the Negro* editorialized, "is the fact that arrogant Europe has been taught a lesson about the 'inferior races.'" Writing about the outcome of the war for the same journal, W. S. Scarborough pointed out that the Japanese "have not stopped to argue with the world as to whether they were yellow or white, red or black; they have simply forged ahead in this battle for their rights in spite of the prejudice against them."[25] Several years later Booker T. Washington, the internationally renowned founder of the Tuskegee Institute and the best-known spokesman for black America, confirmed the significance of Japan's example. An advocate of self-help and vocational education as the best means of overcoming white prejudice, the "Wizard of Tuskegee" told a Japanese editor that "The wonderful progress of the Japanese and their sudden rise to the position of one of the great nations of the world has nowhere been studied with greater interest or enthusiasm than by the Negroes of America."[26]

The feeling of kinship African Americans felt with the Japanese as a result of the war only increased as white Americans recoiled in dread at the new "yellow peril."[27] Even before the war ended, Americans on the West Coast agitated for tougher immigration laws to prevent an anticipated flood of cocky Japanese from muscling their way into California. This flaring of American racism came as a shock to those Japanese who hoped that their country would harmonize the interests of Asia and the West. Shock turned to outrage in 1906, when the San Francisco school board shunted ninety-three Japanese children into a separate school for nonwhite students. Roosevelt, seeing his understanding with Japan threatened by such hysteria, denounced the school board's policy as "a wicked absurdity." The president eventually reduced tensions between the two countries through informal restrictions on Japanese immigration, but not before nationalists on both sides of the Pacific openly talked of war.[28]

Not surprisingly, African Americans readily sympathized with the plight of the Japanese in America. Tokyo's protests over the segregation of Japanese schoolchildren confirmed the fears of West Coast citizens who expected a lightning strike by the recently victorious imperial forces. A year earlier, the *Voice of the Negro* had predicted that Japan would soon "lift the shibboleth 'Asia for the Asiatics'" and advised the administration to sell the Philippines to the Japanese before it was too late.[29] Now, as the crisis in California mounted, several African American newspapers indulged in intemperate editorials urging the Japanese to defend their rights. Some even fantasized about a black alliance with Japan to end racism once and for all. For the most part, however, black commentators, although fiercely critical of the California segregationists, nevertheless predicted that African Americans would once again defend the nation as they had in every previous American war.[30]

Black support for the defiant Japanese did not go unnoticed by other Americans. According to Akira Iriye, of the many letters sent to the government by concerned whites "not a few expressed concern with Japanese collusion with American blacks." "They have a secret committee now negotiating with the Japanese," warned one correspondent, "and if the Negroes of this country [succeed] in forming a secret alliance with Japan it might mean trouble for the U.S."[31] The settlement of the dispute through the so-called gentlemen's agreement restricting Japanese immigration left those predictions untested, but this was not the last time that the government would be warned of a black American–Japanese alliance.

In 1913 a second crisis, this one brought on by California's efforts to restrict Japanese landholding rights, quickly faded as President Woodrow Wilson refused to be stampeded into preparations for war. Diplomacy once again prevailed, but the resurgence of anti-Japanese feeling during the episode further deepened African American sympathies for these targets of discrimination. As would be expected, Booker T. Washington favored a compromise solution that would restrict Japanese immigration to those who were well qualified and educated, but would also permit Japanese already living in the United States to become naturalized citizens.[32] As in the first crisis, however, admiration for Japan's military prowess led some to hope that the United States would finally be chastised for its treatment of nonwhite peoples. Robert S. Abbott, the publisher of the influential *Chicago Defender*, predicted that "The vengeance of the gods finally may be wreaked upon our oppressors . . . through the Providential happenings to fellow sufferers from the Orient who have a flag and navy to demand justice, and not simply ask for it." [33]

As exhilarating as it was to see American bigotry opposed by force, it would have been humiliating to place so much faith in another nation for one's own deliverance. As Abbott's remarks suggest, African American admiration for Japan was tinged with envy. Although it seems possible, as some black publications predicted, that the example of Japan stimulated a renewed commitment to activism on the part of African American leaders, it is more probable that the black elite's open admiration for Japan was conceivable precisely because black leaders had already struck out on a more militant course themselves.

In the years immediately preceding World War I, the collaboration between black leaders and white liberals in the formation of such organizations as the National Association for the Advancement of Colored People (NAACP) and the National League on Urban Conditions among Negroes (the National Urban League) indicated that African Americans also sought to build domestic alliances to solve the deeply entrenched problem of racism in America.[34] The awakened interest in international affairs among African Americans and domestic coalition building could be mutually reinforcing. Black Americans increasingly saw their condition as part of a global system of discrimination that needed to be challenged at home and abroad. Many of the white progressives who worked to reform race relations in the United States were also active in the era's international peace movement. When they turned to foreign affairs, both groups could find common ground in the belief that international peace could not be achieved without an end to colonialism and the militarism that upheld it.

But the potential for disagreement existed in the budding interest many whites showed in the emergence of a republican China. Black internationalists could also welcome China's awakening as a prelude to its casting off white domination. When the Chinese boycotted American goods in 1905, the *Voice of the Negro* noted approvingly that "one way to touch the heart of the white man is to pull his purse strings." [35] When revolution toppled the Manchus in 1911, W. E. B. Du Bois predicted that a reawakened China would further test the myth of white supremacy.[36] But what would happen if Japan clashed with a modernizing China? Black commentators had already shown an inclination to view Japan as the nation best suited to lead the darker races in Asia—"to put her neighbors' feet on the path she has herself irrevocably chosen," as Prime Minister Katsura Taro put it.[37] Would they continue to view Japan as the natural leader in Asia if China rejected the role of student? Would African Americans have to choose one nonwhite nation over another?

For white progressives, that choice was less painful. Taking office in 1913, shortly after the overthrow of the Manchu dynasty, President Wilson hastily recognized the newly formed republican government in Peking. Japanese officials correctly took this as a sign of the new administration's hostility toward Tokyo's designs on China. Wilson also opposed the efforts of American capitalists in China, whom he perceived as gaining unfairly from China's distress. In recognizing the Chinese Republic and thwarting American bankers, Wilson declared himself a friend of China and a foe to all who sought to expand upon the predatory privileges that had been wrested from the decaying Manchu dynasty. Japan, having graduated into the ranks of the powers, had lost its claim on the affections of most Americans.[38]

Although the new president was strongly influenced by missionary reports praising the new regime in China, there was more than mere sentiment behind his view of Asian realities. For those progressives, like Wilson, who fought the "money power" at home, it seemed only natural to wage that campaign abroad as well. In this respect, Wilson's China policy was part of a broader progressive internationalist approach to the conflict between the demands of international capital and the desire for economic progress in the undeveloped world.[39] Employing the economic analysis of social problems common to reformers at the time, Wilson saw little difference between Japan and the other predators in China. Under different circumstances, black American leaders would also have sympathized with the Chinese as victims of European exploitation, but the presence of Japan among the claimants in China cast a different light on the problem.

Despite China's travails, African American editors, academics, and organizational leaders proved too committed to the image of Japan as the leader of the nonwhite assault on colonialism to see it as just another imperial power. For the time being, this problem of allegiance remained of small consequence to domestic politics and the emerging civil rights movement. Support for Japan required little more than an occasional editorial or speech. Black reformers were more concerned with improving conditions at home, in securing the "fair dealing" Wilson had promised them, than with remote events in Asia.

Over the next several years increased discrimination at home during the segregationist Wilson administration demanded the full attention of black American leaders. For most African Americans, the outbreak of war in Europe seemed unconnected to the struggle against racism. As John Hope Franklin has noted, black Americans were more concerned about events in Washington than Paris or Berlin.[40] This is not to say that black leaders ignored foreign affairs altogether. The Wilson administration's intervention in Haiti in 1915 aroused vehement protests from African Americans, whose emotional ties to the first black republic were far stronger than their growing affection for Japan. Moreover, although black Americans had their hands full asserting their rights, they eventually came to recognize the enormous consequences that the European conflict would have for the worldwide struggle against racism.

One of the first analysts to perceive the racial implications of the war was the scholar and cofounder of the NAACP, W. E. B. Du Bois. A brilliant writer, Du Bois possessed an intimidating intelligence that easily earned him the respect and admiration of other civil rights leaders, if not their affection. By the time the war began in Europe, Du Bois, who also edited the NAACP journal *The Crisis: A Record of the Darker Races*, had participated in several international conferences dealing with race issues. As early as 1900, at the Pan-African Congress, he had placed the question of racism in an international context. Like most Americans, Du Bois regarded the outbreak of war in Europe as a great tragedy for humanity, but his position as editor of the *Crisis* also required him to evaluate the effects of the war on the "darker races." In November 1914, four months into the conflict, he concluded that an Allied victory would leave "the colored races no worse than now." But he added, somewhat hopefully, that "considering the fact that black Africans and brown Indians and yellow Japanese are fighting for France and England it may be that they will come out of this frightful welter of blood with new ideas of the essential equality of men."[41]

Writing in the *Atlantic* the following year, Du Bois identified racism and imperialism as the ultimate causes of the European struggle. In blaming the scramble for empire for the war, Du Bois drew on the work of British anti-imperialist J. A. Hobson and anticipated the analysis of Russian revolutionary V. I. Lenin by several years. But his essay, titled "The African Roots of the War," was also noteworthy for what it said about Japan's role in Asia.

By the early twentieth century, Du Bois argued, the ruling classes in the industrial world had placated workers by sharing a small portion of the wealth they had stolen from Africa and Asia and by threatening them with competition by "colored labor." Through this alliance of capital and labor the European nations forged the unity necessary to compete in the increasingly intense race to control economic spheres of influence. Du Bois dismissed the commonly held view that the war had started over rivalry in the Balkans. The contest, he asserted, was really about controlling the "men and materials in the darker world." In large measure, the war was part of "that desperate struggle for Africa." Interest in Africa, "the Land of the Twentieth Century," had escalated, he explained, not only because of that continent's vast wealth, but because it appeared that efforts to subjugate Asia were failing. Japan, according to Du Bois, had blurred the international color line and thwarted dreams of total domination of the world by whites. Although some racists tried to "prove the Japanese 'Aryan' " to win Japan's support against the remainder of the world's nonwhite peoples, the Japanese would have none of it. "[B]lood is thick," he wrote "and there are signs that Japan does not dream of a world governed mainly by white men." "Then too," he continued, "the Chinese have recently shown unexpected signs of independence and autonomy, which may possibly make it necessary to take them into account a few decades hence."[42]

By the time Du Bois penned those words, the war in Europe had spilled out onto the ocean, endangering American shipping and threatening to involve the United States directly. For more than two years Wilson tried to protect American neutral rights through direct negotiation with the belligerents and by offering to mediate between the warring powers. In April 1917, after Germany resumed its unrestricted use of submarines on the high seas, Wilson asked Congress to declare war. African Americans greeted the U.S. declaration of war against Germany with mixed feelings. Although they welcomed a chance to demonstrate their loyalty to the nation once again, they had ample reason to worry that the president's internationalism would not address their concerns. His dismal record on civil rights, including his approval of the extension of segregation to the federal bureaucracy and Washington, D.C., hardly inspired confidence. Wilson had committed the nation's wealth and human resources to the crusade to make the world safe for democracy, but the outbreak of anti-black riots in East St. Louis and other cities, the continuation of segregation in the expanding armed forces, and the president's painfully slow response to an increase in lynchings all suggested that the promised new world order might seem depressingly familiar to most black Americans.

Nevertheless, when Wilson issued his famous Fourteen Points in January 1918, it afforded African Americans some reason to hope that the final peace settlement might address the plight of minorities at home and of the nonwhite subjects of empire worldwide. Although the president pledged to uphold the principle of "justice to all people and nationalities and their right to live on equal terms of liberty and safety with one another," experience had taught black leaders that they would have to assertively present their grievances to the Paris Peace Conference if they were to have any hope of seeing them addressed in the final settlement. To further that end, the NAACP held a mass rally to "bring Africa to the attention of the Peace Conference and the civilized world" and numerous other African American organizations chose representatives to send to the conference.[43] Du Bois's efforts to have the president include several black delegates in the American contingent were rebuffed, but the NAACP managed to send him to Paris to cover the conference for the *Crisis*.[44]

Although African American leaders were far from united in their approach to problems at home, most agreed that the peace conference offered them an opportunity to internationalize the problems of black Americans and other nonwhite peoples throughout the world. Marcus Garvey, the Jamaican founder of the Universal Negro Improvement Association (UNIA), a rapidly growing mass movement, held rallies in support of African liberation and cabled the European governments on behalf of the rights of Africans. Garvey also joined the International League of Darker Peoples, which was organized by wealthy black businesswoman C. J. Walker to advance the interests of colonial peoples at the conference.[45]

At the start of the conference, black leaders had high expectations that Japan, which had fought on the side of the victorious Allies, would champion the cause of racial equality in the final peace settlement.[46] Reporting from the gathering at Versailles, Du Bois rejoiced at the presence of "THIRTY-TWO NATIONS, PEOPLES AND RACES. . . . Not simply England, Italy, and the Great Powers are there, but all the little nations. . . . Not only groups, but races have come—Jews, Indians, Arabs, and All-Asia."[47] A delegation of black leaders including A. Philip Randolph, labor organizer and editor of the socialist *Messenger*, renowned journalist Ida Wells-Barnett, C. J. Walker, and William Monroe Trotter, the Harvard-educated editor and publisher of Boston's *Guardian*, had already been assured by Japanese officials bound for Versailles that Japan would bring the issue of racial discrimination before the conference. Trotter, Wells-Barnett, Walker, and eight others were chosen by the National Equal Rights League, a rival group of the NAACP, to attend the conference, but the State Department refused to grant them passports. Despite this obstacle, the indomitable Trotter shipped out as a second cook on a merchantman and, after jumping ship in France, made his way to Paris, where he met with the Japanese, among others, to discuss the race issue.[48]

It is indicative of the seriousness with which Japan regarded the issue that various statesmen announced their commitment to the principle of racial equality before the start of the conference. Placing the subject in the broadest humanitarian terms, Japanese newspapers proclaimed that it was their country's duty to "insist on the equal international treatment of all races. . . . No other question is so inseparably and materially interwoven with the permanency of the world's peace as that of unfair and unjust treatment of a large majority of the world's population."[49] The Foreign Office and senior government officials on the Advisory Council on Foreign Relations viewed the problem of racial prejudice somewhat more narrowly in terms of national interest. Specifically, they worried that racism would lead the "the United States and the top-raking nations in Europe" to use the proposed League of Nations to "freeze the status quo and hold in check the development of second-rate and lower-ranked nations." Accordingly, the Japanese government instructed its delegates to secure absolute guarantees that the league would contain a provision recognizing racial equality.[50] Shortly after they arrived at Versailles, the members of the Japanese delegation began pushing for inclusion of that principle in the League of Nations Covenant.

It is probably also indicative of the gulf that separated the Japanese delegation from its putative allies that none of the other negotiating teams was prepared to deal with the subject of racial equality. The Americans were concerned primarily with Japan's intentions for the territory it had seized from Germany in the Far East, namely Germany's former sphere of influence in China's Shantung (Shandong) Peninsula and German-held Pacific islands north of the equator. Despite his progressive commitment to a just peace and his incomparable ability to convey his ideals in moving oratory, President Wilson continued to display a persistent tone deafness on the issue of racial equality.

When Baron Makino Nobuaki and Viscount Chinda Sutemi privately broached the subject with Wilson and his adviser Colonel Edward House, the president tried to mollify the Japanese with a vaguely worded clause to be included in the league covenant. The statement, which Chinda judged as "practically meaningless," declared: "The equality of the nations being a basic principle of the League, the H[igh] C[ontracting] P[arties] agree that concerning the aliens in their territories, they will accord them *so soon and so far as practicable*, equal treatment and rights in law and in fact, without making any distinction on account of their race or nationality."[51] Even that wording, which House regarded "as mild and inoffensive as possible," proved unacceptable to the British representative.[52] When Baron

Baron Makino Nobuaki, Japanese delegate to the Paris Peace Conference, 1919. (Library of Congress)

Makino brought the issue before the League of Nations Commission, Lord Robert Cecil sought to table the proposal.

Significantly, Wellington Koo, the Columbia University–educated Chinese representative, indicated his sympathy for Makino's proposal, although he required further instruction from his government. Here was a development that should have alerted observers to the importance that nonwhite nations attached to the inclusion of a racial equality clause in the league covenant. As one of Wilson's confidants later noted, "In this great issue of world policy, it is highly significant that the Chinese, though suspicious of the Japanese in every other way, came here to their support."[53] Colonel House succeeded in postponing a vote on racial equality but only by abandoning the article on religious freedom to which it was appended. Despite his disappointment at having to sacrifice Wilson's much-desired provision on religion, House consoled himself with the thought that in dealing with the racial equality clause he had lifted "the load from our shoulders and plac[ed] it upon the British."[54]

Any goodwill the Americans might have gained by cooperating with the Japanese evaporated the next day, when Wilson distributed a draft of the league covenant to the peace conference without reference to the unsettled matter of racial equality. The same day that the draft covenant made the rounds, the president left for a scheduled trip to Washington. Despite their frustration with Wilson's high-handed tactics, the Japanese recognized that they needed his support to succeed. While he was in Washington, Makino and Chinda met regularly with House to find a solution to the impasse. On the day Wilson left Washington for his return to Paris, the president received a special communication from the Japanese ambassador on behalf of the government in Tokyo. Noting the importance of eliminating discrimination in international affairs, the Japanese once again asked for Wilson's help in crafting a racial equality clause that would be acceptable to all concerned.[55] Shortly after making his presentation to Wilson, Ambassador Ishii Kikujirō spoke publicly on the issue to the Japan Society in New York. In his widely noted speech, Viscount Ishii called attention to the need for ending racial discrimination, but he hastened to add that the Japanese government would not view a racial equality amendment as providing the legal basis for unrestricted immigration to America. Despite its mild tone, Ishii's speech met with immediate opposition from politicians in the western United States.[56]

In contrast, black leaders viewed Japan's support for the amendment as the partial fulfillment of their preconference consultations with Japanese officials. The *Philadelphia Tribune* noted with approval a recent speech by Premier Okuma Shigenobu in the House of Peers recommitting his government to the struggle for equality at Versailles.[57] Assessing these developments, the NAACP's James Weldon Johnson congratulated Japan for throwing "a wrench into the machinery that is grinding out the League of Nations." "She has done this," Johnson explained, "by raising the race issue and forcing it right up to the point where it must be met and met squarely."[58] The Associated Negro Press also reported that black Americans were keenly interested in Japan's efforts at Versailles on behalf of the amendment.[59]

As public discussion of the proposed racial equality amendment intensified, the Japanese delegates tested a revised amendment that avoided the word "race" entirely and called only for the "equality of nations and just treatment of their nationals." This, too, failed to meet with approval from Cecil and Australian prime minister William Hughes. Even House, who appears to have been influenced by senatorial opposition to any mention of "equality" in the covenant, turned Makino down.[60] Despairing of ever winning a private endorsement from the Anglo-American members, the Japanese presented the amendment in the League Commission. Once again, Wellington Koo spoke in support of the measure. During the discussion House passed Wilson a note warning that if the Japanese amendment passed, "it would raise the race issue throughout the world." The president made a last effort to head off a vote by assuring the members that the principle of equality was implicit in the structure of the league. Unpersuaded, Makino called for a vote. The measure received eleven out of seventeen votes. China sided with Japan. Nevertheless, Wilson, as chairman of the commission, ruled the measure defeated on the dubious grounds that it did not have unanimous support. Although Wilson's flaunting of democratic procedure clearly upset Makino, the Japanese delegate contented himself with quietly asking that the minutes reflect the actual vote "for the record."[61]

In killing the racial equality amendment, Wilson provided the Japanese government with further evidence that it could not rely on a League of Nations dominated by the Western powers to protect its interests in Asia. When the conference took up the Shantung problem, the Japanese government instructed its delegates not to sign the league covenant unless Tokyo's claims in China were recognized. Wilson faced a terrible dilemma. Meeting Japan's demands would require him to violate the principle of self-determination, which formed the basis of his vision for a new world order. The president was equally unwilling, however, to see the Japanese quit the conference. Convinced that the Japanese were not bluffing, Wilson made the best deal he could, believing, correctly as it turned out, that better terms could be arranged for China once the league was formed. Within days the dispute was resolved by granting Japan economic control of Shantung. In return, the Japanese recognized Chinese sovereignty over the peninsula.[62]

The Champion of the Darker Races

The president's compromise, reached at the end of the conference, provoked heated opposition in the United States. The American Left, already disillusioned by wartime restrictions on civil liberties and other illiberal government policies, denounced the Shantung bargain as a continuation of the discredited power politics of old. Oswald Garrison Villard, editor of the progressive *Nation* and a founding member of the NAACP, asserted that the "uncompromising demands" on China "more than offset any sympathy" Japan was entitled to on account of the rejection of the racial equality amendment.[63] As the fight over the treaty heated up during the summer, Villard berated the president for permitting the "unconscionable theft of Shantung." Of his "Fourteen Questions for Mr. Wilson," published in July 1919, seven dealt directly with the Shantung decision.[64] Republican opponents of the League of Nations capitalized on the liberals' frustrations by making the "scandal of Shantung" a key element in their campaign against the proposed world body. To highlight what they believed to be a fatal flaw in the covenant, Senate Republicans, led by Wilson's archrival Henry Cabot Lodge, warned that the league might one day require American troops to defend Japan's holdings in Shantung. Wilson denounced such accusations as false and inflammatory, but the damage was already done. The sacrifice of Chinese interests to what many Americans regarded as a rapacious Japan drained away much of the remaining liberal support for the treaty.[65]

In contrast to American liberals, most African American writers identified with Japan as the aggrieved party. Whereas the white press devoted scant attention to the debate over racial equality, African American journals saw the race question as inseparable from the basic issues of war and peace. When word of Japan's defeat on the racial equality matter reached the United States, gratitude for Japan's valiant struggle on behalf of nonwhite peoples far outweighed any doubts African Americans harbored concerning their ally's role in China. However much African Americans opposed imperialism in the abstract, they could not bring themselves to see Japan as a villain in the Shantung controversy. Forced to choose between China and Japan, most African Americans sided with Japan.

Japanese control over parts of China was regrettable, but African Americans claimed to perceive a qualitative difference between imperialism practiced by whites against Asians and imperialism practiced by Asians against Asians. James Weldon Johnson ventured that "Little Japan" might be "the greatest hope for the colored races of the world." Although he acknowledged that the Shantung settlement violated the principle of self-determination, Johnson believed that "on the whole it is better for China to be dominated by Japan than to be dominated by some European government." Given the West's rejection of racial equality, Japan was smart to place little faith in pious pronouncements about self-determination. What mattered, Johnson concluded, was force and power. The Japanese were sure to realize that the quickest way to overcome white discrimination was by ending their diplomatic isolation through an alignment with the "colored peoples of the world." "She may not deem it wise to espouse the cause of these other peoples just now," he concluded, "but the time is sure to come when she will do so. All success to little Japan."[66]

Johnson temporized somewhat during the summer, conceding that "from China's point of view there is good ground for protest." But given the record of Western exploitation in the region, he did not see how the white nations were in a position to complain. Johnson opposed "the whole business of domination and exploitation"; however, if the Europeans insisted on holding on to parts of China, he was "in favor of Japan doing the same thing."[67] Johnson was not alone in detecting more than a whiff of hypocrisy in the Republicans' use of the Shantung question. Among those who shed crocodile tears for China was California's Hiram Johnson, a longtime foe of Chinese immigration. But whereas others perceived talk about the "rape" of Shantung as a ploy by bitter-enders to kill the treaty, the NAACP's field secretary viewed it as a calculated effort to weaken Japan. This seems doubtful. Although Lodge and his allies played to anti-Japanese sentiment in the American public, it does not appear that they had anything more in mind than the humiliation of the president. Historian Thomas Bailey drew a similar conclusion when he noted that China's newfound friends were "more eager to discredit Wilson than Japan, more eager to help the party than to help China."[68]

There were, however, opponents of the treaty who expressed genuine concern for China and who called for an end to Japanese and European imperialism in Asia. For disillusioned former supporters of the liberal peace plan like the *Nation*'s Villard and the *New Republic*'s Walter Lippmann, the Shantung travesty exemplified all that was wrong with the treaty. In marked contrast, Du Bois viewed the rejection of racial equality as the greater defect. Yet despite his disappointment, Du Bois supported American entry into the League of Nations as a necessary step toward preventing "the Great War of Races," which would be "absolutely inevitable unless the selfish nations of white civilization are curbed by a Great World Congress in which black and white and yellow sit and speak and act."[69]

The different perspectives on the Far Eastern question held by Lippmann and Villard on the one hand, and Johnson and Du Bois on the other, provided further evidence of the seemingly unbridgeable gulf that separated even those black and white Americans who opposed discrimination in the United States.[70] White progressives saw Japan as simply another predator intent on plundering China, Korea, and Siberia. They had supported Wilson's call to arms in the belief that the war would be waged to end the politics of the old order. Instead, they found that in one compromise after another the president had succumbed to the unrelenting demands of the imperialists.[71] Many black Americans saw matters differently. The rejection of the racial equality amendment confirmed their belief that only the presence of a nonwhite nation in the councils of the great powers would force the West to confront the issue of racism.[72]

It is a telling commentary on the state of relations between black civil rights leaders and white progressives that the conflicting reactions to the Shantung question went unremarked upon within the NAACP. Disillusioned and weary of crusades, white and black civil rights advocates went their own way, each filing separate grievances and seeking strange new partnerships, Villard with segregationist isolationists, and Du Bois and Johnson with an imperialist Japan.[73]

It is perhaps even more noteworthy that, although they seemed not to realize it at the time, African Americans' admiration for Japan left them all but unable to appreciate China's own struggle against imperialism. As a result of an extensive American propaganda effort during the war, most educated Chinese had been led to expect that the peace treaty would restore Shantung to their control. When they learned that the final settlement merely transferred most of Germany's rights to Japan, students poured into city streets across the country to denounce the treaty. Suspected pro-Japanese officials were mobbed and a boycott of Japanese goods organized. The May Fourth Movement, as these protests became known, marked an important stage in the development of modern China. The Kuomintang (Guomindang or Nationalist) Party, led by Sun Yat-sen in the south, gained new momentum as a result of the demonstrations. The Chinese Communist Party (CCP) also emerged out of the anti-imperialist protests. It would be nearly a decade before this awakening of Chinese nationalism produced an internationally recognized government and almost another ten years before that government challenged Japanese encroachment in China. Eventually, as the competition for influence over China's development intensified, many African Americans, most notably W. E. B. Du Bois, became apologists for Japan. In doing so they unabashedly justified Japan's behavior in China in terms reminiscent of the hollow rhetoric employed by American and European advocates of the white man's civilizing mission. All of that lay ahead, however. In 1919 it was possible to ignore China's aspirations and dream about the unity of the darker races under Japan's leadership.

By 1919 African Americans had developed a worldview that placed their own struggle against discrimination into the context of a global battle against racism. Some black Americans protested against this internationalization of their problems. Others complained that civil rights organizations should not dissipate their limited resources to struggle on behalf of others when so much needed to be done at home. Nevertheless, African American leaders succeeded in creating a foreign policy on the basis of color. They mobilized their constituents at home, petitioned governments, and sought support among those thought to be sympathetic to their interests. In attempting to forge a global fellowship of nonwhite peoples, black internationalists anticipated the surge of liberal internationalism that peaked during the Wilson years. But black internationalists went beyond the new diplomacy championed by the president and his supporters to seek redress for racism in the international arena.

When they identified Japan as a potential ally in the struggle against racism, Du Bois, Trotter, Garvey, Johnson, and other Japanophiles did not simply project their own aspirations onto an unresponsive Japan. In 1904, when the Japanese first stood up against Russia in defense of their interests in Korea and Manchuria, it required some imagination to believe that they were standing up for the great masses of nonwhite peoples as well. Black Americans could enjoy the vicarious thrill of putting white supremacists in their place, but they still looked for signs of Japan's willingness to assume the leadership role that black internationalists envisioned for it. Japan, by way of its actions at Paris, had fulfilled the expectations of African Americans.

In the aftermath of the Versailles conference, some critics accused the Japanese of insincerity in the racial equality controversy. Japan, they alleged, knew that the provision would be rejected, but they persisted in pressing the issue so they could embarrass the Americans and British and extract further concessions from them. Others observed that Japan's treatment of minorities within its own empire fell far short of the ideal they asked other nations to endorse. Moreover, even in its strongest form, the racial equality clause dealt only with migrants from one league member to another and would not directly affect the well-being of minorities within their own country. African Americans recognized the limitations of the Japanese amendment insofar as their own battle against segregation was concerned, but they eagerly welcomed any attempt to enshrine the principle of racial equality into the new code of international justice. Over time, Japan's fight at Paris would achieve almost mythic proportions among black Americans, whereas China's support for the same measure would be all but forgotten.

Wilson understood the symbolic importance of the racial equality amendment to the Japanese, but he feared that its inclusion in the league charter would jeopardize acceptance of the peace treaty by the U.S. Senate. When the president seemed ready to accept Japan's amendment, Colonel Edward House reminded him that even Japan's watered-down clause "would raise the race issue throughout the world." House was referring to the firestorm of opposition he and Wilson expected Japan's measure to arouse in the British empire and on the West Coast of the United States. With the advantage of hindsight, however, we can see that the Americans were mistaken in thinking that the conference was better served by maintaining an embarrassed silence on the principle of racial equality. For although Wilson managed to suppress Japan's amendment in the league covenant, others were raising the race issue worldwide.

[2]

The Rising Tide of Color

Russia's conquest of Europe began with the invasion of Poland in 1932. Moving swiftly westward, the Red troops engulfed Austria, Germany, and France. Benito Mussolini's Italian forces made a valiant stand against the Russian hordes, but they too succumbed under the weight of the Soviet juggernaut. Shortly afterward, a coalition government of Communists and Socialists in Great Britain capitulated. The new Soviet tsar, Karakhan of Kazan, proved nearly unstoppable owing to his brilliant strategy of synthesizing the forces of revolution with the seething resentments of millions of the world's darker inhabitants. Advancing under the "flag of miscegenation," Karakhan enlisted the support of China and Japan, the other country besides Russia "where race is no barrier," and laid siege to North America. Panic spread throughout the United States fueled by revelations of communist plans for an elaborate campaign of sabotage. Karakhan further encouraged fifth-column activities by offering the states of Mississippi and Louisiana to black Americans. Following a fire in New York's Chinatown and a race riot in Chicago, the authorities arrested Gorkus Marvey, president of the Amalgamated Ethiopian Order of the Black Plume, in his New York headquarters and confiscated propaganda literature advocating revolt among black Americans.

Karakhan's stunning victories eventually succeeded in accomplishing what diplomacy had failed to achieve, the unification of the white races. The American and Canadian armies, bolstered by the remnants of European forces, withstood an invasion on two fronts. The U.S. Navy delivered the final blow by defeating and capturing Karakhan in the Battle of the Windward Passage.

The Red Napoleon, as this fictionalized account of the next world war was titled, was the product of the lurid imagination of Floyd Gibbons, a war correspondent for the *Chicago Tribune*.[1] After being serialized in *Liberty* magazine, the masthead of which proclaimed "Our Country, Right or Wrong," *Red Napoleon* was published in book form in 1929. Although some reviewers scoffed at Gibbons's characterizations and dismissed his plot line as "having so large an element of incredulity about it that we are laughing up our sleeves," the *New York Times* found that Gibbons wrote "plausibly and well" and recommended that the book "be read with attention by all pacifists and millennium makers."[2] The *Nation* regarded the story as "pish-posh" but concluded that its depiction of interracial lust and vivid battle scenes had helped boost *Liberty*'s circulation. Moreover, episodes of American vigilantism earlier in the decade convinced the journal's reviewer that "our miseducation in pugilistic nationalism has prepared millions of good ordinary Americans from Gastonia to Centralia, to accept it as gospel truth."[3]

Whatever its shortcomings as literature, Gibbons's warning of an impending race war is noteworthy as a catalog of the racial phobias that afflicted millions of Americans in the postwar era. For black internationalists, as well as white supremacists, World War I marked a watershed in the history of race relations. As pioneering sociologist Robert Park noted in 1923, "The American Negro no longer conceives of his destiny as bounded by the limits of the United States. He is seeking alliances and creating loyalties that transcend the boundaries of our American commonwealth. The Negro, in his racial relationship at least, is internationalist. He is becoming a citizen of the world."[4] Park was referring specifically to Pan-Africanism, but during the 1920s black Americans looked beyond Africa to Japan for assistance. Some black internationalists viewed Japan as an important symbol that destroyed the myth of white superiority. Others believed that Japan would directly aid black Americans and other victims of discrimination by taking up the cause of racial equality in international politics. Even if Japan did not directly champion their cause, black internationalists believed that at the very least Japan's power would force the American government to alter its racial policies or face a future race war in the Pacific. All black internationalists, however, shared a belief that race and racism were determining features in international affairs.

In the 1920s the same signs of colonial unrest that inspired black Americans to look outward for allies caused white supremacists to fear that the world's nonwhite peoples might soon overwhelm the ruling white minority. Americans had already been introduced to the specter of a "yellow peril" by a militant Japan in the first decade of the twentieth century. Those fears soon degenerated into a dread of an emerging alliance of the world's nonwhite peoples against white supremacy. The victory of Russian Communists in 1917 and the support the new Soviet regime gave to revolutionary movements in the colonial world produced further anxiety among white supremacists. Indeed, what worried the *Nation*'s reviewer was the effortlessness with which Gibbons blended the American fear of communist revolution with the almost equally powerful dread of an emerging alliance of the world's nonwhite peoples.

Such concerns were already in evidence when the delegates assembled at the peace conference ending the Great War. The war's devastation had brought down the tsarist regime and raised the first socialist state in its place. As the delegates labored in Paris to isolate the new nations of Eastern Europe from the red contagion, Allied armies sought to aid the Bolsheviks' numerous but disorganized opponents. Having learned from his failed intervention in Mexico's revolution, President Wilson gave his support to the Allies only grudgingly. A small contingent of American troops headed for Archangel (in Russian, Arkhangel'sk) under British command while a larger group, numbering seven thousand, occupied Vladivostok on the Pacific coast. There, among its various missions, the U.S. expedition kept a watchful eye on a much larger Japanese force. When the counterrevolutionary resistance collapsed, the Americans lingered, concerned about Japanese intentions. The Americans finally left Siberia in early 1920, but Japanese troops remained. By the end of Wilson's term, a dispute over control of the island of Yap, new restrictive legislation in California, and a looming naval race had brought American-Japanese tensions to a new high.[5]

In the aftermath of World War I, the fear of communist revolution and apprehension about Japanese expansionism left U.S. officials doubly vexed. Most Americans regarded the victory of either of these forces as a waking nightmare. Many African Americans, however, were happily dreaming in color.

For the darker races of the world, it seemed as though their deliverance might soon be at hand. The Great War had claimed the lives of more than 10 million Europeans. The toll in property was incalculable. To prevail in their struggle against Germany, the British and French had recruited heavily from among their imperial subjects. Britain threw 800,000 Indian troops into the campaigns in Mesopotamia and the Western Front. Another 400,000 Indians formed labor battalions. France filled out its front-line forces with 175,000 Africans. More than 200,000 Chinese and Indochinese served in labor battalions.[6] The United States, although it suffered least from the war, also strained to field an army, protect its empire, and continue supplying its allies. In mobilizing for the conflict, the Wilson administration had called up 367,000 black troops, 50,000 of whom went to France. Most served as laborers, but some, notably the Ninety-second Division—actually an amalgam of disparate units—fought with distinction under French command.[7] The battle to clear the Atlantic sea lanes of German submarines also taxed American resources. To concentrate on the Atlantic theater, the United States shifted its fleet out of the Pacific, where it left American possessions under the protection of the Japanese navy. As part of this arrangement, known as the Lansing-Ishii Agreement, the Wilson administration recognized Japan's "special interests" in China.

The significance of the nonwhite world's contribution to the Allied victory was too great to be ignored. Millions of Asians, Africans, Indians, and African Americans had participated in one way or another, in foreign service or in their own countries, in what appeared to be Europe's fratricidal struggle. In aiding the Allies they had witnessed the Europeans at their most vulnerable. The myth of white supremacy, weakened at the turn of the century by Japan's victory over Russia, suffered a mortal wound on the fields of Flanders. The idealism that buoyed Americans as they entered the war also inspired the nonwhite world. Colonial subjects refused to believe that Wilsonian pledges of self-determination and the rights of free peoples applied only to the white world. Secretary of State Robert Lansing, whom Wilson suspected of reactionary tendencies, sensed the danger in the president's peace program. "The more I think of the President's declarations as to the right of 'self-determination,' the more convinced I am of the danger of putting such ideas into the minds of certain races. . . . The phrase is simply loaded with dynamite."[8]

African Americans were among those who hoped to achieve the same rights that the president promised to the European subjects of the central powers. In 1917 U.S. entry into the war provided new opportunities for black Americans in the army and expanding war industries. The same year, however, a riot against recent black migrants in East St. Louis left forty African Americans dead. There were also fifty-eight lynchings of blacks, and none of the killers were prosecuted. At the same time black conscripts and volunteers learned that the rapidly expanding U.S. Army would continue the practice of Jim Crow segregation at home and in France. Despite these bleak circumstances W. E. B. Du Bois, writing in the *Crisis* in July 1918, urged African Americans to "close ranks" and to defer protests for equal rights until the war was won. Du Bois's editorial drew immediate criticism from his colleagues, who accused him of adopting the conciliatory demeanor of Booker T. Washington to secure a captaincy in the army. More recently it has become clear that Du Bois was under considerable pressure from white members of the NAACP who threatened to withdraw their support from the organization unless he soft-pedaled black grievances for the duration of the war. Moreover, he was under constant surveillance by the government, which had already silenced other critics by prosecuting them under the wartime sedition act.[9]

Du Bois, criticized by onetime supporters and rebuffed by most liberals, nevertheless found reason for hope at the end of the war. The turmoil that alarmed Robert Lansing gave the editor of the *Crisis* cause for grim satisfaction. "This war is an end," he wrote, "and also a beginning. Never again will darker people of the world occupy just the place they had before. Out of this place will rise, soon or late, an independent China, a self-governing India, an Egypt with representative institutions, an Africa for the Africans, and not merely for business exploitation. Out of this war will rise, too, an American Negro with the right to vote and the right to work and the right to live without insult."[10]

Other African American intellectuals reacted similarly to the powerful changes wrought by the war. Hubert H. Harrison, whom Vincent Harding has called the "most important and influential radical black intellectual teacher of the period," deplored the awful bloodshed of the war, but he also told cheering crowds in Harlem that "we find consolation in the hope that when the white world shall have been washed clean by its baptism of blood, the white race will be less able to thrust the strong hand of its sovereign will down the throats of other races." Like Du Bois, Harrison looked for the war to bring "a free and independent Egypt, for nationalities in Africa flying their own flags and dictating their own internal and foreign policies."[11] John Edward Bruce, who for several decades was known to black readers by his pen name "Bruce Grit," also predicted that the war would produce momentous changes in the nonwhite world. "Africa and India, the Blind Samsons, are now awake," he wrote, "the cannons of the allies and the central powers have aroused them from their long slumber. . . . Presently they will burst [their chains] asunder and will stand up like men, and then goodbye to white domination on both sides of the salt pond."[12]

Those Americans who were determined to preserve the racial caste system also sensed the transforming nature of the Great War. Following the armistice in November 1918, black soldiers returning from the front faced increased hostility in many parts of the country. A new wave of lynchings greeted them, with some veterans hanged while still in uniform. Early in 1919 the explosion of several mail bombs transformed the wartime search for subversives into America's first Red Scare. Although the perpetrator(s) remained unknown, most Americans, led by the attorney general of the United States, concluded that Bolsheviks were behind the terrorist attacks. Russian agents were also said to be responsible for the numerous violent strikes by organized labor and were alleged to be fomenting rebelliousness among black Americans. That summer, called the "Red Summer" by James Weldon Johnson, more race riots erupted in U.S. cities. This time, blacks showed a fierce determination to defend their homes from attack. The urban racial violence took a devastating toll in lives and property. Despite the contributions they made to victory over Germany, African Americans could not find peace at home. Once more democracy had eluded them.

By 1920 the Red Scare had died out, a victim of its own excesses as much as anything else. The intense violence of the Red Summer also diminished, although riots occurred sporadically throughout the decade. Gradually, the tumult of postwar reconversion subsided, but many Americans remained on guard for signs of subversion and other challenges to the status quo. Vigilante groups such as the reborn Ku Klux Klan remained strong during the first half of the decade and fed the nativist sentiment that pervaded American society. Faced with a resumption of immigration at prewar levels, much of it from Eastern Europe and southern Europe, Congress passed restrictive measures in 1921 and 1924 to stem the tide. The latter bill greatly reduced the number of entrants overall and tilted the balance in favor of the more desirable "races" from northern Europe. The 1924 law also specifically prohibited Chinese and Japanese immigration to the United States.[13]

The 1924 Immigration Act (sometimes called the National Origins Act) marked the apotheosis of scientific racism in American life. Drawing on many of the pseudoscientific theories that had provided the intellectual justification for imperialism, Congress sought to screen out those peoples it deemed by nature and custom as inherently incapable of assimilation into democratic society. Two of the most prominent scholars who promoted immigration restriction as a means of staving off internal decay were Madison Grant and Theodore Lothrop Stoddard. Grant's *The Passing of the Great Race*, first published in 1916, passed through four editions and numerous reprintings after the war.[14] Surpassing Grant's work in gloom, Stoddard's *The Rising Tide of Color against White World Supremacy* appeared in 1920 and was reprinted seven times in less than two years.[15] Whereas Grant called for opening America's doors only to the most fit, Stoddard warned that immigration restriction was at best a temporary national solution to a danger of global proportions. Assessing the world conditions at the end of the Great War, he declared that unless the superior white races reunited against the darker peoples, Western civilization would drown in a sea of blood. Stoddard lamented the death wish displayed by the white races in the last war and criticized what he believed were the unjustly harsh terms of the Versailles settlement. Unless white leaders extracted the "dragon's teeth sown by Versailles," Europe would plunge into another suicidal conflict to the further advantage of the darker races.[16] Stoddard regarded the Pan-African movement as an indication of "negro race solidarity" and marveled at "the way in which the news of white military reverses have at once been known and rejoiced in all over black Africa; spread it would seem, by those mysterious methods of communication employed by negroes everywhere and called in our southern states 'grapevine telegraph.'"[17] Nevertheless, he doubted that the supposedly primitive African race could mount a challenge to white rule on its own.

The real danger, he believed, lurked in a "renascent Asia." Conceding that at the moment Japan held the upper hand against China, Stoddard, who was apparently determined to invoke every racist cliché in the American lexicon, predicted that "the inscrutable 'sons of Han'" would prevail in a Pan-Asian alliance. Cooperation between Japan and China was likely in any event since both were "fundamentally of the same race and culture."[18] The only hope for the West lay in an orderly retreat from its outposts in Asia and a regrouping around "our outer dikes in Latin American and Africa." Failure to do so would provoke a global race war in which "Neither a Pan-Colored nor a Colored-Bolshevist alliance are impossibilities, far fetched as these terms might sound."[19]

Stoddard, of course, did not think such an alliance was far-fetched. Judging from the success of his treatise, it is safe to conclude that a large number of literate Americans did not believe his predictions to be far-fetched either. Stoddard's warning to the white race was in many respects a repackaging of the "yellow peril" in scholarly wrapping. Even his predictions of a nonwhite alliance led by Asians recalled the earlier era of the Russo-Japanese War. *The Rising Tide of Color* owed much of its success to the mood of despair that permeated much of the West in the immediate aftermath of the world war. In America, and to a lesser degree in Europe, the half decade of economic prosperity before the start of the Great Depression in 1929 helped to alleviate some of the doubts westerners felt about their superiority. Nevertheless, Stoddard's dark forecast of a future imperiled by a nonwhite alliance would prove remarkably resilient in the years to come.

F. Scott Fitzgerald acknowledged the popularity of Stoddard's book, if not its validity, by referring to it in *The Great Gatsby*.[20] Gibbons's *Red Napoleon* retailed Stoddard's scholarly predictions as pulp fiction. But when it came to popularity and longevity, Karakhan of Kazan could not match the power of the diabolical Dr. Fu Manchu. Published during the interwar period, Sax Rohmer's *Fu Manchu* series sold over twenty million copies. It is impossible to say with certainty what message, if any, readers took from these tales of suspense and international intrigue, but even a cursory reading of the plots reveals a consistent theme of the West under assault from what would later be called the Third World. Rohmer's stories drew their inspiration from current events and reflected, intentionally or otherwise, the growing criticism by Asian and African intellectuals of Western science and technological prowess as effective barometers of civilization. In his duel of wits with British foreign agent Sir Denis Nayland Smith, the "yellow-skinned genius" employed an occult non-Western science to wage his struggle throughout much of the colonial world, including India, Egypt, Africa, and Haiti. Although each novel ended with the West prevailing over the sinister doctor, Fu Manchu always escaped to carry on the battle, and the series, another day.[21]

In placing his villain in the context of current events, Fu Manchu's creator could be assured that he would never lack for new plot material. Although the 1920s were relatively quiescent when compared with the great cataclysms of the 1930s and 1940s, observers of foreign events found enough turbulence in world affairs to ward off any feelings of complacency. Indeed, in much of the colonial world rebellion and internal strife ruled the day. In 1919 the General Syrian Congress rejected the trusteeship status thrust on it by the League of Nations and resisted, unsuccessfully, a French invasion. The same year Turkey, built on the remains of the defeated Ottoman empire, repulsed an Anglo-Greek invasion. For much of the 1920s China remained ravaged by warlord rule, but in 1927 Kuomintang armies began their march north to unify the country. During the same period colonial officials in Southeast Asia found themselves contending with emerging nationalist movements. Closer to the United States, Mexico and much of Central America experienced continued political upheaval. There was little in these seemingly random events to threaten the United States directly, but some alarmist officials, including President Calvin Coolidge, claimed to see the "Bolsheviki" behind the turmoil.

Lothrop Stoddard saw another, more menacing pattern to these convulsions. For Stoddard, even the Bolshevik danger became subsumed under the "Rising Tide of Color." He believed that the communist threat, to the extent that it was a threat, owed much of its power to the ability of the Russians to exploit the color line in the world. What worried him most was that some anti-Western force, Bolshevik or Asian, would organize the darker peoples of the world against the white race.

But whereas Stoddard saw a "Rising Tide of Color" in the world, those seeking to free themselves from white domination saw an emerging fraternity of the darker races or, as it would later be called, a "Black Internationale." In the now classic 1925 anthology *The New Negro*, scholar-critic Alain Locke described how the growing color consciousness of African Americans led them to identify with other victims of racism throughout the world. He pointed out, however, that "this wider race consciousness is a different thing from the much asserted rising tide of color. Its inevitable causes are not of our making. The consequences are not necessarily of our making." [22] Obviously there was a world of difference between Stoddard's nightmarish vision of a conspiracy of color and Locke's hope for the liberation of suppressed peoples through an alliance of colonial subjects. That difference, important as it was, should not obscure the extent to which the idea of nonwhite unity as expressed in both ideologies exerted a powerful influence on the minds of Americans, white and black, in the years before World War II.

Like Stoddard, black internationalists tended to mingle economic and racial categories of thought in their analysis of world events. Stoddard feared a possible Colored-Bolshevik alliance, whereas advocates of black internationalism regularly emphasized what they perceived as the mutually reinforcing relationship between racism and capitalism. In 1927 Leopold Senghor, a Senegalese poet and one of the founders of the Negritude school of literature in postwar France, reminded a gathering of the International Congress against Colonial Oppression and Imperialism that France had employed Africans as counterrevolutionary forces throughout the empire. "We have seen," he said, "that during the war as many Negroes as possible were recruited, to be used as cannon fodder. . . . They let our comrades be slaughtered in the first Morocco war before the great War of 1914. They are still being butchered today in Morocco, in the Rif and in Syria. Negroes are being sent to Madagascar. Negroes are sent to Indochina because it is near China which is setting them a splendid revolutionary example." Senghor ended this recital of revolutionary agitation within the French empire with a denunciation of capitalism. "It all stems from capitalism," he exclaimed. "It is capitalism which breeds imperialism in the peoples of the leading countries."[23]

In the United States of the 1920s, a straightforward indictment of capitalism such as Senghor gave was not likely to reach a wide audience, even among African Americans. In this respect, the ideology of black internationalism allowed black leaders, especially middle-class professionals and newspaper editors, to emphasize the racism inherent in imperialism without directly attacking the core American faith in capitalism. The role of discrimination in shaping black neighborhoods also helped influence the tone and content of black ideology. As Alain Locke noted, "proscription and prejudice" had thrown together blacks from all walks of life.[24] Class distinctions might arise in internal debates, but when black Americans faced outward they did so as a group.[25] Du Bois, who was the leading herald of black internationalism, exemplifies this pattern of analysis. Although he offered a biting critique of capitalist expansion in his essay on the African roots of the Great War, he abjured a doctrinally pure socialist analysis for one that highlighted the importance of race in international affairs.[26]

During the interwar period Du Bois did much to promote the idea of nonwhite solidarity as the means to ending racism. In 1919 he had hoped that the League of Nations would become "a Great World Congress in which black and white and yellow sit and speak and act."[27] By the late 1920s Du Bois concluded that the white nations would only be brought to the conference table by a global alliance of nonwhite peoples. When that alliance did not materialize, he created it in the pages of his novel *Dark Princess*, which featured, among other characters, a Japanese who was "quite yellow" with a face that was "a delicately handled but perfect mask."[28] Apart from revealing Du Bois's susceptibility to prevailing stereotypes about the color and inscrutability of Asians, the plot reflected his ambivalence about the relationship between socialism and the liberation of nonwhite peoples. Throughout the novel the African American protagonist struggles to include laboring whites in the alliance against injustice. But in the end the reader is left to believe that the alliance of the darker races will come first.[29]

In the aftermath of the Great War, Harlem radical Hubert H. Harrison also became convinced of the need for black solidarity and a revolutionary Pan-Africanism. Harrison, a former Socialist, abandoned his expectations of an internationale based on class in favor of a "race first" approach to the problems of nonwhite peoples.[30] In part this was a reaction to signs of racism within the Socialist Party.[31] But it was also a rejection of what many blacks regarded as party leader Eugene V. Debs's naive view that African American workers faced the same obstacles as the white working class.[32] "Bruce Grit" also rejected socialism as a solution for the problems of African Americans. After listening to black Socialist A. Philip Randolph, he concluded that "Socialists are themselves divided and there can never be unity in division."[33] More than ever, Bruce believed that unity counted most for blacks. Speaking on the "Destiny of the Darker Races" shortly after the armistice, Bruce predicted that "What is back of the white man's mind at this particular time, if he would only give voice to his thinking, would greatly accelerate a get together movement among the black and colored men of the world."[34] Again in 1919 he emphasized the "great necessity for a closer union and a better understanding between the black and colored races whose destiny is identical." "The white race," Bruce admonished his audience, "is going to dominate as long as the Black and Colored races permit it—and no longer."[35]

Other writers and academics such as James Weldon Johnson and Kelly Miller spread the idea of nonwhite solidarity in the black community. For much of his adult life Miller was affiliated with Howard University as a professor of mathematics and sociology and as dean of the College of Liberals Arts. Although he had previously supported American expansion into Cuba and Puerto Rico, Miller came to share Du Bois's belief that the race question had become a world question. Miller's postwar essays collected in 1924 under the title *The Everlasting Stain* reflected this awareness. "We hope somehow," he wrote, "there is an imminent moral economy in human affairs. The World War has brought together all peoples of all lands and this incidental contact has, of itself, aroused a consciousness of brotherhood and of moral unity."[36] Like Secretary of State Lansing, Miller recognized the explosive impact of Wilsonian rhetoric on the nonwhite peoples of the world: "There exists among modern statesmen and publicists the complaisant delusion that they can indulge in universal declarations of the rights of man, while the ears of the weaker people are too dull to hear and their minds too feeble to understand. But when Pandora's box is once opened, it can never be closed."[37] According to Miller, Japan had played a leading role in bringing about this revolutionary change in the nonwhite world. As the "foremost section of the Asiatic peoples," Japan was now "speaking with authority for the yellow races." "They have already put the world on warning," Miller declared, "that the intolerant spirit of the white race can never be accepted as the final basis of peace on earth and good will among men."[38]

In the 1920s the creation of the International Council of the Women of the Darker Races further testified to the black bourgeoisie's interest in the plight of the world's nonwhite peoples. Organized in 1923 as an offshoot of the National Association of Colored Women, the International Council included such prominent African American women as Josephine Turpin Washington, a writer and Tuskegee teacher; Mary Church Terrell; Mary McLeod Bethune; and Genie Hope, wife of college president John Hope. The group's constitution called for a membership of "one hundred fifty American women of color and fifty foreign women of color." The founders committed themselves to "mutual international cooperation and sympathetic understanding in every forward movement among women and children of the darker races of the world, for the dissemination of knowledge of peoples of color the world over that there may be a larger appreciation of their history and accomplishments."[39] Although its program was far from radical, the council, which survived until 1929, provided further evidence of the growing awareness among black Americans of the connection between their condition and the fate of colonial peoples worldwide.[40]

Committed to cooperation with other peace groups, the International Council of the Women of the Darker Races was too genteel a gathering to voice any concern about the possibility of a future race war. But other black leaders, as we have seen, openly expressed their fear of racial conflict on a global scale. Kelly Miller's identification of Japan as a natural ally in the battle against racism repeated an important theme in the ideology of black internationalism. But this perception of Japan as a leader in the liberation of nonwhite peoples was not limited to black Americans. Lothrop Stoddard also saw Japan posing "as the champion of the colored races," but he dismissed the Japanese performance at the Paris Peace Conference as a cynical and empty gesture.

Pearl S. Buck, the daughter of China missionaries who would later gain renown as the author of *The Good Earth*, approached the issue of nonwhite solidarity from the opposite direction but reached a similar conclusion about the possibility of a race war. Outraged by the racism practiced by whites in China and the United States, Buck wrote a master's thesis in 1925 warning that the Japanese and the Indians were urging the Chinese to join them "in the final struggle which will eventually come against the white race." It was not too late to avoid a race war, she believed, if Americans purged themselves of their prejudices and helped to establish world politics on a foundation of equality and justice.[41] Those who welcomed an emerging fellowship of the darker races as a means to liberation, those who feared it, and the small number of white liberals like Pearl Buck who worried that a race war would be retribution for the sins of white supremacists shared an important assumption about the importance of color in the world. Although Miller, Stoddard, Buck, Bruce, and Du Bois disagreed over who would lead the "Asiatic peoples," all assumed that color created a natural affinity among Asians.

That message deeply disturbed A. Philip Randolph and Chandler Owen, the socialist editors of the *Messenger*. Randolph had attended a gathering with Japanese representatives at C. J. Walker's house and delighted in the controversy Japanese delegates created at Paris when they raised the racial equality issue, but his socialist ideology permitted few illusions about Japan's ultimate aims in Asia. In 1918, following Japan's intervention in Siberia, Randolph warned black Americans "not to be appealed to on the basis of color." Japan, he added, was "more imperialistic than Prussia."[42] Randolph had little patience for an analysis of world affairs based on race. Significantly, the *Messenger* declared that "the only fairly scientific production which we have ever seen from the pen of Dr. Du Bois was an article in the May issue of the *Atlantic* entitled 'The African Roots of War.'"[43] Once again, in 1919, Randolph pleaded with readers to view world politics in terms of class not color. "Japan, though a nation of color, will fight socialists as savagely as any other nation," he explained. "It is not color, but reaction and capitalism which are clashing with radicalism. . . . Japan does not want Asia for the Asiatics she wants Asia for Japan. Both Japan and China are colored too. Color is no issue unless it is yellow gold."[44]

The stridency with which Randolph preached his message suggests the extent to which Japan occupied a favorable position in the thoughts of many internationally minded black Americans. Further evidence of its appeal could be found even farther to the Left on the political spectrum. In 1919, not long after the founding of the Communist Party, United States of America (CPUSA), Cyril Briggs, an immigrant from Nevis in the West Indies, launched the African Blood Brotherhood, a group of former socialists whose leaders soon migrated into the CPUSA. As Briggs later explained, he was attracted to the party because of the national minorities policy of the Russian Bolsheviks. "My interest in communism," he said, "was for the national liberation struggle, not economic struggle."[45] Briggs, who was also editor of the *Crusader*, a Harlem-based militant journal, adapted this theme of national liberation to African American circumstances by fusing ideas of race pride with radical socialism in his attacks on the establishment. In doing so Briggs firmly highlighted the issue of race, thereby avoiding, at least initially, the mistakes of the Socialist Party. Not long after Randolph flayed Japan for its invasion of Siberia, however, the *Crusader*

A. Philip Randolph and Edward P. Morrow, labor mediator and former governor of Kentucky, ca. 1926. (Library of Congress)

boldly declared that in the event of a conflict between the United States and Japan or a possible clash with Mexico, African Americans were duty bound "NOT TO FIGHT AGAINST JAPAN OR MEXICO." "The Negro who fights against either Japan or Mexico," Briggs wrote, "is fighting for the *white man* against himself, for the *white race* against the darker races and for the perpetuation of *white domination of the colored races* . . . in opposition to the principle advocated by Japan of Race Equality."[46] Briggs later adopted the Communist Party's view of Japan as one of the imperialist "robber nations," but perhaps nothing demonstrates more clearly the malleability of black internationalism in the 1920s than the ease with which even left-wing African American leaders, Randolph excepted, rhetorically attached themselves to Japan.

Although black Americans, particularly intellectuals, remained enamored of Japan in the 1920s, developments in other areas of the globe generated more enthusiasm and interest in the broader African American community. As Sudarshan Kapur has shown, it was during the 1920s that the unfolding drama of the Indian independence movement captured the attention of black Americans. Fascinated by the spiritual strength of the courageous Mohandas Gandhi, African American readers followed the Mahatma's campaign of nonviolent resistance against British rule in numerous periodicals. Gandhi's saintly demeanor and his opposition to India's caste system struck responsive chords among African Americans who had developed their own theology of liberation to combat a rigid caste system based on color. Black Americans were less united on the applicability of Gandhi's philosophy of nonviolence to their own condition. But even this debate over the merits of nonviolence in America helped to keep alive the black community's growing interest in India. During the interwar period, as numerous writers and speakers admonished their audiences to "watch the Indian people," African American and Indian leaders traveled across continents to meet and exchange ideas and support.[47]

African Americans' identification with the peoples of East Asia and India helped to distinguish their internationalist ideology from the more traditional concern of other Americans with the country of their birth. Nevertheless, affection for Africa and the Pan-African idea remained at the core of black internationalist thought. Du Bois played a crucial role in organizing the Pan-African Congress in 1919, and he fervently believed that African Americans were the vanguard of the African liberation movement. Miller, like Du Bois, also saw African Americans as "the most advanced section of the African race." As such, they were "the best qualified to utter the voice of two hundred million people in the continent of Africa and scattered over the face of the globe."[48]

Writers like Du Bois and Miller did much to promote Pan-Africanism among the black elite and middle classes in the United States. But the most influential mass leader to advocate the vanguard strategy for African liberation was the Jamaican-born immigrant Marcus Garvey. As founder of the Harlem-based Universal Negro Improvement Association (UNIA) and publisher of the *Negro World*, Garvey hoped to redeem Africa for the children of the diaspora. His recipe for African liberation was a mixture of capitalism and black nationalism, spiced heavily with the pomp and regalia of an African empire just waiting to be created. Although Garvey left much to be desired as a business manager, the UNIA established branches throughout the country. Launched in Jamaica in 1914, the Garvey movement by the end of the war had generated great enthusiasm among African Americans with its appeal to racial pride, self-help, and solidarity. Indeed, the organization's rise was so swift and startling that its leader soon attracted numerous enemies. Du Bois considered Garvey a demagogue. He denounced the UNIA's emigration schemes and thought that the numerous titles the Jamaican bestowed on loyalists, such as "Duke of Uganda," were ludicrous. Nevertheless, Du Bois later admitted that during the 1920s his own Pan-African movement suffered directly because of Garvey's mass appeal. A. Philip Randolph and officials in the NAACP likewise condemned Garvey for abandoning the cause of black equality in America for what they regarded as the pipe dream of an African homeland for all African Americans.

Despite these bitter disagreements over the prospects for full citizenship in America, Garvey and his detractors shared an internationalist perspective on the race question. Like his opponents, Garvey believed that Americans (and West Indians) had a special role to play in the liberation of Africa. And like his critics, Garvey's speeches and publications contained frequent references to events involving subject peoples around the globe. Garvey also sought to forge connections with independence movements elsewhere in the world by sending telegrams to movement leaders, by soliciting foreign support for the UNIA's various enterprises, most notably the Black Star Steamship Line, and by inviting representatives from other countries to share the podium with him at his numerous conventions.

Garvey's militant rhetoric and his strong following among the most disaffected African Americans alarmed U.S. officials, who in the calmest of times were inclined to attribute any sign of black protest to foreign sources, and earned him the dubious distinction of being caricatured in *Red Napoleon* as the subversive "Gorkus Marvey." The UNIA, with its strong internationalist program, quickly attracted the attention of agents from several of the nation's intelligence and security agencies including J. Edgar Hoover's Federal Bureau of Investigation (FBI), the Office of Naval Intelligence (ONI), and the army's Military Intelligence Division (MID).

Although Garvey often welcomed Indian guests and offered warm praise for Gandhi's movement, American agents were understandably more concerned by the UNIA's connections to another, more powerful representative of the darker races, Japan.[49] On numerous occasions Garvey and his associates held Japan up as a model for African Americans. Like other black internationalists, Garvey predicted that unless the great powers addressed the issue of racism in international affairs, there would be no peace in the world. According to the MID, shortly after the armistice Garvey told an audience at Bethel AME Church in Baltimore that "We, like Josephus Daniels, believe that the next war will be a war of the races, and I believe that the war will start between the white and the yellow perils." Garvey's reference to Daniels, a prominent southern newspaper publisher and Wilson's secretary of the navy, further demonstrates how both apprehensions of a rising tide of color and black internationalism could start from the same premise of an Asia united under Japanese leadership.[50]

In the same speech Garvey proposed that "Negroes should make no

Marcus Garvey, 1923. (New York World-Telegram and Sun Collection, Library of Congress)

compromise with either the white men or the yellow men." "We have become the balance of power," he boasted, "in between the white men of Europe and the yellow men of Asia." In addition to revealing his tenuous grasp of geopolitical realities, the Jamaican's assertion that black Americans held the balance of power between Asia and the West implied that he regarded both sides in the predicted war between the races with equal suspicion. But such was not the case. Although he insisted that African Americans had to rely on themselves, Garvey and his followers were much more likely to present Japan as an interested supporter and potential ally, especially after the Paris Peace Conference. In early 1921 Dr. J. D. Gordon, vice president general of the UNIA, told a Los Angeles audience of 1,800 not to countenance or assist the Anti-Alien Land Law and Anti-Japanese movement. According to one report, Gordon said, "the Japanese are our best friends because they injected into the peace conference the equality of races without regard to color, and now this country is trying to prevent them having what they won and what the allies gave them."[51]

When Garvey turned his attention to foreign activities, he put most of his energy into establishing a foothold in West Africa and fund-raising and organizing in the Caribbean. The visionary provisional president of the "Empire of Africa" reached out to the Japanese as well. Garvey tried to purchase ships for his struggling Black Star Steamship Line from several unnamed Japanese, but these efforts were unsuccessful.[52]

Despite the fruitlessness of these contacts, U.S. intelligence officials remained concerned about the UNIA's connection to Japan. In particular, the ONI maintained close surveillance of UNIA activities on the West Coast. J. J. Hannigan, the district commandant of the navy's intelligence office, reported that several Japanese were using the UNIA to organize a "Colored Peoples Union" of African Americans, East Indians, and Mexicans in Seattle, San Francisco, and Los Angeles. According to Hannigan, Japanese delegates reportedly had attended UNIA meetings in New York as well.[53] In early 1922 Hannigan informed the director of naval intelligence that the "Hindu revolutionary movement has definite connections with the Negro agitation in America. And both of these movements have [been] leaning, at least for political reasons, to Bolshevik Russia." He acknowledged that many people "know of the race movement and place little importance to it as they do to other things that are going on in the world, such as the Mexican situation, the German-American situation, the Russian Bolshevik agitation, and the negro movement." Hannigan found such complacency dangerous. "[A]ll of these things are growing," he warned, "and behind all is the Japanese hand playing the powerful yet silent note."[54]

Hannigan's reports and those of other intelligence agents revealed, and no doubt exaggerated, a persistent effort on the part of UNIA members to establish informal alliances with other governments and liberation movements. Although little came from these contacts, Garvey's highly popular movement helped to raise African Americans' awareness of international events. Surveillance of the UNIA showed that when its members looked outward, their views were shaped by a core faith in the solidarity of non-white peoples. In this way, the steady stream of intelligence reports flowing into Washington provided yet another means by which the anxiety created by the rising tide of color seeped into the consciousness of white official-dom. Not long after Hannigan filed his reports, Garvey was convicted and jailed on charges of fraud relating to the UNIA's business activities. With Garvey in prison, the movement dwindled and fragmented only to be revived, as will be seen, in a somewhat different form in the 1930s.

Hannigan's reports of pro-Japanese sentiment in the UNIA and his own predictions of pending conflict provide a startling counterpoint to the interpretations of international events being presented in the major white-owned newspapers and journals of the same period. One would never know from the ONI field reports that diplomats from the United States, Japan, Great Britain, and the lesser powers were attending an arms limitation conference in Washington or that the leaders of Japan and the United States had established a system for cooperation and consultation in East Asia. While officials in Washington and Tokyo were hailing a new era in American-Japanese relations, black Americans and U.S. naval officers remained convinced that the two countries were on the verge of war.[55]

The Washington Conference of 1921–22 developed out of the unsettled conditions in East Asia following the defeat of Germany and the overthrow of the tsarist regime in Russia. Following World War I, the Japanese had been surprised by the international condemnation of their seizure of Shantung and their venture in Siberia. Moreover, Japanese imperialism provoked protest at home and further hindered Prime Minister Hara Kei's ability to chart a course for Japan in the postwar era. At the same time Japan faced the financial challenge of keeping pace with the U.S. naval program begun during World War I. Hara concluded that Japan would have to find a different means of protecting its economic interests on the mainland without antagonizing the United States and Britain.

Secretary of State Charles Evans Hughes was also interested in ending the naval race, finding a way of cooperating with Japan in Asia, and protecting America's limited interests in China. For Hughes this meant ending the Anglo-Japanese alliance, which Americans believed encouraged Japanese aggressiveness in China, and preserving what he believed was America's commitment to open economic competition in China. He did not expect the great powers to abandon the privileges they enjoyed in China, but he did hope that they would agree not to expand them at China's expense. The secretary believed that in the long term the foreign powers in China would relinquish their rights once a recognized national government emerged. At present, however, the worsening factional strife in China convinced Hughes that he could not expect a unified government to appear any time soon. The secretary thus sought only to make sure that competition in China did not disrupt the more important American-Japanese relationship.[56]

African Americans greeted the announcement that Britain and the United States had called a naval arms conference with suspicion. They sensed, correctly, that America was attempting to restrain Japan in the aftermath of its successes during the Great War. The summoning of a conference fulfilled the predictions made by black Americans that the white nations would try to regain the ground they had lost in the European struggle. "But if they expect Japan is going to disarm when Europe has its eye on Asia," Garvey told his supporters, "they make a big mistake, they have a second thought coming."[57] John Houghton, a correspondent for the UNIA's *Negro World*, told readers that the conference was "A diplomatic shroud to veil certain ignorant people so as to give Europe a chance to repair its naval forces and to prepare the minds of Europe for certain propaganda—'White supremacy and the Rising Tide of Color.'"[58]

The NAACP's James Weldon Johnson regarded the conference in similar terms. Noting the curious presence of China at an armaments conference, Johnson concluded that "the chief purpose in calling a conference is not to place a limitation on armaments but to place a limit upon the influence of Japan in the Far East."[59] In a later column he told readers of the *New York Age* that although Japan had sometimes been unjust toward China, the Chinese could be faulted for never seeking cooperation with Japan. He seconded the view of K. K. Kawakami, a Japanese correspondent, that China had adopted a "'Nagging attitude'" toward Japan. Indeed, his discussion with Kawakami reminded Johnson of an earlier conversation he had with an unnamed Japanese. On one occasion, Johnson recalled, his Japanese acquaintance had declared: "'The Chinese are like some of your colored people in the United States. We try to get an understanding with them that we must plan and work together, but every time we do they run and tell the white folks.'" With apparent approval Johnson noted: "This remark not only gave me a side light on the Japanese-Chinese situation, but it was an amazing revelation of the insight of the Japanese observers."[60] Despite the odds Japan faced, Johnson predicted that "when the results of the Arms Conference are weighed it will be found that the most vital victories were won by the polite and smiling but nevertheless keen and watchful little men from Japan."[61] Du Bois, who complained that "insidiously and carefully prepared propaganda [was] making the white world think that the only enemy of China is Japan," was more worried about the outcome of the conference.[62]

James Weldon Johnson, ca. 1900–1920. (NAACP Papers, Library of Congress)

This tendency of black Americans to side with Japan during the Washington Conference dulled their sensitivity to Chinese aspirations. African Americans were not wholly indifferent to China, rather they assumed that racial affinity would eventually overcome artificial Japanese and Chinese differences. Marcus Garvey told his followers that "white capitalists have gone into China and have poisoned the minds of the Chinese against themselves and against the Japanese. They have been subsidizing certain Chinese to fight among themselves, to divide up their soil into two republics. They have subsidized the Chinese to reject every proposal of Japan to cause them to believe that the Japanese hate them and want only to take away their country." Eventually, Garvey argued, the two peoples would see their true interests. Once that happened there would be an "Asia for the Asiatics."[63] The Associated Negro Press's correspondent likewise predicted that Japan and China would "bury the hatchet" at the conference, because Japan was "mindful of the background of color."[64]

A. Philip Randolph, of course, deplored such views for their lack of scientific rigor. The editors of the *Messenger* were almost alone among black intellectuals in arguing that the real story of the conference was that Japan, Great Britain, and the United Sates were "forming a joint program against Russia, Germany," and other nations in Europe, "along with assassinating glances at India, Egypt, China and other undeveloped countries." The spreading threat of socialism in Europe, he explained, drove the three capitalist powers (America, England, and Japan) together. "Confronted by the red terror of democracy and socialism they are ready to unite against the common enemy without regard to nationality, race, creed, or color."[65]

Historians have assessed the outcome of the Washington Conference in terms that more closely fit those of Randolph than Du Bois or Johnson. Although black internationalism tended to be more flexible than socialism, owing to its ability to accommodate categories of class and race into its analysis of world affairs, it appears that in this instance the prominence given to race in the deliberations at Washington misled black internationalists as to the significance of the decisions made there. The Anglo-Japanese alliance was replaced by a four-power consultative agreement (which included France) to preserve each nation's insular possessions. Nine nations also agreed to "respect the sovereignty, the independence, and the territorial and administrative integrity of China."[66] Like the four-power agreement, the nine-power treaty did not contain any mechanism for enforcement. Japan's position in China was bolstered by private assurances from former secretary of state Elihu Root that nothing in the treaty compromised existing Japanese holdings in China. Americans, particularly those active in the growing internationalist organizations and peace movements, were most pleased with the five-power treaty limiting the number of capital ships (battleships, battle cruisers, and aircraft carriers) for the four powers and Italy. That treaty also placed restrictions on military fortifications in the Pacific west of Hawaii and north of Singapore, thereby conceding naval supremacy to Japan in the western Pacific.

Although Japanese and American naval officers criticized the naval treaty for jeopardizing their respective nations' security, the diplomats in both countries were more hopeful about the outcome of the conference. Japan forfeited its close alliance with Britain but found broader acceptance for its policies in the larger international community. The terms of the nine-power treaty left Japan in a strong position to dominate China's economic development. Hughes had also accomplished his aims. During the conference Japan committed itself to completing its withdrawal from Siberia, reached an agreement on Shantung with China, and removed the danger, however remote, of an Anglo-Japanese alliance against the United States. Most important, the China irritant had been removed from the American-Japanese relationship, opening the way, Hughes believed, for a "new era of good feeling in the Far East." [67]

The Chinese delegates concluded otherwise. Protesting that the great powers had cavalierly settled their disputes without considering China's position, they denounced the final agreements. Another demonstration erupted in Shanghai, and the Soviet Union, which was not represented at the conference, capitalized on Chinese disillusionment by strengthening its ties to Sun Yat-sen's revolutionary Nationalist Party.

Although black internationalists had misjudged the intentions of the great powers at the conference, their special perspective on world politics gave them a greater sensitivity to the ways in which American racism could affect government policies. The Washington system that Hughes devised received its first blow not from a revived Chinese nationalism, but from the resurgence of racist xenophobia in the United States. Much to the secretary's dismay, the National Origins Act of 1924 prohibited Japanese and Chinese from migrating to the United States. Hughes warned Congress against gratuitously insulting Japan, but his pleas were drowned out by the demands of Americans who continued to view the world in terms of color. The 1924 law also weakened the position of Japanese officials who promoted cooperation with the West and reminded the Japanese people that despite their achievements, white Americans viewed them as undesirable.[68]

African Americans reached the same conclusion. Even newspapers that supported immigration restriction to increase economic opportunities for African Americans argued against singling out any group on the basis of race. The *Chicago Defender* illustrated its opposition to anti-Japanese measures with a front-page cartoon showing a brick labeled "Land Shall Be Sold to Caucasians Only" bouncing off a Japanese and striking a black man. "Perhaps It Wasn't Intended for Us," read the caption, "But ———."[69] The *Defender's* position, though not unanimously endorsed by African Americans, represented the majority view. In previous instances of discrimination against the Japanese, the black press had tended to side with the immigrants. As the *Indianapolis Freeman* had explained in 1913, "Race proscriptive measures do not sound good to Negroes, and for reasons known." California's anti-Japanese measures seemed doubly hypocritical to African Americans because, despite the prejudice they faced, the immigrants had begun to succeed economically. "The Big sin committed by the Japanese," asserted the *Baltimore Afro-American*, "and that which made them so obnoxious to white California, was their thrift and progress."[70] This analysis of anti-Japanese prejudice resonated with black Americans because many also believed that they faced discrimination because whites feared black economic success.

When discussion of the plight of Japanese immigrants surfaced in the black press in the period 1900–24, it was derived mostly from second-hand sources. In this respect, black American opinions about the Japanese were similar to African American perceptions of Japan's foreign policy. At a time when white-owned wire services and newspapers were extending their coverage to Asia, the black American press lacked the resources to post regular correspondents abroad. Newspapers and journals carried occasional reports from African American travelers to Japan or China, but for the most part black American journalists had to take stories from other sources and present them from the African American point of view.

If Japan remained something of an abstraction for African Americans, a challenge to the myth of white superiority and an ally in the struggle against racism, the Japanese in America were only slightly more familiar. As late as 1940, fewer than 75,000 African Americans out of a total population of approximately 13 million lived in Los Angeles, Oakland, and San Francisco, the centers of Japanese immigration. This meant that most African Americans derived their opinions on the Japanese in America from secondhand sources such as journalists, who were also unlikely to have direct contact with their subjects. In the instances where Japanese and African Americans interacted, it is difficult to determine how or if that experience influenced the views of black Americans outside California. One social survey completed in the 1920s indicated that African Americans and Japanese in California coexisted on a friendly basis in one transitional neighborhood. But as Quintard Taylor notes in his study of black Americans in Seattle, little has been written about the interaction of nonwhite groups in urban areas. In Seattle, African Americans lived in a racially mixed neighborhood with Filipinos, Chinese, and Japanese. Taylor found fragmentary evidence that Japanese and Chinese businesses were less discriminatory toward black Americans than those owned by whites. But he also noted that although the main Japanese-owned newspaper vigorously opposed anti-Japanese restrictions, it rarely commented on discriminatory measures against the city's smaller black population.[71] A study of Japanese Americans conducted in the mid-1990s concludes that although "they lived mixed in geographically with lots of non-Japanese, most Nisei [second-generation Japanese] inhabited a separate social world, effectively segregated from any intimate contact with the non-Japanese people around them."[72]

African American contacts with Chinese in America were only slightly more frequent than interaction with Japanese. As late as 1940 the largest group of Chinese, 17,782, lived in San Francisco, which was home to only 4,846 African Americans. Nevertheless, in the 1870s black Americans on the West Coast had joined in anti-Chinese protests, largely out of fear that the new laborers threatened their job opportunities. Black Americans were also well aware that plantation owners in the South sought to replace black labor with Chinese labor after the Civil War. "Better Shanghee than Timbuctoo!" asserted one white proponent of this scheme.[73] According to David Hellwig, despite the attempts of white businesses to pit one group against the other, black American leaders frequently recognized the similarities in the way the Chinese and African Americans were treated and opposed discriminatory measures.[74] One example was Horace Cayton Sr., a prominent Seattle editor, who welcomed Chinese immigrants into the Pacific Northwest as a means of developing the region's economy.[75]

But African Americans also had judged the Chinese as a people apart, "a class of people who use no common dictates of reason while among us, who are pagans in religion, inhuman in their traits, most scurrilous when their feelings are irritated, illiterate in intellectual education and of the doctrines of morality, and lastly wholly incompetent to become true citizens."[76] Even after the Chinese Exclusion Law of 1882 ended fears that coolie labor would drive down the wages of black workers, African Americans continued to see the "celestials" as incapable of assimilation. In 1911 Booker T. Washington doubted that "any other portion of the population remains so thoroly [sic] foreign as is true of the Chinaman."[77] More than a decade later, in 1922, the *Chicago Whip* complained that the Chinese "come into this country and retain eating sticks, sandals, and queues for many years and they always think as Chinese."[78]

On occasion, black American leaders noted the unwillingness of Japanese and Chinese to mix with African Americans. T. Thomas Fortune reported that during the Louisiana Purchase Exposition in 1904, "a high Japanese official" declared that "'High class Japanese and Chinese desire to associate exclusively with white people. We wish the colored people would let us alone.'" Fortune attributed this rebuff to the "weakness of human nature that causes the darker races to war among themselves and to desire to curry favor with those who, for the time being are dominant in a given environment." But he went on to say that on his Asian sojourn he found no evidence of prejudice when he visited Japan and China.[79] Civic leader Mary Church Terrell complained to a Japanese delegate to the Washington Conference that Japanese were quick to snub blacks. In her memoir, however, she acknowledged that since the Japanese had so many troubles of their own, it was understandable that they would be reluctant to associate with ostracized African Americans.[80]

According to Roger Daniels and Harry Kitano, African Americans in California resented the Japanese because they rejected any attempt to classify them as Negroes.[81] The *Chicago Defender* bitterly denounced Ozawa Takao when he sought citizenship on the grounds that Japanese were racially part of the white race. "Chink and his cousin the smooth slippery Jap, have been taught to scorn the Race or lose the little footing they may now boast," complained the editors.[82] In 1922, two years after the Supreme Court ruled against Ozawa, the *Defender* continued to complained that Japanese longed to be considered white.[83] Black Americans were also concerned with evidence of prejudice among Chinese. Principal places of contact for African Americans and Chinese were the small businesses run by the latter. A frequent complaint voiced in black American newspapers was that Chinese restaurant and club owners discriminated against black patrons to keep their white customers happy.[84]

As this brief summary suggests, African American views of Chinese and Japanese immigrants were hardly uncritical. David Hellwig has persuasively argued that although African Americans opposed race-specific proscriptions, they frequently succumbed to the same ethnocentrism as white Americans.[85] It is significant that much of the hostility directed toward Asian immigrants stemmed from a belief that either Japanese or Chinese were betraying the common interest they shared with black Americans as people of color. Moreover, even after the Ozawa case, most black Americans held the Japanese in higher esteem than the Chinese. In part it appears that black American leaders responded favorably to the interest in African American life displayed by visiting Japanese such as K. K. Kawakami. But Japan's status as a great power and its campaign for racial equality at the Paris Peace Conference almost certainly account for the greater empathy and admiration African Americans displayed for the Japanese. In contrast, China's disorganization and prostration before the white powers elicited mostly scorn from African Americans.[86]

Given the infrequent interaction between these peoples, it is probable that international events did more to shape African American images of Chinese and Japanese than did domestic contacts. Even glaring cases of prejudice toward black Americans on the part of Asians were outweighed by major developments abroad. In January 1927 the nationally distributed *Pittsburgh Courier* reported that the Bamboo Inn, a famous Chinese after-hours club in Harlem, had recently barred black patrons from one of its early morning affairs. "That colored people have made the proprietor wealthy is a well known fact," complained the *Courier*, "and that the Oriental employees of the inn have constantly slurred their colored guests is another well known fact."[87]

This gross insult did not prevent the same journal from rejoicing at the widespread panic caused by the northward movement of Chinese Nationalist forces under Chiang Kai-shek. A month after the Bamboo Room snubbed Harlem's revelers, the *Courier* explained that the Europeans "talk no longer of 'teaching the Chinks a lesson.' All they hope to do now is to keep the Chinese from murdering the missionaries and merchants who are wildly flocking to the treaty ports for protection. The Chinese have grown too powerful to be bulldozed any longer by white imperialists." According to the *Courier*'s editor, China's awakening was part of a larger international movement. "The defeat of Russia at the hands of Japan dealt white supremacy a heavy blow in the Orient and the imminent ousting of white imperialists from China will deal it even a heavier blow." Having learned the lesson that only the weak are enslaved, China was "going methodically and efficiently about the business of freeing herself. Some day India will do the same. Some day Africa will do the same!"[88]

In applauding Chinese militancy, the editor of the *Pittsburgh Courier* struck a defiant pose without actually endorsing the use of violence by black Americans to obtain equal rights. By identifying with independence movements abroad, black opinion makers fostered the idea of black internationalism and employed a rhetoric that in tone and substance would appeal to a broad range of readers in the African American community. The *Courier* used events in China, such as the murder of an American woman, as a mirror held up to white society at home, an example of "the great law of compensation" in action. In the South, black women were routinely "attacked shot and butchered" yet no marines came to their defense.[89] China's awakening under the tutelage of Bolshevik agents also served as a warning to white America of the perils of racism. Adopting the vocabulary of the militant Left, the otherwise safely middle-class *Courier* declared:

> All over the world the forces of imperialistic exploitation are being chal-
> lenged by the enlightened and militant students and workers. . . . Every-
> where throughout the world, wherever articulate groups can be found
> the revolt is on. Due to the fact that the big imperialist nations are white
> nations while the exploited ones are, in the main, colored, the contest is
> resolving itself between white and colored peoples, with one exception.
> That exception is Russia, which some people claim is not a white but a
> Mongolian nation.[90]

A more striking example of the malleability of the ideology of black internationalism would be difficult to imagine. In one deft passage, the *Courier* glossed over Japanese imperialism in Asia, inducted Russia into the ranks of the colored nations, and implicitly associated black interna-tionalism with communism. The paper further predicted that if the Na-tionalists "allied with Soviet Russia, win China, it will be difficult to pre-vent India, French Indo-China, the Dutch East Indies and Burmah [*sic*] from raising the red flag. This would mean not only the winning of inde-pendence by these subject peoples, but it would also mean the extension of Communism over two-thirds of humanity."[91] Two decades before Ameri-cans became familiar with the domino theory in international politics they knew the same phenomenon by another name. What African Americans hailed as the emerging unity of the darker races, their white compatriots saw as the "Rising Tide of Color."

[3]

Class or Color?

After the Imperial Navy destroyed the American fleet at Midway, the Pacific became a highway for the advancing Japanese forces. The conquest of Hawaii enabled the Japanese to launch an invasion of the West Coast of the United States and to establish bases for bombing the Midwest. As expected, Japanese efforts against the more powerful foe benefited from the uprising of ten million black Americans led by Marcus Garvey. The beaten Americans sued for peace after a successful attack on New York. In the wake of their victories, Japanese emissaries gloated as a humbled Lothrop Stoddard participated in the negotiations.

•

This depiction of the next war, taken from Sato Kojiro's *A Fantasy of War between Japan and the United States* (1921), was one of a growing number of "invasion scenarios" to appear in Japan in the interwar period. The prevalence of such war fantasies is one measure of how American allusions to a rising tide of color fed countervailing worries of a "white peril" in Japan after World War I. As John Stephan has noted, most efforts in this genre carried the same "literary baggage (destruction of the U.S. Pacific fleet, seizure of Hawaii, uprisings of American minorities, and so forth)."[1] But Japanese expressions of solidarity with other nonwhite peoples were not confined to the realm of fiction.

During the Paris Peace Conference, Japanese delegates and journalists fought a losing battle to gain official recognition of the equality of all races in the League of Nations Covenant. That failure, followed by the flaring of a brief crisis in U.S.-Japan relations over land tenure in California, as well as American opposition to Japanese policy in China and Siberia, led many nationalists to see war as inevitable. The limitations placed on Japanese naval strength by the Washington Conference, the severing of the Anglo-Japanese alliance, and the exclusion provisions of the 1924 Immigration Act weakened the standing of pro-Western statesmen and appeared to confirm the worst fears of staunch nationalists. In the 1920s these ultra-patriots redoubled their commitment to Japan's mission as the liberator of Asia's nonwhite peoples. In practice, however, Japanese nationalists concentrated their attention on expanding Japan's domain in Asia, often justifying their actions by exposing the racial hypocrisy of Western countries. In this way, Japan's "double patriots," as one historian called them, produced a rhetorical defense of Japanese imperialism that simultaneously rebuked the West and appealed to the world's colonial peoples.

Japanese propaganda also appealed to many African Americans. Black internationalists continued to see Japan as an important symbol of racial progress and a potential ally against racism. Indeed, by the end of the 1920s black Americans' admiration for Japan was so prevalent that apparently even Tokyo's renewed aggression in China might not weaken its appeal in the black community. The onset of the Great Depression and the resulting growth of the Communist Party in black communities posed another challenge to African American support for Japan. At the same time that they helped organize black workers, CPUSA members denounced Japanese foreign policy for its exploitation of China and its hostility to the Soviet Union. Could black Americans work with the Communists at home but reject the party's views on international affairs? In the 1920s no such dilemma had presented itself. But during the strife-filled 1930s the growing appeal of the CPUSA and the harsh reality of Japan's aggression in China compelled black internationalists to answer a question of fundamental importance. What mattered most in world affairs, class or color?

For Japanese policymakers, the answer to that question seemed deceptively easy. During the 1920s new nationalist associations and quasi-secret organizations proliferated almost as rapidly as war fantasy literature. Existing societies expanded their activities in response to the perceived challenge to Japan's interests. In the latter category the most important organization to achieve notoriety in the interwar period was Kokuryūkai. Founded in 1901 by Uchida Ryohei, the coleader of a Nationalist society that engaged in intelligence work in China before the Sino-Japanese War, Kokuryūkai (literally the "Amur River Society") took its name from the Japanese term for the river on the Russian-Manchurian border. The Chinese knew the same river as the Black Dragon (Heilung-chiang), which is how the Japanese identified it when writing in the Chinese characters called Kanji. The Western press translated the group's name as the Black Dragon Society.[2] Although the name Black Dragon Society conjured up images of a Fu-Manchu–like conspiratorial organization dedicated to world conquest, the group was neither secret nor committed to a global crusade. Instead, Kokuryūkai used public rallies and propaganda to pressure Tokyo into defending what Nationalists believed was Japan's rightful claim to Manchuria.

As part of its propaganda effort, Kokuryūkai published the *Asian Review*, an English-language monthly on Japanese politics and economics. In the first edition the *Review*'s editors explained that the journal's purpose was to "interpret the true Japanese ideals to the world." They denied Japan's imperial ambitions in Asia, proclaimed their desire to see "our colored brothers of all shades of opinion to present a united front" on racial equality, and blamed Americans and Europeans for inciting anti-Japanese agitation in China and Korea.[3] In subsequent issues, the editors gave considerable attention to the maltreatment of African Americans. The *Review* labeled lynching America's "greatest stigma" and carried numerous stories on violence committed against black Americans.[4]

Japanese interest in the plight of black Americans was well known to African American leaders. Journalists for the *Asian Review* in the United States gathered statistics on lynching and mob violence provided by the NAACP and the Tuskegee Institute, reported on rallies held by Marcus Garvey, and reprinted an interview with Garvey originally published in the *Asahi Shimbun*, one of Japan's largest dailies.[5] Black American newspapers completed the circle by informing their readers of Japanese interest in their plight.[6]

Kokuryūkai's condemnation of white terrorism in America may well have been sincere, but it served the interest of the Japanese government to remind Americans of their own failings. Indeed, it appears that the *Asian Review* enjoyed the support of the Foreign Ministry precisely because it could address controversial subjects with a bluntness that diplomats avoided. Listed among the journal's many supporters were former foreign minister Ishii Kikujirō; Baron Makino, recently vice chief of the Japanese delegation at Versailles; and Vice Minister for Foreign Affairs Hanihara Masanao, Navy Minister Admiral Katō Tomosaburō, Foreign Minister Uchida Yasuya, and Prime Minister Hara Takashi.[7]

Skepticism concerning the editors' intentions seems warranted in light of the journal's position on the delicate issue of minorities and subject peoples within Japan's own empire. Despite its self-proclaimed duty to serve as the voice of the world's downtrodden, the *Asian Review* reverted to the time-worn practice of blaming unrest within the Japanese empire on outside agitators and foreign propagandists.[8] Under different circumstances, such feeble explanations might have appeared unconvincing to black leaders who had so recently seen similar accusations used to justify the mob violence of the Red Summer. But Japan's criticism of American racism, its support of racial equality at Paris, and its status as a victim of racism outweighed whatever transgressions the Japanese committed in Asia.

If African American leaders seemed unwilling to investigate Japan's policies in China and Korea too closely, they were also disinclined to probe too deeply into Japanese racial attitudes. Of course, any attempt to discuss the racial views of a large population must remain at the level of broad generalization. Nevertheless, if black writers and other commentators had delved beneath the surface rhetoric of Japanese officials, they would have encountered ideas about race relations that were bound to leave them uneasy. Underlying Japanese attitudes toward other peoples in this era was a powerful belief in the purity of the Japanese race. Even before Japan became an expansionist power, various ethnic groups such as the Ainu of Hokkaido and the Okinawans faced discrimination in employment and government policies. The Burakumin, a group once associated with "unclean" trades such as leather tanning, faced segregation and economic hardship despite the absence of any distinguishing cultural or ethnic features. The stigma attached to membership in this group, like the taint whites associated with color, was passed from generation to generation.[9]

The myth of Japanese purity and Japan's advanced level of industrial development combined to convince many nationalists that they had a duty to mediate between the less advanced societies of Asia and the Western world. In times of conflict, such as the Sino-Japanese War, the tension between the self-image of Japan as leader of Asia and the perception that industrial development made Japan the most "white" of the colored peoples produced startling consequences. When Japanese woodblock artists glorified their nation's victory over China, they depicted Japanese soldiers with round eyes and European features. The Chinese, in contrast, were presented as unmistakably Asian, with slanting eyes, broad flat noses, flying pigtails, and wild-looking visages, much as they were in Western caricatures. As Donald Keene has aptly suggested, it was as though the Japanese were viewing the Chinese with Western eyes. During the Russo-Japanese War illustrations portrayed the Russians and Japanese as almost identical, that is, as white.[10]

The elusiveness of racial identity and the uses to which race could be put for ideological purposes were demonstrated by the Reverend Sydney Gulick, an American educator in Japan and a close friend of journalist K. K. Kawakami. Gulick, who devoted his career to the ideal of American-Japanese comity, sought to allay American fears by explaining that "the intermarriage of whites and Japanese is not analogous to that of whites and Negroes. . . . Caucasians and Japanese are, to begin with, much closer. The Japanese race already has much white blood." High-class Japanese, Gulick assured readers, "could easily pass for an Italian or Spaniard." To demonstrate his point, Gulick, apparently without fear of giving offense, used his friend Kawakami as an example. The Japanese journalist was married to a white American woman and the couple had two lovely daughters, both of whom, according to Gulick, looked white.[11] Japanese efforts to pass for white seemed fulfilled in 1930, when the Union of South Africa agreed to treat Japanese members of the business community the same as their European and American peers.[12]

Meanwhile, as Japan expanded its empire onto the Asian mainland, Japanese officials produced stereotypes of their new subjects that paralleled depictions of the other in Western texts. Government documents described the Koreans as "lazy, who use their extra money for gambling and sake, and make no effort to improve themselves." Schoolchildren derided Chinese as cowardly "Chinks." Even those who ostensibly worked to improve relations between different peoples found it difficult to break free of racial stereotypes. Following passage of the 1924 Immigration Act, Abe Isoo, a leading Christian Socialist, expressed an understanding of American reluctance to live with the Japanese in their midst. After all, Isoo explained, how would Japanese like to have "filthy Chinamen of the lowest class," with all their unpleasant smells and customs, in the middle of Tokyo?[13]

Japanese nationalists' perceptions of their nation's special role in Asia produced a hierarchical view of the region's inhabitants that mimicked the Social Darwinism of the West. Publicly, Japanese imperialists endorsed a policy of "racial harmony" as the best means of developing Manchuria and Korea. By the late 1920s, however, they had contrived a division of labor that placed the Japanese, as a more advanced race, in command of the region's lesser peoples whom they governed. This scheme, originally devised for Korea and Manchuria, was later expanded to include the rest of China, Micronesia, and Southeast Asia.[14]

Black American writers and other commentators occasionally criticized Japanese imperialism, but with the exception of Randolph's *Messenger*, they were more likely to emphasize Western prejudice toward Japan and the part Japan played in threatening the idea of white supremacy. During the interwar period black Americans traveling to Japan reported on the graciousness of their hosts, contrasting such treatment with the discrimination they faced at home. Dignitaries such as W. E. B. Du Bois, James Weldon Johnson, and Robert Russa Moton, Booker T. Washington's successor at Tuskegee, as well as schoolteachers and sightseers, received warm welcomes in Japan.[15] Skeptics would later point out that individual instances of hospitality hardly amounted to convincing evidence of Japan's commitment to racial equality. Indeed, the readiness of the Union of South Africa to treat Japanese as honorary whites proved that even the most racist of nations could play the role of benevolent host when trade or affairs of state were involved. Nevertheless, whatever their private thoughts on the subject, black visitors publicly used their experiences in Japan to confirm the favorable impressions already gained from their associations with Japanese journalists in the United States.

The willingness of black leaders to overlook policies that belied Japan's claims to leadership of the world's nonwhite peoples illustrates the persistence among African Americans of a worldview that race was the determining variable in international politics. In the 1920s neither the Socialist Party nor the newly formed CPUSA made many converts among black Americans. Prominent African Americans rejected socialism and the Socialist Party after World War I. By the mid-1920s even A. Philip Randolph concluded that it was hopelessly naive to think that race did not matter in labor relations. After leaving the party, but not completely abandoning socialism, Randolph committed himself to movements that were controlled by African Americans.[16]

For most African Americans, the idiom of race offered the best means of explaining world affairs. Black resistance to other theories of international relations continued even after the global economy collapsed and Japan seized Manchuria. The newly established Nationalist government of China under the leadership of Chiang Kai-shek was one of the first victims of the worldwide depression that began in 1929. As will be recalled, the early stages of the Kuomintang's campaign had thrilled African Americans as much as it alarmed Western residents in China.

In 1927 Chiang suddenly halted the Northern Expedition long enough to turn on his communist allies before they had the chance to eliminate him. The subsequent white terror routed but failed to exterminate the "Reds," as they became known to American journalists, and the Communists regrouped in the hills of the southeastern province of Kiangsi.

Chiang's forces resumed their march northward. By 1928, through a combination of negotiation and fighting, the Nationalists achieved at least nominal sovereignty over China south of the Great Wall. The United States, which had the least to lose in China, became the first government to relinquish tariff control to the newly established government in Nanking. Chiang still faced the daunting task of bringing his ambitious military chieftains to heel, the Kuomintang was a swamp of factionalism and intrigue, and China's economic prospects, even with tariff autonomy, seemed bleak. Nevertheless, Chiang's apparent willingness to accommodate American and European interests in China made him far preferable to the Communists. U.S. aid and investment began to arrive, while numerous technical advisers from the United States and the League of Nations lent their support to the reconstruction of China after more than a decade of warlord rule.

By 1931 Chiang Kai-shek had begun to expand the Nationalist movement into Manchuria, an area lying outside of his control. The Japanese, who considered this region vital to their economic and military security, perceived Nationalist activity as a violation of the treaty rights they had assiduously accumulated in Manchuria since their war with Russia. On 18 September 1931 Japanese troops took it upon themselves to preserve Japan's control over this crucial territory. Staging an explosion on the Japanese-owned South Manchurian Railroad, the soldiers of the Kwantung Army retaliated against this Chinese "provocation" by seizing the city of Mukden and commencing larger military operations in Manchuria. As the Kwantung Army expanded its conquest of Manchuria, the Western powers, paralyzed by the depression, remained uncertain how they should respond. Finally the League of Nations sent an investigating team to Manchuria.

In Washington, President Herbert Hoover and Secretary of State Henry Stimson disagreed over what steps to take, with Stimson more eager to intervene diplomatically than the president. Hoover and a significant number of American diplomats privately recognized the importance of Manchuria to Japan. They also conceded that the region had never really been under the control of the Chinese central government since the fall of the Manchu dynasty in 1911. Stimson countered that Japan's actions threatened to torpedo the Washington Conference system and destroy the efforts of those who had sought to establish a process for peaceful change in international affairs. Seconding that view, liberal peace groups such as the Women's International League for Peace and Freedom urged the administration to stop Japan.

In the end, the administration did little more than voice its opposition to Japanese aggression and issue unimpressive threats. In January 1932 Stimson notified Japan and China that the United States would not recognize any infringement on its treaty rights or any violation of Chinese sovereignty brought about by force. The Hoover-Stimson nonrecognition doctrine failed to deter the Japanese. That same month the Japanese navy attacked Shanghai, the center of Western influence and prestige in China. The United States responded by sending additional ships and marines to the area, but the Japanese eventually withdrew of their own accord.

Stimson's final bid to save the Washington Conference system appeared in a letter to the chairman of the Senate Foreign Relations Committee, William Borah. The secretary explained that a violation of one of the terms of the Washington Conference treaties would release the United States from any obligation to abide by the other treaties. In other words, the United States would be free to build its navy beyond the limits imposed at Washington. This too was a hollow threat. In the end China had only American words to comfort it, whereas Japan now had Manchuria.[17]

Stimson's defense of the Washington Conference system and his insistence that China should be left to work out its own destiny struck many African American commentators as the height of hypocrisy. According to these observers, America's own record of imperialism in the Western Hemisphere and the Pacific made it an unlikely guardian of propriety in international affairs. As Du Bois acidly observed in the *Crisis*, "The United States (which stole a large part of Mexico, invaded Nicaragua and Santo Domingo and raped Haiti, annexed the Philippines and Porto Rico, dominates Cuba, because of her economic interests and investments) is now explaining the Golden Rule to Japan."[18]

China was also judged to be unworthy as an object of concern. Chiang's rightward move during the Northern Expedition and his toleration of a continued Western presence in China, including the humiliating practice of extraterritoriality, deprived the Nationalists of African American sympathy. "The Chinese have become a kind of 'uncle Tom' of Asia," declared the *Baltimore Afro-American*. "As we see it," the paper's editors explained, "Japan is kicking China in the pants to make it stand up and be a man."[19] In keeping with the prevailing belief in the solidarity of nonwhite peoples, the *Philadelphia Tribune* stated that Japan was actually helping its Asian "cousin" to throw off the yoke of white oppression. China's prostration before the West made it Japan's "manifest destiny" to rescue Asia for the Asians, argued the *Chicago Defender*.[20]

Appalled by such opinions, African American Communists argued that, as exploited workers, black Americans should rally to China's defense against the present "robber war of Japanese imperialism." A decade removed from the African Blood Brotherhood and his earlier enthusiasm for Japan, Cyril Briggs now warned black Americans that "the only way in which we can win our freedom is by uniting with the working class of all races." Briggs alluded to the problem Communists faced in overcoming the appeal of black internationalism to many African Americans when he reminded readers that as "colonial peoples," their true allies were found among workers of all races. Briggs lumped Japan with the other oppressors of China, Britain, France, and the United States, and argued that it sought to destroy the one true hope for black American toilers, the Soviet Union.[21] To be persuasive, however, Briggs needed to undermine Japan's reputation among African Americans. Reeducating blacks to view international relations from a communist perspective would be no easy task. In 1932 black perceptions of China as an Uncle Tom and white hostility to Japan convinced many African Americans that race, not class, still mattered most in international politics.

Shortly after the Manchurian crisis receded from public attention, African Americans had a new opportunity to demonstrate their fraternal concern for other members of the darker races. In 1932 Mohandas Gandhi launched a hunger strike to protest a British plan to divide the Indian population into separate electorates based on caste. The Mahatma's insistence on the unity of the Indian peoples and his determined opposition to the segregation of his country's "Untouchables" resonated among African Americans for obvious reasons. Although black leaders continued to debate the applicability of Gandhi's methods of peaceful resistance to America, all of them warmly supported his battle against India's Jim Crow system of segregation.

Gandhi's defiance of Britain, his apparent willingness to risk everything in the liberation of his people, contrasted sharply with the images most African Americans had of Chiang Kai-shek in China. "There is today in the world but one living maker of miracles," enthused Du Bois, "and that is Mahatma Gandhi. He stops eating, and three hundred million Indians, together with the British Empire, hold their breath until they can talk sense. All America sees in Gandhi a joke, but the joke is America."[22]

In addition to the *Crisis*, such major black American periodicals as the *Chicago Defender, Pittsburgh Courier, Atlanta Daily World, New York Amsterdam News*, and *Norfolk Journal and Guide* covered the drama unfolding in India. The amount of space black editors used to provide an African American perspective on the Manchurian crisis and the Gandhian saga suggests that most journalists believed that readers would attach considerable importance to distant events even as blacks were struggling to survive during the bleakest period of the Great Depression. The Gandhian message of resistance, organization, and dignity, hammered home through numerous editorials, could also be heard on the street corners and in the public halls of America's major cities.

Most prominent among the numerous groups proffering programs for alleviating the plight of black Americans were the representatives of a revived Communist Party. In times of relative prosperity, the great majority of African Americans evinced little interest in attaching themselves to a political party that would only push them further to the fringes of American society. But after a decade of meager gains and following the onset of the depression, more blacks were willing to give the party a second look. Because they were employed primarily in service industries and nonunionized unskilled jobs, black Americans suffered disproportionately during the depression. The sudden and devastating economic contraction also swept black shop owners and landlords out of business at an alarming rate. CPUSA officials sought to take advantage of this new opportunity to recruit blacks by adjusting and readjusting their message to appeal to what they believed were the special needs of this oppressed class. These adjustments were often clumsy, however, and the party's doctrinal oscillations left observers baffled.

During the early years of the depression the CPUSA, following the lead of the Communist International (Comintern) in Moscow, endorsed the idea of black secession into a separate nation in the heart of the Black Belt. As Mark Naisson has shown, the overall message from Moscow concerned the need to place the special circumstances of black Americans in the forefront of the party's agenda. In effect, African Americans would not be joining the party so much as the party would be joining them. At the local level this resulted in a heavy emphasis on integration. To drive home this point, the CPUSA engaged in showy trials of white party members who resisted complete integration with black members on terms of social equality. At the same time, however, the CPUSA's theoretical attachment to a separate black state hung around its neck like an albatross. Most African Americans hotly denounced the idea, which resembled nothing so much as the black homelands later created in South Africa, as ludicrous. George Padmore, a West Indian member of the Comintern, recalled: "In the face of the implacable hostility of all sections of the Negro population, from middle-class to workers, from radicals to conservatives, the 'Black Belt State' proposal proved a heavy flop." [23]

Despite Moscow's strategic blunder, the CPUSA continued to make inroads into black communities during the depression. The willingness of party members to place themselves in life-threatening situations to organize southern sharecroppers and their tireless efforts on behalf of urban workers more than compensated for the Black Belt state. As the publisher of the *Baltimore Afro-American* explained, "The Communists appear to be the only party going our way, for which Allah be praised." The party's highly visible defense of the Scottsboro Boys, a case in which nine young black men were accused of raping two white women, and Angelo Herndon, a black activist arrested on charges of fomenting insurrection, did even more to win the support of many black Americans.[24]

But what party workers gained through their initiative, Moscow forfeited, at least in part. No sooner had the Comintern relegated the idea of a Black Belt state to the dustbin of history, then Moscow further alienated black Americans by seeming to profit from the Italian conquest of Ethiopia. Black Americans possessed a deep affection for the East African kingdom because of its storied place in African American theology and because the highland nation had maintained its independence during the European scramble for Africa. By 1934, however, Benito Mussolini's fascist empire was menacing Ethiopian independence. Determined to avenge Italy's humiliating defeat in 1886 at the hands of the Abyssinians (now Ethiopians), the fascist dictator launched an invasion from neighboring Italian Somalialand in October 1935.[25]

The crisis galvanized the African American community as no other international event had done up to that time. Pro-Ethiopian activism among black Americans took many forms. Street rallies and fund-raising drives were the most visible constructive actions. Less helpful was the rumble that occurred between African Americans and Italian Americans following a heavyweight boxing match in which champion Joe Louis (the Brown Bomber) defeated his Italian opponent Primo Carnera.[26]

During Ethiopia's hour of peril various black protest groups beseeched the League of Nations to halt Italian aggression. This public diplomacy proved unavailing. In truth, black American leaders expected little help from the white nations of Europe. They did, however, hope that the Soviet Union, which had so vehemently denounced imperialism in the past, would take the lead in demanding action from the league. Here too they were disappointed. The Soviets' best chance to place the issue before the League of Nations came in May 1935, during the long period of diplomatic tension that preceded Italy's invasion. Although Russian representative Maxim Litvinov presided over the opening of the league's session, he studiously avoided any reference to Italy's intimidation of Ethiopia. Stunned by the Russian's silence, Walter White, the NAACP's executive secretary, cabled Litvinov to ask, "Has Russia abandoned its alleged opposition [to] imperialism. . . . Does your anti-imperialism stop at black nations?"[27]

Injury followed insult when the *New York Times* alleged that Russia sold oil and other raw materials to Mussolini's war machine. Infuriated by this apparent betrayal, but also somewhat relieved, one suspects, to be able to distance itself from the communist state, the NAACP denounced Soviet opportunism.[28] Combining its disdain for the now moribund idea of a separate black state with its outrage over Russia's betrayal of Ethiopia, the *Crisis* asked:

> They swear by all that's holy that such a plan of plain segregation is *not* segregation, but who can predict what they will say tomorrow or next week? Anyway, we maintain that the mere existence of the proposal proves that the idea of separateness is uppermost in the minds of the Red brain-trust and not the idea of oneness. And in advancing this theory of separation, the Communists are hand in hand with the southern ruling class which they so delight to lambaste. But since the Moscow masters are opportunists in the matter of war profit, who would dare to criticize the American followers for opportunism in a little thing like segregation? Who indeed, except the segregated American Negro?[29]

In the aftermath of the Ethiopian debacle, a significant number of black members left the CPUSA and African American enrollment stagnated. Moscow's perceived betrayal of Ethiopia and its dogmatic support for a Black Belt state would have destroyed the party in African American communities, such as Harlem, had it not been for the tireless efforts of local party members to rally to the cause of Ethiopia. Moreover, local officials continued to devote most of their attention to the core issues of jobs and wages. The CPUSA survived but it did so by forming popular front alliances with black religious and civic organizations previously condemned as "agents of the bourgeoisie."[30] For the moment, however, the Comintern's policies had gravely injured the efforts of African American Communists to propagate a socialist perspective on international affairs.

Ethiopia received little aid from the outside world during its brief struggle against Italy. Nevertheless, African Americans found it instructive to compare the response of the nonwhite world, in terms of moral support, to the deafening silence emanating from the League of Nations headquarters in Geneva. The *Pittsburgh Courier* informed its readers that Gandhi had appealed to his countrymen to contribute money to a Red Cross mission to

Ethiopia. The paper also quoted the Mahatma's declaration that "Although India is under British rule she is a member of the League of Nations. She is fully entitled to assist another nation even in a non-combatant way."[31] Even more significant was columnist George Schuyler's praise for Gandhi. The irreverent Schuyler had once written for Randolph's *Messenger*, but he found his true calling and a wider readership among black Americans when he began deflating the reputations of the black elite. The *Courier* columnist had at first chided African American admirers of Gandhi with the observation that "whenever a big leader begins talking about 'God' taking a hand, he is either insincere or ignorant." But Schuyler soon changed his mind. Moved by Gandhi's public defense of Ethiopia, the usually cynical Schuyler now hailed the Indian leader as "a brilliant English-trained attorney." "Gandhi's moral alignment with Ethiopia in the present crisis may well halt Mussolini," he predicted.[32]

India's moral support failed to halt the Italian invasion, but in the weeks before the onslaught, rumors that other countries were preparing more substantial aid for Ethiopia abounded in the African American community. The expectation that Japan might aid the East African kingdom rested on the general assumption of shared interest between those two independent nonwhite nations as well as on the more concrete evidence of increasingly closer trade relations. By the mid-1930s 80 percent of Ethiopia's imports came from Japan. In 1933 Tokyo announced that the daughter of a Japanese prince planned to marry one of Emperor Haile Selassie's nephews. (Italian protests subsequently forced the cancellation of the marriage.)[33]

In 1935, as international tensions grew, the African American *Indianapolis Recorder* told readers that Japanese, Chinese, and Egyptians were volunteering to fight for Ethiopia. The *Pittsburgh Courier*'s special correspondent to Ethiopia reported that Ethiopian pilots were training in Japan. Even more encouraging were the efforts of several thousand student members of Kokuryūkai to prod Tokyo into the war on Ethiopia's behalf. Newspaper editors and diplomats in Rome talked ominously of an impending alliance of the darker races. The Japanese press and some officials responded with threats to punish Italy for its racist pretensions to superiority.[34]

Yet Japan, despite its growing interest in the Ethiopian trade, failed to intervene when Italy attacked the African kingdom. African American enthusiasm for Japan persisted, however. In November 1935 Leonard Robert Jordan (who also went by the name Robert O. Jordan), a Jamaican merchant seaman with experience in Japan, launched the Ethiopian Pacific

Movement in Harlem. Jordan, a former member of Garvey's UNIA, created the organization to foster an alliance between the darker races, starting with the superpatriots of the Black Dragon Society. The Ethiopian Pacific Movement gained few recruits from among Harlem's destitute citizens, but the attention it attracted, most notably from members of the U.S. government's internal security agencies, far outweighed its modest size.[35]

The Ethiopian crisis was a turning point in the development of black internationalism. As John Hope Franklin has noted, "Almost overnight even the most provincial among Negro Americans became international-minded."[36] For some, fascism in any form became the enemy. A small number of black American volunteers subsequently joined the Spanish Civil War to defend the doomed republic from General Francisco Franco's fascist legions. For others, the plight of Ethiopia heightened their sensitivity to the perceived color scheme in world affairs. James McIntyre, an associate of Marcus Garvey, wrote that after the sordid display by white capitalist and communist countries, peoples of African descent would best be advised to "pick a page from the book of Japan with its united and phenomenally progressive people."[37]

W. E. B. Du Bois, a year removed from his editorship of the *Crisis*, explained the significance of the African situation to readers of the influential journal *Foreign Affairs*. Waxing poetic, the scholar warned that if Italy conquered Ethiopia, "the whole colored world—India, China, Japan, Africa in Africa and in America, and all the South Seas and Indian South America—all that vast mass of men who have felt oppression and insults, the slavery and exploitation of white folk, will say: 'I told you so! There is no faith in them even toward each other. . . . Japan was right. The only path to freedom and equality is force, and force to the utmost.'" Du Bois also declared that "an understanding between Japan and China will close Asia to the white aggression, and India need no longer hesitate between passive resistance and open rebellion."[38]

The effects of the white world's betrayal of Ethiopia would also provoke Africans into rebellion against their colonial overlords. "Japan is regarded by all colored peoples as their logical leader," Du Bois continued, "No matter what Japan does or how she does it, excuse leaps to the lips of colored thinkers." As if to demonstrate his point, Du Bois explained that Japan's domination of Formosa, Korea, and Manchuria was no different from Europe's plundering of Asia "except for this vast difference: her program cannot be one based on race hate for the conquered, since racially these latter are one with the Japanese and are recognized as blood relatives. . . . Conquest and exploitation are brute facts of the present era, yet if they must come is it better that they come from members of your own or other races?"[39]

Du Bois, of course, already thought he knew the answer to that question. Over the next several years he would cling to this perception of Japan's role in China. Japan's rapprochement with Italy on the eve of the Ethiopian War, its prompt diplomatic recognition of Rome's conquest, and its refusal to recognize the Ethiopian government in exile did not alter his views.[40] Du Bois might have surmised, as did the new editors of the *Crisis*, that Japan's empire in Asia made it an unlikely source of comfort to victims of imperialism elsewhere. He might also have concluded that Japan's refusal to support international sanctions against Italy was part of a quid pro quo in which Rome recognized Tokyo's puppet state of Manchukuo.[41] Instead, he remained firm in his belief that Japanese imperialism was different. Even Japan's full-scale invasion of China below the Great Wall would fail to shake him from this conviction.

Du Bois's emphasis on the role of race in foreign affairs and his belief that racial affinity would prevail in the war between Japan and China came just as the American academic community was beginning to demolish the whole foundation of pseudoscience on which modern ideas of race rested. As early as 1928 Edward M. East had answered Lothrop Stoddard, Du Bois, and all others who either dreamed or fretted about a union of the darker races. "The Japanese and the Chinese despise each other," he insisted, "and both feel superior to the brown and black, and the Hindu had more caste tabus [*sic*] than either."[42]

Still the belief in the future solidarity of nonwhite peoples persisted. In 1936, the year Italy completed its conquest of Ethiopia, Ralph Bunche, a young Howard University political scientist and future diplomat, once more tried to bury the idea. Bunche intended his monograph, *A World View of Race*, as an attack on the very concept of race. He directed some of his strongest criticism against Stoddard and the Pan-Africanists. Referring to the frequent predictions of a global race war, Bunche declared: "Such beliefs are as fantastic as they are misleading. They assume that both white and black peoples of the earth have a common fundamental interest in the color of their skin. They ignore completely the class, tribal, religious, cultural, linguistic, nationalistic and other differences among both black and white peoples." In what was almost certainly a reply to Du Bois, Bunche added that "They carefully avoid the fact that for either a white or black man it is scarcely more pleasant to be exploited and oppressed by privileged members of one's own race than by members of some other." Bunche then made it clear that he discerned a pattern of a different sort emerging from the chaos of the depression. Race issues were beginning to merge with working-class issues. "Throughout the world," he declared, "the issue between the working and owning classes is sharpening."[43]

Bunche's monograph was part of the growing academic assault on the idea of race as a scientific category that gained momentum in the 1930s.[44] Although African Americans applauded these efforts to undermine the intellectual foundations of racism, they recognized that race, however imprecise a term, was still an important factor in world affairs. Racism had existed before scientists had given it their blessing, and it would continue after the science of race was discredited. Academic refutations of race as a biological category did not translate into independence for India or the African colonies. Biologists and social scientists might find race to be a socially constructed term of little analytic value, but as long as people of European ancestry held the inhabitants of Asia and Africa in subjection, black internationalists still found it useful to view the world in terms of color.

Black internationalists' belief in the emerging unity of the darker races thus continued to flourish in the early 1930s, and with it the widely held perception of Japan as leader. It had survived a challenge from the communist Left and thrived in the void created by liberal internationalism's failure to address the issue of race in world politics. As Penny Von Eschen has shown, in the aftermath of the Ethiopian conquest black Americans began to fill that void by fashioning their own broadly based internationalist movement against colonialism and fascism. Led by former Comintern member George Padmore, the movement blended communist doctrine with an emphasis on the role of race in world affairs. This new movement included black activists across the political spectrum and found its organizational expression in the Council on African Affairs (CAA).[45] The CAA's emphasis on race in international affairs and its focus on anticolonialism, especially in Africa and the West Indies, made the council an appealing home for black internationalists. But the CAA's support of a popular front against fascism created a dilemma for black Americans who continued to find some advantage in defending Japanese foreign policy. Black internationalists could support the CAA's attack on racial capitalism in the regions of the African diaspora, but many of them remained unwilling to accept a view of world affairs that made little distinction between Italy, Nazi Germany, and Japan.

The inability of the emerging anticolonial movement to break the intellectual ties that held black internationalists to Japan became evident in 1937, when skirmishing between Chinese and Japanese troops outside

Peking escalated into a full-scale invasion of China below the Great Wall. Once again large numbers of African Americans defended Japanese actions as necessary and even salutary for China. Foremost among them, of course, was W. E. B. Du Bois. Recently returned from a world tour that had included stops in Japan, Manchukuo, and Shanghai, the prolific commentator produced a series of columns for the *Pittsburgh Courier* in which he explained how China's turmoil made it necessary for the Japanese to impose order so the Chinese might one day progress to the point where they would be free from the threat of European imperialism. Du Bois described the special attention he received from government officials and assured readers that his warm reception in Manchukuo and Japan resulted from the Japanese sense of a "common brotherhood, a common suffering, and a common destiny" with twelve million black Americans. War, especially modern war, was a nightmare, Du Bois conceded, but one needed to ask if the Chinese in Manchukuo were better off under Japanese rule than they had been when left to the devices of corrupt warlords.[46]

Du Bois was critical of Japanese capitalism, but he believed that private capital had been used to benefit the public more in Manchukuo than in other colonial regions he had visited. Based on his brief visit, he concluded that Japanese imperialists were preferable to others in one crucial respect: the Japanese did not impose a color caste system on their subjects.[47] Although he reported on mining production in Manchukuo, Du Bois did not explain why Chinese wages for the same jobs came to a fraction of those earned by Japanese. Nor did he wonder about the grossly disproportionate numbers of injuries and deaths suffered by the Chinese working in Japanese enterprises. Instead, he abandoned any pretense of rigorous analysis and leaped to Japan's defense.[48]

In the autumn of 1937, following the outbreak of war below the Great Wall, Du Bois again attempted to explain the "mad muddle" of the Chinese-Japanese conflict. Japan sought to save China from Europe, he argued, but China "preferred to be a Coolie for England rather than acknowledge the only world leadership that did not mean color or caste." Du Bois added bitterly that the same "spirit that animates the 'white folks nigger' in the United States" motivated the Chinese to scorn Japan's guidance. He further admonished readers not to be fooled by American propaganda. Hate for Japan, not love for China, motivated white Americans, he asserted.[49]

Du Bois remained firm in his defense of Japan against what he perceived to be the racially motivated hostility of the West. When the U.S. State Department protested Japanese actions, Du Bois dismissed its com-

W. E. B. Du Bois in Japan during his controversial tour of Asia, December 1936. (Asahi Shimbun Newspapers)

plaints as mere hypocrisy. Characteristic was his cabled reply to an invitation from the American League against War and Fascism to endorse a meeting "for democracy and peace." "Am bitterly opposed to present effort of American and English capital," he explained, "to drive this nation into war against Japan[.] Such miserable war would be based on color prejudice and would put forward as false friends of China a nation which fought the opium war and is today the most ruthless exploiter of Chinese labor and a nation that passed and maintains the Chinese Exclusion Act."[50]

The *New York Age* agreed that "China will yet come to bless the day that she was beaten by Japan."[51] In contrast, the larger *New York Amsterdam News*, a pro–New Deal paper, argued that Japanese fascism was no different from the Italian variety, and, as far as the editors were concerned, communism was little better.[52] The *News*'s columnist, Adam Clayton Powell Jr., the young pastor of Harlem's venerable Abyssinian Church and an emerging figure in the African American protest movement, insisted that Japanese aggression in China was part of the rising tide of fascism in the world. Powell was disturbed that fascism's ultranationalism was destroying the natural ties that bound peoples of different nations. Comparing Japan's attack on China to recent violence in Haiti, he lamented that "The deed that shakes us more than even Japan's atrocities in China is the slaughter of Black Haitians by their lighter skinned brothers in Santo Domingo." Rather than choose between an internationalism based on either color or class, Powell hoped that "with a solidarity of race and with a unity of workers of all colors, pray God fascism shall not come."[53]

Although Powell refused to see Japan as the champion of the darker races, he did not hesitate to criticize the Roosevelt administration for its inconsistent response to Italian and Japanese aggression. "We have recently read the thundering denunciation of Japan by our own President Roosevelt," he observed. Yet the president, the pope, the British, and the French "were strangely silent during the dark days of Ethiopia's plight, but I said then, and I say now, one cannot fight the fascist menace in Spain and not in Ethiopia, in China and not in the South. Fascism must be fought everywhere."[54]

The editors of the *New York Amsterdam News* saw a valuable lesson for African Americans in the way the Chinese in America rallied to the aid of the imperiled Nationalist regime. Writing under the provocative heading "The Chinese Are Not Negroes," they made an unflattering comparison between the Chinese reaction to Japan's invasion and the African American response to the invasion of Ethiopia. The paper noted that there were slightly less than 250,000 Chinese in America and approximately 13 million African Americans. But when Ethiopia was attacked, "Negroes talked, held lots of wordy mass meetings, waved flags, and then left Ethiopia to the gods. In other words, we raised very little money. To date, however, the Chinese people of this country (both those born here and in China) have dug into their pockets for over one and a half million dollars."[55]

Adam Clayton Powell Jr. rounded that figure up to nearly two million dollars. Writing on a theme that his congregants must have found familiar, he complained that black Americans had money for a Joe Louis fight and other forms of entertainment but little for Ethiopia or other worthy causes. He ended his sermon with the rueful observation that if it were not for the help of "white angels," such vital organizations as the NAACP and the Urban League would cease to exist.[56]

Despite the *New York Amsterdam News*'s editorial position on the "China incident," as the Japanese called it, many Harlemites refused to view Japan as simply another fascist power. They were even less inclined to give the United States the benefit of the doubt on matters of foreign policy. As the *News* observed, "The Chino-Japanese war (or isn't it a war?) is the topic not only of the headlines, but also of the street corners. A trio of curbside debaters were heard the other day applauding the way Japan is showing the white world that 'if they can gobble up China and everywhere else, Japan can do some gobbling too.'"[57]

Some of the paper's readers took a similar position. "I for one am color conscious before I am class conscious and as such I am backing the Japanese," explained one of them. "These people, little brown men, alone have the courage, guts and brains to face the occidental nations and proclaim an Asiatic Monroe Doctrine. The Chinese to the contrary are the 'Uncle Toms' of the Far East. They have no respect for themselves, as is evidenced by their allowing foreign nations to establish their own courts of justice within China." "I am reliably informed," he added, "that parks have been established in Shanghai with signs reading 'Chinese not allowed.'"[58] According to another reader, the Chinese "like the Negro . . . places his hopes and security in the hands of the great white race." The Japanese, on the other hand, "know why these great humanitarians are trying to stop the cruel Chinese war. The market must be saved for white posterity and the ultimate destruction of Japan. If Japan goes down," he warned "every black man's right will go down with her."[59]

For Powell and the editors of the *New York Amsterdam News*, the course was clear: "we must aid China, Loyalist Spain, the Jew in Germany, the Haitian, the anti-Lynch Bill, the remaining Scottsboro victims and the plight of the jobless. In any land where the cry goes up 'To arms for freedom!' We must answer."[60] But to list those causes placed members of the anticolonial Left at a disadvantage in their campaign to sway black opinion against Japan. Because the president had kept a Sphinx-like silence during the recent filibuster of an antilynching bill, unemployment in Harlem lagged far behind that of white communities, and the administration had eased restrictions on the admission of Jewish refugees, some believed that the government was more concerned about the welfare of white foreigners than black citizens. Whereas Powell saw the Asian conflict as linked to the battle against fascism in Europe and lynch law in the South, black admirers of Japan found it possible to compartmentalize these different struggles because the Roosevelt administration did likewise. Even Powell admitted that both the president's reticence on the antilynching bill and the administration's weak response to the Ethiopian crisis and European fascism contrasted sharply with the U.S. response to Japan's invasion of China.[61]

It seemed to many black Americans that the United States was spoiling for a fight with Japan. As one reader of the *New York Amsterdam News* warned, "We are egging for a war! . . . What reason did we have for waking sleeping Japan? . . . It is time that the races holding others in subjection look forward to another day and make their peace with the weaker and less offensive brother."[62] William Pickens, a columnist for the Associated Negro Press and a former field secretary for the NAACP, advised Chiang Kai-shek to deal directly with Japan instead of relying on European aid and blamed the white press for spreading "anti-Japanese feeling" by distorting the news from China.[63] Another of the *News*'s readers reached a similar conclusion about reports from the war front. "I don't say that Japan is fighting the black man's battle in China," he conceded, "but what will Buddhism do to China and the Chinese that Christianity hasn't done to Africa and the African. . . . It is the Christians who do the lynching in the south. They are Christian senators who upheld lynching in Congress. So what's more wrong with Japan? My New Year's resolution is: I won't be fooled by one-sided propaganda."[64]

Defending Japan involved little risk or effort and offered the emotional satisfaction of siding with a nation that challenged white supremacy. It is also conceivable that the reaction of some African Americans to Japan's invasion of China said more about how they perceived their own circumstances than what they thought about Asian politics. After all, it took little imagination to see in China uncomfortable parallels to the segregation and discrimination black Americans faced at home. As divided as African Americans might have been over the Sino-Japanese War, they shared a tendency to view that struggle in abstract terms. The two belligerents assumed symbolic stature, representing qualities that African Americans either admired or disdained. In this respect their reaction to the war, which seemed barely grounded in the realities of the conflict, resembled that of the larger white population.

For liberals such as Powell, the Chinese were battling the same forces that oppressed blacks in the South. Those African Americans who praised the Japanese for their martial spirit and their willingness to challenge the white world condemned the Chinese for their docility and for permitting parks in Shanghai to be posted with signs reading "Chinese not allowed." Although there were exceptions, the admirers of Japanese militancy were more likely to belong to or sympathize with African American–led protest and nationalist organizations.[65] In praising the Japanese and ridiculing the Chinese, they were criticizing both black liberals and African American Communists for appearing to depend on white Americans for their own liberation.

Although few black Americans were prepared to actively support Japan, the ranks of those who continued to regard it as the champion of the darker races were much larger. Contemporary observers certainly believed this to be the case. Not long after the Japanese invasion began, the *Pittsburgh Courier* expressed bewilderment at the extent of African American interest in the war. According to the paper's analysis, the outcome of the conflict was unlikely to affect African Americans. If China won, Europeans and Japanese would be expelled from the mainland. The West would attempt to recover its losses in China by "a more intensive exploitation of Africa." "We may deplore such exploitation," explained the *Courier*, "but it will scarcely touch us, except that fear of a land-seeking Japan might scare America into better treatment of us." If Japan won, Africa would suffer the same increase in exploitation, but Japan would be less of a threat to the United States, "In which event our actual status remains unchanged." "There is not the slightest indication that either China or Japan has any particular interest in the fate of colored Americans one way or the other," added the editors. "So beyond the natural human curiosity and sympathy, there seems to be little reason for any Negro getting excited over the outcome."[66]

Two months later the *Courier* abandoned its aloofness to applaud Japan's humbling of the West in China. "With Japanese troops parading in Shanghai last week, the white Powers definitely lost 'face,'" the editors observed. "England, France, the United States and the others were told who was boss in Asia and they couldn't do anything about it. At least there is ONE part of the earth no longer ruled by white imperialism."[67] A week later the paper adopted a cautionary tone. It admonished readers not to be "foolish enough to believe that Japan is fighting YOUR battle: that her conquest in China helps you in some way." Japan was allied with Hitler's Germany and Italy. That alliance should be sufficient to convince African Americans that "Japan is fighting its own battle. No one is fighting for you except YOURSELF."[68]

This message was more in keeping with the independent stance of *Pitts-*

burgh Courier publisher Robert L. Vann. Since 1932 Vann had urged black citizens to bargain more shrewdly with their votes and to avoid becoming dependent on either major party. By 1937 he was growing concerned that black Americans had bound themselves too tightly to a Democratic Party that remained insensitive to their needs. Vann may well have feared that sympathy for Japan foreshadowed another form of misplaced loyalty that could be equally, if not more, damaging to African American political interests.[69]

Communist Party members also worried about the extent of pro-Japanese sentiment in the African American community. The CPUSA attempted to convince blacks that it no longer sufficed to view the world in terms of color alone, but this proved to be a hard sell. "Is Japan the Champion of the Colored races?" asked the CPUSA in a 1938 pamphlet. The answer according to such "outstanding Negro Communists" as Cyril Briggs and vice presidential candidate James W. Ford was a resounding no. "Peace loving humanity the world over stands aghast at this, the latest crime of the Japanese warlords against a peaceful nation. But the deepest disillusionment is felt by the millions of colored peoples in America, Africa, and Asia who once regarded seriously Japan's claim to leadership of the colored world." The CPUSA tried to convince black Americans that when Japan joined Hitler, "who loudly proclaims his contempt for the Negro," and Mussolini, "the assassin of Ethiopians," in the anti-Comintern pact, it relinquished any claim to speak for the downtrodden. "Manifestly," the pamphlet continued, "the key to the understanding of the present world conflict cannot be found in the simple but dangerous formula of a fight between colored and white races for a world supremacy."[70]

It was clear, however, that many black Americans viewed the world on those terms. Speaking to the biannual convention of the CPUSA, Pettis Perry, a delegate from Los Angeles and a member of the National Negro Congress, conceded as much when he said, "if Negroes can be convinced of the similarity of the struggle of the people of Ethiopia with that of the Spanish and Chinese people, they would take a greater interest in the struggle against fascism."[71]

The extent of black sympathy for Japan troubled those who sought to enlist African Americans into a worldwide antifascist alliance. J. H. Linn, a Harvard graduate and Chinese journalist, attempted to win Harlem's support for a boycott of Japanese goods. In an address to the International Liberal Club on Seventh Avenue, Linn insisted that "The Japanese are not the friends and defenders of the darker races." Describing the subordinate position of Koreans and Formosans in the Japanese empire, he added that

Tokyo's alliance with the Nazis and Italian fascists proved that they were unconcerned about the plight of nonwhite peoples. Summing up the liberal internationalist position, Linn warned: "Today the greatest problem in the world is how to maintain peace. Japan and the other fascist countries are breaking the peace and threatening democracy. Negroes must not allow themselves to fall into the trap of Japanese propaganda that they are friends of the Negro and will help them."[72]

The tone of Linn's appeals revealed his concern that he was waging an uphill battle for the minds of Harlem. In fact, the same night he gave his address, two blocks away Masao Dodo [sic], New York correspondent for the *Tokyo Nichi Nichi*, was defending his country's actions to Harlem's Association of Trade and Commerce. According to the press report of the meeting, Dodo was asked to speak "because of the interest Harlemites have manifested in the current Sino-Japanese war." George Harris, a former publisher of the *New York News*, introduced Dodo with the observation: "This community is deeply interested in the issues involved in the orient. The main issue is the parity of all non-Nordics with the Nordic nations. A Monroe Doctrine is now being established by Japan in Asia. Upon its success will rest the freedom of Africa as well as Asia."[73]

Dodo likewise framed his arguments in the familiar idiom of black internationalism and justified Japan's actions in terms that were calculated to resonate with his audience. "Japan is the only colored nation that challenges the domination of the entire globe by the white nations," he explained. Referring to the Monroe Doctrine, Dodo made it clear that Japan was behaving as other nations had, except for one crucial difference. "The greatest sin the Japanese committed," he declared, "was that of being born colored." Japan had tried to help China, he insisted, but "Because the Chinese government under General Chiang refused to concur with Japan in its determination to remain free of white domination, Japan invaded China."[74]

Dodo clearly knew how to reach his audience. According to the *New York Amsterdam News*, "From the various questions asked by persons in the audience it was clear that most of those present sided with Japan in the present imbroglio with China." The members of the Association of Trade and Commerce were said to favor Japan "solely because it is a nation of colored people, according to the opinions voiced." On the other hand, they opposed the boycott of Japan and criticized the "black Reds" who sought to involve the United States in a war against Japan. Feeling for Japan ran so strong that Arthur Schomburg, curator of the 135th Street branch of the Public Library and a renowned bibliophile and collector of Africana materials, declared, "If Japan will help the darker people to gain equal opportunities I am ready to shoulder arms for Japan now."[75]

In another time, the spirited reactions of African Americans to the Sino-Japanese War could have been interpreted as a healthy sign that black Americans encouraged free thinking and vigorous debate in their community. For many black Americans, however, unity was more desirable than debate. There were enough schisms in the black community already. They did not need to add the Asian conflict to the list of issues that prevented them from forming a unified front. Nevertheless, a month after Linn's and Dodo's presentations, a contributor to the *New York Amsterdam News*'s weekly guest editor column admitted that "The Ruthless invasion of China by the Japanese and their tactics have sharply divided Negro opinion." Hodge Kirnon, a self-described intellectual and lecturer, wrote that although some black Americans condemned Italy's invasion of Ethiopia and Japan's attack against China, "The other group regards Japan's action as a necessary means towards a desirable end, namely full manhood status and freedom for the Negroes of the world and the colored races in general. They see in Japan's domination of China an essential step, however Machiavellian, for her future role as leader and liberator in the predicted clash of color." For Kirnon, such views amounted to "childish fancy." Japan would not risk its wealth and power to eliminate "color prejudice and its comitant [*sic*] evils" in Ethiopia, South Africa, America, or the West Indies. Kirnon thought he knew why black Americans deluded themselves into sympathizing with Japan. "The passionate desire to see some arrogant white imperialistic nation crushed by some colored group has led many astray," he explained, "by masquerading the joy of revenge with much special pleading and all forms of circuitous reasoning to prove that the success of Japanese imperialism will be the means of our racial salvation."[76]

In upbraiding his fellow Harlemites for placing their faith in Japan, Kirnon urged them to exchange their "childish fancy" for an interpretation of world politics based on hard calculations of power and national self-interest. The cynicism implicit in Kirnon's realpolitik was likely to register with black Americans frustrated by the opportunism and inconsistencies displayed by liberal internationalists and the leaders of the international communist movement. At the same time, however, his icy contempt for those who sympathized with Japan was unlikely to win him many converts.

The *Pittsburgh Courier* had tried to make the same point a year earlier when it said that the conflict in Asia would not affect black Americans. But that assertion seemed to contradict one of the main themes in the development of black internationalism. The new imperialism of the late nineteenth century and the concurrent institutionalization of racism in the United States had encouraged African Americans to see their own predicament as part of a larger phenomenon in world politics. For three decades leading black intellectuals, journalists, and civic leaders had promoted a view of international affairs rooted in the assumption that the darker races of the world shared a common enemy in the form of white supremacists. Working from that premise, they concluded that the nonwhite peoples of the world had a natural interest in promoting solidarity among the darker races. Japan had played a major role in the development of this ideology. It became a model for other nations to emulate and a leader in the fight to make racial equality a guiding principle of international affairs.

Now African Americans were being told that the weakening of white supremacy elsewhere in the world was of no consequence to them. Even the editors of the *Pittsburgh Courier* seemed unconvinced by their argument. They cheered Japan for having caused westerners to lose face in China and predicted that if Japanese expansion in China were checked, there would be a reckoning between the United States and a land-hungry Japan. In that case, the American government might come to perceive an important connection between equal rights, black loyalty, and national security. But this prescient analysis was lost in the *Courier*'s haste to make what it deemed to be the more important point, namely that African Americans need not concern themselves with the struggle in Asia.

In this respect the *Courier* differed from the leaders of the emerging popular front against racism and colonialism like singer-activist Paul Robeson and Adam Clayton Powell Jr., both of whom argued that black Americans had a stake in the outcome of the China incident. All, however, were dismayed to find that a significant number of black Americans warmly defended Japanese policy. Press reports, newspaper columns, and editorials suggest that African American support for Japan was large enough and certainly vocal enough to concern black leaders who sought to enlist their constituents in the emerging popular front against fascism. As international tensions mounted throughout the world, this reservoir of passive support for Japan could prove troubling for leaders of organizations like the NAACP and the CPUSA that continued to operate within a system dependent on white Americans. As will be shown, the sympathetic response of many black Americans to Japan soon attracted notice in Congress and in the government's intelligence and security agencies.

In the depression decade the attention African Americans gave to the cause of Indian independence and the unprecedented outpouring of popular support for Ethiopia demonstrated the continuing vitality of the ideology of black internationalism. The ongoing debate over Japan's invasion of China showed that the belief in the emerging solidarity of the darker races retained its appeal for black Americans. Although black internationalism suffered a blow as a result of the Sino-Japanese War, it continued to be a potent force among internationally minded African Americans. By early 1938 there appeared to be no shortage of blacks willing to defend the merits of Japan's case in formal and informal debate. In fact, the Lincoln University debate team did just that when it upheld the affirmative in its annual forensic competition with the Students Literary and Debating League in Brooklyn. The evening's topic read: "Resolved: that Japan is justified in intervening in China." Given the state of opinion in the black community, the outcome of the contest seemed especially appropriate: the two teams battled to a draw.[77]

[4]

The Rise of the Black Internationale

The international crises that brought the world to the brink of war in the summer of 1938 left American observers and internationally minded commentators bewildered and groping for explanations. How had the promising system of the 1920s collapsed so quickly, and what did its demise portend for the nations of the world? There was, of course, no shortage of opinions on either subject. Newspapers, magazines, scholarly journals, and countless volumes were devoted to analyzing the world situation and recommending the best means of averting war or keeping America out of war should peace prove unattainable.

Many African Americans in the foreign policy public had begun to participate in this debate, particularly as it touched on the danger to peace posed by Nazi Germany. For black New Dealers and more radical Leftists, Japan forfeited the sympathy it had earned at Versailles and as a result of the 1924 National Origins Act when it joined Germany and Italy in the anti-Comintern pact in 1936 and invaded China the following year. Yet many black internationalists continued to defend Japanese actions, and to varying degrees they argued that Japan's victories benefited all of the darker races, including the Chinese. According to this view, as Japanese power increased, the European grip on Asia would loosen until eventually the white imperialists would be driven from the East entirely. The liberation of the remainder of the colonial world would follow naturally in the wake of the European exodus from Asia. Viewed from this perspective, the gathering clouds over Europe seemed to promise a brighter future for the nonwhite peoples of the world.

"I haven't the slightest interest in Europe or its institutions," wrote George Schuyler in April 1937, "the quicker they destroy themselves, the better it will please me. As long as they remain up, we remain down. Hence my inability to fathom Negroes who favor world peace." Several months later Schuyler declared that if war should erupt, "I am anxious that it be long, bloody, and exhausting. Therein lies the hope for the oppressed millions of Africa, India, China, and the islands of the sea."[1] Not content to wait for the outbreak of war in Europe, Schuyler had already started his own global conflict in the pages of the *Pittsburgh Courier*. Writing under the name "Samuel I. Brooks," the talented and prolific journalist treated readers to weekly installments of *Black Internationale*, an adventure-filled tale of African liberation and global race war. Like the *Fu Manchu* series, *Black Internationale* could be regarded either as a pleasant diversion or as social commentary. Schuyler claimed to prefer the former. Calling his story "hokum and hack work of the purest vein," the "Black Mencken" declared that he "deliberately set out to crowd as much race chauvinism and sheer improbability into it as my fertile imagination could conjure. The result vindicates my low opinion of humanity."[2]

However disparaging Schuyler might have been of his own work, it is evident that he took *Black Internationale*'s theme of black liberation emerging out of world war seriously. In his pulp fiction (a sequel titled *Black Empire* appeared in 1938), Schuyler created a brilliant but ruthless black protagonist named Dr. Henry Belsidus and placed him in command of a global conspiracy to destroy white supremacy. But in the political commentary published under his own name, Schuyler saw Japan as the destroyer of white dominance. Like many other black internationalists who perceived Japan as the victim of Western prejudice, Schuyler enthusiastically defended Japanese actions in China. At one point the *Pittsburgh Courier* refused to publish a series of columns it had commissioned from him because they were so vigorously pro-Japanese.[3] Undeterred, Schuyler found an outlet for his views in the pages of the NAACP's *Crisis*. Significantly, he chose to title his controversial analysis of world events "The Rise of the Black Internationale."

Schuyler began by tracing the roots of the present international color line back to the "astounding technological mutation" that occurred in Europe in the second half of the nineteenth century. Following the era of conquest, Schuyler explained, white overlords tightened their control over the darker races through intimidation and indoctrination. "Then the triumph of Japan over Russia in 1904 roused hope among colored people that the balance of power might again shift to their side." World War I produced many important changes, weakening Europe and encouraging "new ideas of solidarity in the world of color." "Dark colonial emigres schemed and planned in the salons and cellars of London, New York, Paris, Bombay, Batavia, Singapore and Cairo." The interwar ferment of the 1920s bore fruit in the tumult of the 1930s. "Mahatma Gandhi electrified the world with Non-cooperation. White people were *not* united, the colored world learned, and there were flaws in the armor of imperialism." According to Schuyler, the black man found reason for hope in every act of a defiant Japan. "He sees erstwhile haughty whites cowering in the shell-holes of Shanghai, a British ambassador machine gunned on the road to Nanking and an American gunboat bombed to the bottom of the Yangtze River without reprisal from a Caucasia become panic-stricken and paralyzed." The New Negro had arrived, proclaimed Schuyler. "He is aware the balance of power is shifting in Africa, in India, in Malaya, the Caribbean and China. . . . Everywhere he is on the march, he cannot be stopped and he knows it."[4]

Years later, in his autobiography, Schuyler applauded his own foresight for having predicted in that article the postwar wave of decolonization. But although none could match his riveting prose style nor capture quite so vividly the image of a white world crouching in terror, there were many observers, white and black, who sensed the dramatic changes under way in the world. As had been the case since the late nineteenth century, the interplay between American racism and black internationalism continued to work itself out. Whereas Schuyler saw cause for hope in Japan's displays of power in China, particularly in the allegedly accidental sinking of the navy patrol boat USS *Panay*, U.S. military officials brooded over the ominous precedent created by Japan's challenge to white people's prestige in Asia.[5]

Less than a year after publication of "The Rise of the Black Internationale," the war Schuyler had hoped for finally began when Germany invaded Poland in September 1939. France and Britain promptly declared war on Germany, but the Soviet Union, in a stunning reversal, entered into a nonaggression pact with the Nazis and took the Baltic states and Poland as its share of the spoils. The *Pittsburgh Courier*'s P. L. Prattis welcomed the conflict. Ignoring Japan's attack on China, Prattis stated that he preferred to see whites "mow one another down" rather than "have them quietly murder hundreds of thousands of Africans, East Indians and Chinese."[6] In white publications the mood was somewhat different: weary resignation at Europe's folly and a sense of grim foreboding tended to be the dominant responses. In one controversial article, famed aviator Charles Lindbergh warned Americans that the real loser in the European war would be the white race. Writing in the November *Reader's Digest*,

George S. Schuyler, July 1941. (Photograph by Carl Van Vechten;
Van Vechten Collection, Library of Congress)

Lindbergh asserted that the rising tide of color, the alliance of "Mongol, Persian, and Moor," must be met by an alliance of the white nations, including Germany—"a Western Wall of race and arms which can hold back either a Genghis Khan or the infiltration of inferior blood." He considered the Soviet Union to be among the colored nations of the world, leading at least one historian to suggest that Lindbergh was really offering a prescient warning of the Cold War yet to come. But the Lone Eagle's call to arms, titled "Aviation, Geography and Race," borrowed too heavily from the rhetoric of white supremacist thought to be passed off as a geostrategic analysis of the costs of war in Europe. His reference to "White ramparts," his fear of "racial suicide," and his warning that as a result of the European war, "all foreign races stir restlessly" betrayed an obvious familiarity with the writings of Lothrop Stoddard.[7] Certainly black readers believed that to be the main message. Labeling Lindbergh's views as "claptrap," the *Chicago Defender* and the *New York Amsterdam News* summarized his message as a warning that "the world war is a threat to the domination of the world by the white race, since it may give the black, yellow and brown races a chance to usurp the top spot now held by 'Nordics.' "[8]

As Lindbergh feared and Schuyler hoped, Japan, emboldened by Europe's distress, sought to press its advantage in China at the expense of Europeans and Americans. In 1939 Japanese troops occupied Tientsin and infuriated westerners by strip-searching men and women as they left the international compound. Reacting to the outrage expressed in the white press, Mabe Kountze, writing for a new *Chicago Defender* feature titled *Streamlined History*, argued that there was more to American indignation than a desire to protect the honor of white women. "Let no man believe that Japan started the degradation of white women in Asia," she wrote. "There were Ninevahs and Babylons in Asia and many of the islands whose inside stories are yet to be published." Japan's real offense, she explained, was that in causing white women to lose face, the Japanese sought to "smash all white prestige in Asia." Kountze predicted that if Japan's campaign proved successful, the white world would suffer a devastating blow. Stimulated by Japan, Asia and Africa would be roused from their slumber. "It is plain to everyone," she asserted, "that should these two giants awaken simultaneously and be launched into a war of conquest under the direction of Japan—well, who knows what?"[9]

That was a question the editors of the *Chicago Defender* did not wish to contemplate. Indeed, they clearly wished that it had not been asked in the first place. Followed to its logical conclusion, Kountze's reasoning was bound to lead to conjecture over black American loyalty in the event of conflict. Underneath her column the editors appended a disclaimer stating that her views were not necessarily those of the *Defender*. Beneath that they printed an extraordinary editorial note explaining that in future installments of *Streamlined History* "we hope to arrive at the logical conclusion that America is still the best and offers the best to people of all races, creeds, and colors."[10]

It would appear that by 1939, the editors of the *Defender* were as uncomfortable with the pro-Japanese position of some African Americans as were the editors of the *Pittsburgh Courier* who earlier had suppressed Schuyler's columns. It is unclear, however, what prompted these journalists to distance themselves from their more radical scribes. Perhaps they feared a loss of already small advertising revenues or they did not wish to invite attention from the government. They might have found the anti-American tone of the columns too strong for their personal taste or feared that their readers would. Regardless of their motivation, the *Defender*, especially after the Ozawa case in the 1920s, saw little to admire in the Japanese empire.

Nevertheless, as George Schuyler, W. E. B. Du Bois, James Weldon Johnson, William Pickens, authors of numerous letters to the editor, and street corner lecturers indicated, the image of Japan as the champion of the darker races remained an important element in the worldview of black internationalists. Some expected an actual alliance between Japan and other nonwhite peoples, while others saw Japan as a model, a powerful contradiction of white supremacist thought and an inspiration to colonial peoples. In either instance, the image was positive. For black internationalists, color was crucial in world affairs, economics important but secondary. During the 1920s this worldview had seemed to explain much, especially in the immediate aftermath of the Paris Peace Conference.

The Ethiopian crisis reconfirmed this perspective and awakened millions of previously unconcerned African Americans to the ways in which the system of discrimination at home appeared to be replicated abroad. Proponents of a view of world politics based on race always encountered the most difficulty, however, in trying to fit Asian developments into the pattern predicted by their theories. Here, black internationalists seemed on firmer ground when they inverted the relationship between race and economics, that is, when Western opposition to Japanese expansion in China was perceived as an attempt to save China for European exploitation. But black internationalists were unwilling to live with this dilution of their theory of international politics. Race entered the picture, they believed, in the form of a heroic Japan seeking to uplift and develop China, endeavoring to make a cringing Uncle Tom stand on his own two feet.

Japanese propagandists said much the same thing, of course, but they had less success in convincing the Chinese of their benign intentions. For their part, black internationalists seemed unaware of how their explanations of Japanese behavior echoed Tokyo's propaganda. They were likewise undisturbed by the way in which their rationalization of Japanese imperialism mirrored the traditional justifications of Western colonialism. By 1939 black internationalists were defending imperialism as a means of racial liberation. Black internationalists also seemed unaware of the way in which their defense of Japanese actions in China led them to an unwitting association with some of the most reactionary groups in the United States. Much as Ralph Bunche and others, including American Communists, had predicted, by emphasizing race as the crucial factor in international politics, black internationalists had accepted the terms of debate handed down by Adolf Hitler. The results were not edifying.

Apart from black internationalists like Du Bois, Schuyler, Kountze, and the intrepid street corner orators in Harlem, the only voices raised in defense of Japan at this late date came from a dark corner of the American political arena not usually known for its hospitality to blacks. Included among the unsavory figures who argued Japan's case were Father Charles Coughlin, the "Radio Priest" whose once strong Social Justice movement had degenerated into an anti-Semitic, anti-Communist fringe group; William Dudley Pelley, founder of the fascist Silver Legion; and Fritz Kuhn of the German-American Bund. Although each leader embroidered his interpretations of international affairs with his own distinctively bizarre touches, all agreed that Japan was fighting Bolshevism in China and was thus deserving of American support.[11]

Black internationalists did not regard international communism as a source of evil in the world or even as a grave threat to the interests of African Americans. They did view black Communists as misguided souls who traded one form of white domination for another. Thus, black internationalists were quite willing to attack their opponents as traitors to the cause of African American liberation by labeling them "black Reds." Similarly, George Schuyler thought that the best way to rebut Claude McKay, the black communist poet, was to refer to him repeatedly as "Comrade McKay."

W. E. B. Du Bois, as might be expected, was something of an exception. The elderly scholar could still manage kind words for Japan and the Soviet Union in the belief that any nation that posed a threat to British and American imperialism could not be all bad. Du Bois had always been known for his fierce independence of mind, but in the changed political climate of the late 1930s, his outspoken sympathy for Japan became a political liability for those black organizations still dependent on white support.

Early in 1939 Du Bois received a letter from Waldo McNutt, a consumer advocate, questioning the scholar about his views on Japan. McNutt, who described himself as a supporter of the NAACP's campaign for an antilynching bill, explained that during a recent visit to Washington "a number of liberals in Congress interested in this legislation asked me if it was true, as has been rumored, that you are receiving funds for Japanese propaganda work in this country." [12] McNutt pointed out the similarities between Du Bois's recent speeches and Japanese propaganda and referred to a recent issue of the *China Weekly Review* that named him as having pro-Japanese sympathies. McNutt ended his letter by asking Du Bois for a clear statement of his views so as to dispel the rumors once and for all. Indignant at the suggestion that he was a paid propagandist, Du Bois shot back: "I have never received a cent from Japan or from any Japanese and yet I believe in Japan. It is not that I sympathize with China less but that I hate white European and American propaganda, theft and insult more. I believe in Asia for the Asiatics and despite the hell of war and the fascism of capital, I see in Japan the best agent for this end." [13]

Although Du Bois was quick to pounce on anyone who questioned his intellectual integrity, he seems to have been slower in realizing how his public defense of Japan was received by those most willing to support the cause of civil rights at home. Du Bois's belligerence, to say nothing of his almost reflexive echoing of Japanese propaganda, was hardly calculated to assuage McNutt's concerns. Moreover, as Reginald Kearney has shown, Du Bois did receive financial support for travel in Japan from Tokyo. [14] That assistance, in the form of reduced fares for press representatives and a free pass from Kobe to Tokyo, was hardly enough to sway Du Bois, who was already predisposed to be friendly toward Japan. Nevertheless, rumors persisted that black writers had been bought out by the Japanese government. During the next year, after the Japanese reissued his novel *Fire in the Flint* under the title *Lynching*, NAACP secretary Walter White spent an inordinate amount of time trying to quash unfounded allegations that his organization was in the pay of the Japanese. [15]

On the eve of Pearl Harbor, black internationalists had reached a crossroads in East Asia. One road, that taken by members of the Left, bypassed

Tokyo and led toward an antifascist alliance that regarded Japan as part of the larger threat posed by Nazi Germany. The other route led to closer identification with Japan's coprosperity sphere in Asia. In the late 1930s the most radical black internationalists chose the latter course. Before long they found themselves headed up a blind alley inhabited by a sullen group of Silver Shirts and anti-Semites.

African Americans who sympathized with Japan, even those who went so far as to actively support what they perceived as the champion of the darker races, were hardly unique in viewing Japanese imperialism as a form of liberation. Hundreds of thousands, perhaps even millions, of colonial peoples thrilled to Japan's intimidation of once haughty whites. Of these, thousands eventually shouldered arms for Japan when the opportunity arose. In part, pro-Japanese feeling among the colonial peoples of Asia was a simple matter of calculated self-interest. The new conquerors were poised to drive out the Europeans, and, if for no other reason than that, they seemed deserving of some thanks. But initially many colonial peoples were genuinely attracted to the message of liberation put out by Japanese propagandists.

In numerous official statements and publications, Japanese representatives heralded the ideal of an "Asia for the Asiatics." Emphasizing the supposed commonality of Asian values, these propagandists criticized what was perceived as the West's selfish individualism and attacked the obvious hypocrisy embedded in Western racial policies. Japanese officials promised to replace the foreign values of the West with an Asian coprosperity sphere based on principles of cooperation and equality. In addition to Japanese patriotic societies, special organizations such as the People's Renovation Society in China were created to spread the pan-Asianist message through encouragement of cultural understanding. In areas not yet under Tokyo's control, such as Indonesia and the Philippines, Japanese agents managed to convince many nationalists that colonial liberation could be accomplished through the creation of the new Asian coprosperity sphere.[16] By the mid-1930s an anti-Japanese Indonesian nationalist observed that "as far as I can make out, the whole Islamic population of our country is now pro-Japanese!"[17]

Japan's power of attraction was not as strong in the United States, but a pro-Japanese movement did develop in black communities where conditions often resembled those found in European colonies. In the 1930s a small number of African Americans formed their own organizations and professed their loyalty to Japan. Although these groups were carefully watched by government security and intelligence officers, most white Americans did not learn of their existence until after the outbreak of war with Japan.

Several months after the attack on Pearl Harbor, the most vocal pro-Japanese leaders were arrested on charges of sedition and draft evasion. These sensational cases received considerable attention in the white press and created the impression that Japanese agents had been recruiting black Americans before the start of hostilities. The evidence gathered by officials in the various government intelligence and security agencies, although incomplete, points to a different conclusion. The material contained in government intelligence reports confirms the pervasiveness of Japan's image as champion of the darker races among those blacks who felt the most estranged from American society. Perhaps even more interesting is the extent to which these reports show how the pro-Japanese movement among disaffected black Americans appears to have been a self-generated affair.

Federal investigators had been aware of pro-Japanese sentiment in the African American community as early as 1919. Following the arrest and deportation of Marcus Garvey in the early 1920s, government surveillance became more concerned with the spread of communism among black Americans. After a decade of quiescence, however, intelligence and internal security officers began receiving new reports of a growing pro-Japanese movement in the industrial centers of the Midwest.

In October 1933 a Japanese presenting himself as "Major Takahashi Satakata," a reserve officer in the Japanese army, attempted to organize a splinter group of the Temple of Islam, the recently formed African American religious group, into a new movement called "The Development of Our Own." To assist his entry into the black community, Takahashi claimed connections to the ultranationalist Black Dragon Society.[18] Major Takahashi, acting as an emissary from Japan, attempted to recruit black Americans into an alliance of nonwhite peoples under Japanese guidance.

The Development of Our Own was chartered in Michigan in 1933 as a fraternal self-improvement organization, one of its activities being a producers' and consumers' cooperative. Major Takahashi hoped to attract new members from the Temple of Islam, whose founder Wali Farrad had recently vanished. But although the Development of Our Own shared the Nation of Islam's emphasis on self-reliance, only a small number of Black Muslims enrolled. Several months later, in December 1933, Major Takahashi was arrested in Detroit for having entered the country illegally.

Immigration officials quickly learned that the major was actually Nakane Naka, a Canadian citizen. Born in Tokyo, Nakane lived in British

Columbia from about 1903 to 1922, when he moved to Tacoma, Washington. Three years later he disappeared without leaving a forwarding address or settling his outstanding bills. Nakane continued his marginal existence until apprehended by federal authorities in 1933.[19] His arrest was widely reported in the press, and a brief summary of his activities in the black community of Detroit appeared in the May 1938 edition of the *American Journal of Sociology*. The article, an investigation of the growth of the Nation of Islam in Detroit, briefly mentioned a Major Takahashi "who sought to lead the Moslems to swear allegiance to the Mikado." The author noted that Takahashi attracted only a few converts and following his deportation "this schismatic movement came to naught."[20]

"Major Takahashi's" career ended almost before it had begun. Even before immigration officials could dispose of the troublesome Nakane, however, federal authorities were on the trail of another Japanese operative. As federal investigators soon learned, their new quarry's energy and organizational abilities far surpassed those of the hapless Major Takahashi.

In September 1933 a navy recruiting officer in Kansas City, Missouri, notified the director of naval intelligence that a Japanese citizen had recently arrived in the area with the purpose of "organizing among negroes an Anti-White Race Movement." The navy's informant, who was described as "the best posted man in this city on racial matters," also reported that the new movement was building on the remnants of Garvey's UNIA organization in the city and that it had already "stripped local communistic bodies of practically all their negro members."[21]

A month later an army intelligence report verified the existence of such an organization in the Kansas City area but offered a decidedly less ominous interpretation of this new phenomenon. In a special report on what was identified as the "Pacific Movement," Major J. M. Moore, acting chief of staff for intelligence in the army's Seventh Corps Area, referred to three "alleged Japanese" who were holding meetings in the Kansas City area. Moore described them as warning black Americans that "within two years the colored races must fight the white for self-determination, and that American negroes should be ready to support Japan on call by training their young men in modern weapons, especially aviation." Membership in the Pacific Movement cost twenty-five cents. Enrollment in the proposed aviation school required another twenty-five-cent payment. "While still watching this matter," Moore reported, "I think now it is simply a racket." He admitted that other intelligence officers held differing opinions but doubted that anyone would learn much more about the organization. "The 'Pacific Movement' has almost as many investigators as it has members," he complained. These included the "Immigration Service, Secret Service, Dept. of Justice, and Kansas City Detective Squad, while the Navy is in full cry." Exasperated, Moore ended his report with a plea for better coordination among intelligence agencies so future investigations could be conducted more effectively.[22]

As Moore indicated, for a subversive organization the Pacific Movement of the Eastern World (the group's full name) maintained an unusually high profile. In November the *Kansas City Journal Post* reported that the Twin City Baptist alliance denounced the new movement as a threat to the interests of blacks. The ministers warned that "if the Japanese or any other races are behind the movement, as obviously is implied and stated, there is a grave danger of more trouble and disadvantages than any possible good that might come to our group out of it."[23]

A subsequent report by Major Moore confirmed that the Pacific Movement organizers were meeting with hostility from area ministers and reasserted his original assessment of the movement's real purpose. Referring to his previous special report, Moore informed his superiors that three new organizers— a Japanese, a Filipino, and a Chinese—had supplanted the group's previous leaders. The new group declared that the first organizers were not "really official, but that they themselves are ready to replace the unofficial membership cards issued by their predecessors for an additional charge of a nickel." "The new trio," added Moore, "have twice been thrown bodily out of colored churches as they tried to speak." Moore enclosed a membership card for the organization and repeated his previous conclusion that "This 'movement' is considered a small racket to get small sums from the credulous."[24]

Despite Moore's evaluation of the Pacific Movement as a small-time confidence game, reports on the organization continued to circulate within the government's uncoordinated intelligence bureaucracy. Over the next several months news from various informants created the impression that the movement was taking hold throughout the Midwest. Organizers were said to boast of 60,000 members in Chicago, 30,000 in Detroit, 20,000 in St. Louis, and 12,000 in Kansas City. "The idea," according to one army report, "is that Japan is the international leader of the colored races—yellow, black and brown in the forthcoming challenge of the colored races to white supremacy and the duty of the colored population in white territory is to strike in the rear the white overlords when Japan is assailed by any white power."[25] Two months later, the War Department received more information on the Midwestern activities of the Pacific Movement of the Eastern World, including the name of a second operative who was presumed to be Japanese. According to the assistant chief of staff for intelligence in the Sixth Corps Area, about 150 members of the movement were drilling at the Odd Fellows Hall on South State Street in Chicago on Friday nights. Participants shared about twenty rifles and followed U.S. Army drill regulations in anticipation of an inspection by "some unknown personage thought to be the Japanese, Dr. Ashima Takis."[26]

A month later a Japanese professor believed to be Dr. Ashima Takis and "understood to be a representative of the Imperial Japanese Government" was sighted in Pittsburgh trying to create a new movement among the city's black population. Called "The Society of Our Own," the new organization urged black Americans to unite behind Japan as the leader of the darker races of the world. Takis was identified as a former student at Johns Hopkins University in Baltimore, Maryland, who espoused similar ideas to black Americans in Chicago in 1932.[27]

Who was the mysterious Dr. Takis and for whom did he work? Although he had attracted the attention of numerous federal and local intelligence operatives, the inspirational doctor's first encounter with federal agents came when he was interrogated by inspectors from the Pittsburgh branch of the U.S. Immigration Office. According to his statement, the secretive Japanese agent was actually a Filipino named Policarpio Manansala whose many talents included a flair for creating false identities and a penchant for misrepresenting himself to everyone he met, including his wife. During his interview he admitted to having used at least four aliases while in the United States, including Dr. Ashima Takis and Dr. Koo.

Given his habitual lying, it is difficult to reach any firm conclusions about Manansala's activities in the United States. But external evidence and his own detailed statement support the view that the Pacific Movement of the Eastern World operated as a small-time racket to separate African Americans from their money. During his interrogation Manansala stated that he was born in the Philippines, served in the U.S. Navy during World War I, and was discharged on 27 November 1921, after which he worked on numerous ships as a cook. In the early 1930s he lived in Baltimore, Philadelphia, Pittsburgh, and Cleveland. In 1932 he arrived in Dayton, Ohio, where he received a letter inviting him to lecture to the Indianapolis branch of the UNIA. Manansala explained that he stayed in Indianapolis one month and then was sent to different branches of the organization including one in Chicago. While in Chicago he stayed at the Filipino Community Center under the name of Ashima Takis. He subsequently fell in with several unnamed persons who asked him to help organize African Americans for political purposes. Manansala said that he accepted the job, which "led me to go from one city into another." In February 1934, after serving thirty days in a Cincinnati workhouse for petty theft, Manansala returned to Cleveland and then moved to Pittsburgh.

At the time he was interviewed, Manansala was employed as a cook by a Mr. Smith, but he had not lost his unique sense of civic duty. Manansala claimed that he helped his current employer organize blacks in the city under the auspices of a group called the Society of Our Own. Asked why he continued to represent himself as a Japanese citizen, Manansala explained that assuming a Japanese identity gave him more credibility with his African American audience. "If I say I am a Filipino they say 'How can you teach us if you don't know anything too.' I have more influence by saying that I was a Japanese and using a Japanese name."

Noting that Manansala's followers actually referred to him as "Dr. Koo," immigration officials wanted to know how he came to be using "neither a typical or recognized Japanese name." Unperturbed, Manansala, alias Dr. Takis, alias Dr. Koo, said that a Chinese by the name of Dr. Koo had given a talk at a YMCA shortly before his own arrival in the city. "He spoke about the Manchurian situation," Manansala explained, "and the people thought I was that guy. So when they saw me they asked me 'Are you Dr. Koo?' and I said 'Yes.' So they always called me Dr. Koo. After a few days I told them I am not Dr. Koo and my name was Ashima Takis. I also was married under that name. My wife even thinks I am Japanese." [28]

Shortly after meeting with immigration officials, Manansala was briefly held by Pittsburgh police. No charges were made, however, and he was promptly released to pursue his unusual career. The ease with which Manansala resumed his activities disturbed the army's intelligence officer in Pittsburgh, who complained that the Immigration Office had closed the case after it had "unquestionably established his citizenship." Immigration authorities dismissed the Society of Our Own as a "racket," but the army's field representative continued to believe that Manansala was "a dangerous individual and is exciting the colored population with ideas of Japanese Government support in their behalf." He obtained corroboration for his theory from an unusual source, the local branch of the Communist Party.

Alarmed by Dr. Koo's popularity, Pittsburgh Communists sought to combat what they believed was Japanese propaganda by publishing a pamphlet on "Japanese Imperialism and the Negro People." Addressed to "All Workers—Negro, Japanese, Chinese and White," the booklet began with the warning that "A Japanese professor, who is a representative of the Japanese government, is conducting a pernicious campaign of propaganda in Pittsburgh, proposing an organization for the Negro people known as 'The Society of Our Own.' "[29]

In April 1935 the Justice Department obtained information indicating that Manansala had left Pittsburgh for New York. According to an agent of the department's Division of Investigation, in March a Dr. Takassi had begun recruiting Harlem residents for a group called the "Pacific Movements, Inc.," "the purpose of this organization being to stir up the Negroes in this country against the government." "Dr. Takassi," the report continued, "promised the protection of the Japanese for negroes both here and abroad if the negroes fight 'Uncle Sam' here in time of war which he referred to as 'being behind the door.' " Takassi claimed to have 45,000 adherents in Detroit, 15,000 in Newark and Jersey City.

Additional reports on the Pacific Movement trickled into federal intelligence and security offices during 1935, including one from the American Vigilant Intelligence Federation, a Chicago area not-for-profit organization committed to "Vigilant Intelligence—Intelligent Vigilance." Responding to this latest warning about the movement, Lieutenant Colonel C. K. Nulsen, the executive officer of the army's MID, explained that "Although we have from time to time had news of the 'Pacific Movement,' there is nothing to indicate that any great success has been attained by its organizers." Nulsen summed up nearly four years of army surveillance with the observation that the Pacific Movement "seems in many instances to be the means of making a slight profit by enrolling colored people in an organization which has for its ostensible purpose the amalgamation of all other races against the white."[30]

For the next three years army surveillance of the Pacific Movement appears to have lapsed. In June 1939 that interlude was interrupted by news that Manansala had returned to Pittsburgh the previous autumn. According to a report in the *Pittsburgh Courier* of 29 October 1938, Dr. Itake Coo (Manansala), "the guiding figure" of the Pacific Movement in America, had returned to the city after a five-year absence to recruit blacks for a colonization venture in Africa. Coo, acting as a spokesman for the Japanese government, offered free transportation from Los Angeles aboard Japanese ships, seventy-five acres, a house, farm implements, and livestock to anyone willing to participate.

The *Courier*'s reporter noted, however, that although Coo stated that applications "similar to passports in substance" were already available, the "learned native of the Land of the Rising Sun" neglected to tell his audience that Japan did not own any territory in Africa. Asked about this oversight and the prospective colonists' destination, Coo answered "somewhere about the Gold Coast." Despite his own uncertainty about the location of this new colony, Coo "urged that Negro delegates be sent to Japan for inspiration and instruction." Ending in "a burst of oratory," the "dynamic oriental scholar" cited Lothrop Stoddard's *Rising Tide of Color* to "prove that Japan was destined to organize all the dark races of the world and lead them in a grand triumph over the whites."[31]

The army intelligence officer for the region transmitted to the War Department a copy of the *Courier*'s account of Coo's meeting together with a summary report identifying Coo as "Ashima Takis, alias Policarpio Manansals [*sic*], alias Ashima Nicomesiki Pacificae, alias Ashima Takis Kinnosuki, alias Adaci Kinnosuki, alias Dr. Takis, alias Dr. Koo."[32] This latest account of Manansala's activities contained nothing to alter the general staff's previous assessment of the Pacific Movement as a profit-making venture of little significance to the government's internal security.

In 1939 Major Takahashi (Nakane Naka) also returned to the United States. Nakane entered the country illegally in January and began to reorganize the remnants of the Development of Our Own into a new group to wrest control of the society from his wife. The second act of this farce lasted only about as long as the first. Immigration authorities closed the show on 22 June, when they arrested Nakane for illegal entry and attempting to bribe an immigration officer. The former "Major Takahashi" was convicted on September 28 and sentenced to three years in federal prison.

As of 1939, the available intelligence records indicated that neither Nakane nor Manansala, and hence the Pacific Movement of the Eastern World, was supported by the Japanese government. For the time being, federal officials could treat the existence of pro-Japanese movements in the black community as a minor annoyance. Once the influence of Japanese agents was ruled out, Manansala and Nakane assumed the more familiar aspect of small-time confidence men. The willingness of these opportunists to feed off the desperation of others would not have distinguished them from the scores of schemers and racketeers who moved through American communities donning titles and changing identities as easily as other people changed clothes.

Compared to Manansala, of course, Nakane was an unimaginative novice. Whereas Nakane merely borrowed a military rank and claimed affiliation with a Japanese society, Manansala, the Filipino who posed as a Japanese with a Chinese-sounding name, acquired an entirely new nationality for himself. Misrepresentation was perhaps an even more common phenomenon in black communities, where the practice of "passing" for white or, in some cases, as an Indian prince was openly discussed in newspapers and films. But Manansala had not changed his identity to gain entry into white society; rather, he had become Japanese to win the confidence of black Americans. Here was compelling evidence of the positive image of Japan in the African American community.

Government surveillance indicated that from New York to Kansas City a small but solid core of African Americans were willing to commit a portion of their meager resources to an organization they believed to be sponsored by a foreign power. Manansala and his henchmen found their converts among the most alienated members of American society. As numerous reports indicated, many of the members of these societies were former Garveyites who had escaped the poverty of the West Indies only to find themselves mired in the depression-racked slums of America's industrial cities. Others migrated from the rural South, trading one form of poverty for another, their conditions made bleaker by harsh winters and crowded slums. A small number, according to informants' reports, were economically better off. All perceived of themselves as subjects more than citizens. Having given up on ever finding relief from discrimination and economic hardship in America, their ties to the United States had unraveled almost completely.

As Ernest Allen Jr. has shown, the Pacific Movement, the Development of Our Own, and related groups combined black nationalism and millennialism in an effort to build on the remnants of Marcus Garvey's UNIA.[33] The similarities between Garvey's movement and those launched by Nakane and Manansala are significant. The UNIA had expanded rapidly during a period of economic hardship after World War I. Garvey, it will be remembered, also hailed Japan as a model and potential ally during a time of rising tension between Tokyo and Washington. By the mid-1930s, in the midst of depression and growing apprehension over conflict with Japan, a group of African Americans once again looked across the Pacific for assistance. But there was also an important difference between the Pacific Movement and the UNIA. Garvey's followers had attended meetings and listened to speeches identifying Japan as a friend of the downtrodden members of the darker races. In the 1930s the followers of the Pacific Movement and its various offshoots joined organizations they thought were led by Japanese. In doing so, they took a step beyond Garveyism and purchased membership cards in the Black Internationale.

[5]

Dissent or Disloyalty?

While the remnants of Marcus Garvey's UNIA were joining what they believed were Japanese-sponsored organizations, representatives of the African American elite were making more direct contact with Japan and the Japanese. W. E. B. Du Bois's trip to Japan, Manchukuo, and China in 1936–37 stirred the most controversy because of his editorial defense of Japanese imperialism, but other black Americans traveled across the Pacific during the same period. Robert Russa Moton, head of the Tuskegee Institute, and a small group of officials from the school visited Japan as part of a tour abroad. Writer and NAACP executive James Weldon Johnson attended a conference in Kyoto. Charles M. Thompson of Howard University and Benjamin Mays of the Negro YMCA also visited Japan for conferences in 1937. Except for Du Bois, these travelers avoided political issues and limited their comments to favorable observations on the sophistication of Japanese art and culture, the refined manners of the people they met, and the beauty of the countryside. Warmly welcomed and well treated during their visits, these prominent black leaders could not help but be inspired by the images they retained of life in an independent powerful nation ruled by people of color.[1]

Between 1937 and the Japanese attack on Pearl Harbor, black American interest in Japan became more controversial. In 1938 the administration of Franklin D. Roosevelt applied increased pressure on Tokyo with the hope of curtailing Japanese aggression. As the United States began to aid Nationalist China and impose trade restrictions on Japan, observers on both sides of the Pacific predicted that war was almost inevitable. The sense of foreboding increased measurably when Tokyo joined the Rome-Berlin Axis following the German conquest of the Low Countries and France in

1940. Responding to the deepening crisis and sense of national emergency, the U.S. government called for conformity and consent from its citizenry. But instead of closing ranks as in World War I, blacks continued to battle for their rights as American citizens.

At the same time they sought to overturn racism at home, African Americans stepped up their rhetorical attacks on colonialism and racism in international affairs. In these tense circumstances many government officials came to view the rising campaign of African American protest and agitation as a sign of disloyalty. Black Americans' intellectual and emotional attachment to Japan added to this misperception and convinced Japanese, Chinese, and U.S. officials that in the event of war, African Americans in large numbers would oppose their own government.

One of the more important contacts between Japanese and African Americans who did much to nurture the perception that blacks would side with Japan in a war was Hikida Yasuichi. An admirer of African American culture, Hikida lived in the United States from 1920 until he was repatriated with other Japanese diplomats in early 1942. Although he worked briefly as an interpreter for the Japanese consulate in New York in 1941, Hikida spent most of his time in the United States employed as a cook at a private residence in Bedford Hills, New York. The FBI found his limited means of support suspicious, in part because he purchased a life membership in the NAACP during that period. Records in the Japanese Foreign Ministry described Hikida as a part-time or nonregular employee (shoku-taku), but it is not clear when he was hired.

Given the available evidence, it is difficult to determine if Hikida acted as a paid propagandist for the Japanese government for most of his stay in the United States or if he decided to employ his knowledge of African American life and personal contacts with black leaders in the service of his country only after political relations between Japan and the United States began to deteriorate. Following the outbreak of war between the two countries, Hikida's contacts with leading civil rights activists and his career as an African Americanist proved embarrassing to black leaders and subsequently contributed to the erroneous but damaging perception that mainstream civil rights organizations were in the pay of the Japanese.

Hikida's study of black Americans appeared to begin innocently enough. In the early and mid-1930s he translated Walter White's *Fire in the Flint* into Japanese and drafted a manuscript titled "A Japanese Sees the Negro American." As a result of his literary endeavors and his regular attendance at meetings of the Urban League, NAACP, and Association for the Study of Negro Life and History, Hikida became friendly with White, Du

Bois, and Howard University historian Rayford Logan. In 1936 he helped Du Bois make arrangements for his trip to Asia. He also displayed an unusual degree of influence for a cook by providing him with the names of officials and business people to contact in Manchuria and Japan, which resulted in Du Bois's special treatment in Japan.

Hikida also tried to encourage black leaders to provide funds for sending African American students to Japan and expressed a desire to create an Information Research Center of Negro Race and Culture in Japan.[2] Beginning in 1938 he was invited to speak about Japan's China policy to numerous black audiences in New York, Philadelphia, and Pittsburgh, where he also attended a gathering at the home of *Pittsburgh Courier* publisher Robert Vann. Hikida later reported that his defense of Japanese policy was well received by black Americans except for one lively session when he mistakenly showed up at the meeting place of Harlem's Communists.[3]

In 1940 Hikida offered Rayford Logan a $1,200 advance for a manuscript on "The Applications of the Monroe Doctrine." Logan, who had written a history of American diplomacy toward the Haitian Republic, declined the offer and gave a copy of Hikida's proposal to the State Department. As he later recalled, Hikida "probably expected me to conclude that Japan had as much right to set up a 'Monroe Doctrine' for Asia as the United States had for the Western Hemisphere." He added that "while I believed Japan's claim to a 'co-prosperity sphere' in Asia was at least as valid as the hegemony of the United States in the Western Hemisphere or the continued 'Rape of Africa,' I was then and am still fundamentally a universalist rather than a regionalist. Most important of all, I was convinced that Negroes in the United States had nothing to gain from allying themselves with the cause of Japan."[4]

Logan had accurately judged Hikida's intentions. In the autarkic 1930s, references to the Monroe Doctrine as a precedent for the construction of regional blocs had become a commonplace among the have-not nations seeking to carve out their own spheres of influence. In April 1934 Amau Eiji, a Foreign Ministry spokesman, declared that Japan opposed any attempts on the part of China to involve other nations in its dispute with Tokyo. Despite some confusion about the statement's status as official Japanese policy, Amau's declaration that Japan was solely responsible for the peace and progress of Asia was quickly perceived as an assertion of an Asian Monroe Doctrine.[5] By the end of the decade Japanese academics were providing scholarly justification for Amau's pronouncement by comparing Tokyo's "Asian Monroe Doctrine" with the original.[6] In this regard, Hikida's offer to Logan fit the broader purposes of Japanese pro-

Rayford Logan. (Moorland-Spingarn Research Center, Howard University)

paganda, but, as Logan understood, Hikida's more immediate target was black America.

Logan's encounter with Hikida illustrates a dilemma Japanese propagandists faced in trying to capitalize on the pro-Japanese sympathies of African Americans. Most black Americans were quite willing to criticize what they saw as American hypocrisy in Asia, but that did not mean they were ready to join the Black Internationale. At the time Hikida approached him, Logan was heading the recently established Committee for the Participation of Negroes in National Defense, a Washington-based group that employed traditional pressure group tactics to improve the status of blacks in the United States. In January 1941 A. Philip Randolph escalated the pressure on the federal government by organizing the March on Washington movement to demand equal access to war industries for blacks. Meetings between Randolph, and NAACP executive secretary Walter White, and President Roosevelt culminated in the issuance of Executive Order 8802 banning discrimination in defense industries and the creation of the Committee on Fair Employment Practices. Although black leaders did not succeed in desegregating the armed services and enforcement of the executive order remained a problem throughout the war, the Committee on Fair Employment Practices was hailed by African Americans as an important accomplishment.

As long as black Americans believed that their conditions might be improved through organization and protest, they were not likely to jeopardize their chances of success by aligning themselves with a potential enemy of the United States. In early 1940 Randolph had lumped the belligerents—including Japan and Russia—with England and France, but a year later he concluded that "England's Fighting Our Cause."[7] Black public figures like Randolph, White, and Logan did not ignore the international dimensions of racism. All recognized the parallels between the conditions of black Americans and nonwhite colonial subjects around the world and believed that nonwhite peoples had a common interest in banding together to overthrow imperialism and promote racial equality. Logan, White, and Randolph were fully committed to achieving equality for blacks in the United States and to ending imperialism in all of its forms.

As Penny Von Eschen has noted, the emerging anticolonial alliance among African Americans blurred the distinctions between liberals and the radical Left to produce a movement committed to ending racism in the United States and capitalist exploitation in the colonial world. Black internationalism was undergoing a transformation that made it possible to reconcile the competing worldviews based on race and class. But Japan, which had been so important to the development of an African American perspective on world affairs, continued to complicate this transformation. The problem was twofold. First, leaders of the new coalition had to convince black internationalists to jettison Japan. Second, they had to convince U.S. officials that black Americans did not harbor strong feelings of loyalty toward Japan.

White, Logan, and others met the challenge by devising an interpretation of events that allowed them to continue to emphasize the place of race in world affairs and at the same time put a safe distance between themselves and their constituents on the one hand and Japan on the other. The new black internationalism would highlight the role of racism in the coming of the Pacific war, but it would also condemn Japan for betraying the interests of the nonwhite peoples and seeking to use their trust for its own national purposes. For leaders like Randolph and White, who were never attached to Japan, this maneuver was executed without difficulty. It remained to be seen if large numbers of black Americans were also ready to see Japan dethroned as the champion of the darker races or if U.S. officials and other interested parties would understand that black Americans no longer sided with Japan in its conflict with China.

By the time Logan delivered a copy of Hikida's offer to the State Department, Chinese sources had already alerted U.S. internal security officers to the possibility of Japanese propaganda activity among black Americans. In December 1938 the *China Weekly Review*, a journal subsidized by the Chinese government, had alleged that Du Bois worked for the Japanese. That report circulated in Congress and no doubt reached the relevant officials in the security establishment. Americans with close contacts to the Chinese government took black American support for Japan as a given. In April 1939 Ernest Price, a founder of the Committee for Non-Participation in Japanese Aggression, solicited the help of renowned black singer Marian Anderson for a benefit concert in the hope that her participation would counter "the prevalent and mistaken notion among negroes [that] Japan was fighting a righteous war in China against white imperialism."[8]

In 1939 the FBI received a report, titled "Japanese Propaganda among the Negro People," written by an American hired by the Chinese government. The report cited articles in the several black newspapers that criticized U.S. opposition to Japanese actions in Asia, including a *Baltimore Afro-American* editorial defending Japan's right to an "Asiatic Monroe Doctrine." Du Bois, Logan, and NAACP field secretary William Pickens were all identified as pro-Japanese. The author also reported that "Enlightened negro leaders" had told him that "between eighty and ninety per cent of the American colored population who have any views on the subject at all, are pro-Japanese as a result of the intensive Japanese propaganda among this racial group."[9]

Propagandists were especially active among African American college students and members of the intelligentsia. According to the 1939 report, China could count on some assistance from black Americans, including Walter White and Frances Williams, labor division secretary of the Negro YWCA, but support among the masses remained thin. The Chinese government's informant explained that because "Negroes are essentially spiritual and emotional," Japanese propagandists succeeded by cleverly "basing their arguments on the negroes' hatred of white superiority, rather than on any moral, political or economic planes." Black leaders friendly to China recommended an extensive campaign directed at African Americans to counter Japanese efforts, but the informant concluded that black political influence on U.S. policy was too weak to justify spending large sums on the project.

In calling attention to black Americans' sympathy for Japan, the author of this report highlighted an important difference in Chinese and Japanese interactions with African Americans. Whereas Japanese traveling to the United States moved freely about the country, Chinese visitors stayed close to "the beaten track." There were no Chinese equivalents to Hikida Yasuichi or the Japanese journalists who corresponded with James Weldon Johnson, W. E. B. Du Bois, and others. China's disinterest in courting black American support resulted, at least in part, from expedient decisions about the best way to use its resources to influence U.S. policy. But Chinese images of African Americans were also important. The recipients of the report on Japanese propaganda would have found nothing surprising in the matter-of-fact manner in which black Americans were characterized as "essentially spiritual and emotional." Despite repeated claims made later during the war that "the Chinese had no word for prejudice," many Chinese officials viewed Africans and black Americans as racial inferiors.

In Chinese culture, as in the West, blackness was associated with slavery and inferiority. By the late nineteenth century Africans and African Americans were commonly depicted in Chinese accounts as unintelligent and licentious, fit for little more than physical labor.[10] Interestingly, in light of black Americans' depiction of China as an Uncle Tom country, one of the most widely read American novels in China was a translation of Harriet Beecher Stowe's *Uncle Tom's Cabin*. Lin Shu, a famous Chinese translator, prefaced his account with a comparison of China's exploitation with that of American slaves. Lin's notes make it clear that he was less concerned with the plight of black Americans than with the danger facing China. By the early twentieth century Chinese nationalists frequently scolded their compatriots into action by bemoaning that "We Chinese are less than black slaves."[11] In much the same way that African Americans had created stereotypes of the Chinese as compliant lackeys of white imperialists, many Chinese officials had come to view black Americans as powerless to change their condition and too submissive to even try.

By the late 1930s, as China defended itself against Japanese aggression, Chinese officials and representatives in the United States had become aware of the pro-Japanese views espoused by prominent African Americans, but they showed little inclination to understand how their own prejudices and their silence on matters of concern to black Americans might have contributed to those views. To counter Japan's inroads into the black community, individual Chinese occasionally spoke to community groups, but the Nationalist government did not make a concerted effort to appeal to African Americans generally. Instead, Chinese officials used their access to the U.S. government to try to silence their opponents. They probably believed that this approach promised the surest results with the least amount of effort, but it also meant that before the attack on Pearl Harbor, little was done to create a more positive image of China among African Americans. Consequently, Japan, almost by default, retained its stronghold on the black American imagination.

In the meantime, as the confrontation between Tokyo and Washington intensified, Japanese intelligence officers were taking a fresh look at the black community's potential as a source of assistance. By late 1940 Japanese officials were beginning to reassess the value of their various propaganda efforts. The New York consulate concluded that "while cultural propaganda and enlightenment, no doubt, contribute toward the promotion of amicable relations between Japan and America, the cost is prohibitive." It was recommended that Japan end its cultural campaign in favor of "widening the intelligence net and its personnel." In particular, the New York consulate sought firmer contacts with "members of the press and persons influential in American politics and business."[12]

U.S. officials learned of this shift in Japanese intelligence activity almost immediately. As is well known, American code breakers regularly intercepted and read Japan's diplomatic message traffic as part of an operation code-named MAGIC. Over the next several months American intelligence officers followed Japanese efforts to recruit informants and agents nationwide. Of particular interest is a message sent from Los Angeles on 9 May 1941 reporting on local attempts to "establish outside contacts in connection with our efforts to gather intelligence material." These included "use of white persons and Negroes, through Japanese persons whom we can't trust completely." After summarizing other activities in the area, the dispatch ended with the vague report, "We have already established connections with very influential Negroes to keep us informed with regard to the Negro movement."[13]

The following month MAGIC revealed that Foreign Ministry officials wanted to learn more about the possibility of spreading propaganda among African Americans as a means of disrupting internal security in the United States. In particular, they suggested that Japanese representatives in America report on the feasibility of training black agents and contacting "leaders and agitators in both left and right wings."[14]

During the summer of 1941, U.S. counterintelligence and internal security officials continued to piece together the disparate elements in Japan's propaganda campaign among African Americans. In July the army's MID sent FBI director J. Edgar Hoover a report warning that "Japanese and Communist press agents are releasing news in all available negro publications and in some cases, Communists or Communist sympathizers are employed on the editorial staffs of these papers." The army's informant, an African American, also stated that he had been asked by a Japanese editor to write press releases for black papers.[15] In August, the *Hour*, a privately published and self-described "confidential bulletin," warned that Japanese agents were at work in Harlem. The article, which noted that the Japanese were thus far unsuccessful, came to the attention of Director Hoover in mid-September. Several days later Hoover dispatched a copy of the article with routine instructions to investigate the story to his New York field office. As Robert Hill has noted, there was no sense of urgency in the director's request.[16]

The reasons for Hoover's apparent unconcern seem clear. The FBI was already watching African American newspapers for seditious material, and the *Hour* had taken pains to note that the Japanese were making little headway in Harlem. The evidence available to U.S. intelligence and security officers in the months before Pearl Harbor provided a hazy picture of foreign influence among black Americans. As MAGIC intercepts indicated, Japanese espionage recruitment in black communities did not begin until mid-1941. No evidence has been found that in the short time remaining before the outbreak of war they achieved any success in recruiting black Americans as agents.[17] After 7 December 1941 Japanese diplomats were quickly interned, thus ending opportunities for further intelligence, espionage, or propaganda activities in black communities.

Japanese-directed fifth-column movements also seemed an unlikely possibility. U.S. officials were aware of the various Garveyite factions, but the army's MID, the ONI, and the FBI had already dismissed them as small-time rackets with limited appeal among the most downtrodden African Americans. It could be argued, however, that these groups did not have to be in direct contact with Japanese agents to disrupt the ongoing mobilization of American manpower and economic resources.

Nevertheless, as the case of Mittie Maud Lena Gordon indicates, federal officials did not regard the various Ethiopian movements as a serious problem. On 2 August 1941 Mittie Maud Gordon was arrested in Chicago for counseling young black males to resist the peacetime draft, which had been in effect since the previous year. A devoted Garveyite, Gordon had joined the Pacific Movement of the Eastern World after meeting a Japanese "major" named Takis. Subsequently she became convinced that Takis sought to defraud the group's members, so she reorganized the association into the Peace Movement of Ethiopia with the intention of "repatriating" her followers to Liberia. Gordon advised her adherents that as Liberian citizens they would not have to register under the Selective Service Act and continued to boast of her contacts to Japan. In late August her case was referred to a federal grand jury, which returned a decision of "no bill." The case against Gordon was dismissed following her promise not to interfere with the draft.[18]

During the remainder of the year the army remained far more concerned about the black press's criticisms of discrimination in the armed forces than about Japanese infiltration of African American groups or publications.[19] As the country edged closer to war, U.S. military officials were beginning to realize that the miserable state of America's race relations could become a national security problem. This recognition did not, however, mark the beginning of racial enlightenment on the part of the defense establishment. It simply meant that military officials viewed the security implications of American race relations as a domestic problem that could be resolved internally through the application of government pressure on the offending African American publishers.

African Americans knew from experience how suddenly government circumspection might give way to persecution. Yet black leaders and journalists would not and could not dampen their criticism of the U.S. government's racial practices either at home or abroad, as the black citizenry was in no mood to tone down its disapproval. Abandoning a program of agitation and protest would leave leaders without followers and newspapers without readers.[20] On the eve of war with Japan, African American newspapers continued to battle discrimination in the military. But they also continued to denounce the country's policy in Asia. Black Americans did not have be under the influence of Japanese propagandists to perceive parallels between the Greater East Asia Co-Prosperity Sphere and the Monroe Doctrine or to recognize that state and federal laws discriminated against the Japanese on racial grounds. In calling attention to these issues, black journalists' ultimate goal was to force the U.S. government to see how its own racial policies contributed to international conflict and thereby demonstrate how discrimination at home contributed to dangers from abroad. Others, however, might just as easily read into these arguments a defense of Japanese imperialism.

The potential for misunderstanding was heightened by the widespread use of black internationalist imagery and rhetoric. By the late 1930s the place of Japan in the ideology of black internationalism had become so pervasive that even those African Americans who saw class antagonisms as the dominant motif in international politics were obliged to make at least a passing reference to Japan's role in disproving white supremacy and its symbolic leadership of the darker races, if only to show how Tokyo's leaders had forsaken the cause. The nature of this dilemma is nicely illustrated in several articles that appeared in two of black America's most important weeklies on December 6, 1941, the last day of peace between Japan and the United States.

The first *Baltimore Afro-American* in December carried two editorials on the Far Eastern crisis. In his regular column, Ralph Matthews, who also served as editor of the paper's Washington edition, confided to readers that "At the risk of being cited for treason," he was forced to agree with Japanese premier Tojo Hideki's charges that American and British capitalists were manipulating China's resistance to Japan for their own benefit. "From where I sit," Matthews observed, "it makes little difference whether a Chinese coolie is kept on starvation rations by Japs or the British, or, for that matter, by his own Chinese warlords and mandarins." "I also fail to see," he added, "where any great democratic principle is at stake in this struggle unless the war now brewing has as its purpose the improvement of the social and economic conditions of the people involved." According to Matthews, "the most important element in this whole Far Eastern crisis is not so much one of material spoils as it is the first challenge of the darker race to the white man's right to rule the world." After a brief summary of "Nordic" conquests, he explained that "Japan, therefore, must be crushed — not to save democracy, not to halt aggression, not to preserve the sanctity of international law, or to carry the four freedoms to the oppressed peoples of the Orient, but to keep intact the idea of Nordic invincibility and to roll back for another century the rising tide of color." Revealing his familiarity with Charles Lindbergh's controversial warning to the white world, Matthews predicted that the "alleged democracies" might ally with Adolf Hitler to stem the dark tide. "To the white man," he asserted, "Hitler's bid for world domination is only a diversion compared to the menace of Nippon."[21]

In the second editorial the *Afro-American* declared, "in fighting Japan our own hands are not clean." The editors warned that in the event of war, Japan expected to exploit American disunity "brought about by this nation's refusal to give full citizenship to its colored people. . . . Candor compels us to admit that disunity increases in a national crisis. Look at Ireland and India. What will happen in case the United States is invaded as it was in 1812, no one can say." Sounding only slightly less ominous, the editors next inquired into the "mystery" of why the United States insisted on a Monroe Doctrine but denied Japan similar leadership in Asia. Citing the litany of American transgressions against the darker peoples of the world, the *Afro-American* argued that many people asked why "we who have slaughtered the reds and the blacks, have so suddenly become Christian Crusaders for the yellows of China. They ask, with some truth, aren't we more interested in Chinese trade than in Chinese salvation?"[22]

P. L. Prattis, editor of the *Pittsburgh Courier*, likewise saw the lure of the China market as a driving force in American policy. He ridiculed the Chinese for wanting "whites to boss them rather than Japanese." The Chinese were a nation of Uncle Toms who "would rather flunky for the whites than allow the Japanese to set up a 'Monroe Doctrine' for Asia."[23]

J. A. Rogers, also writing in the *Courier*, found such sympathy for Japan to be sorely misplaced. Its current rulers, he argued, were a bunch of "cut-throats and robbers," who exploited their own laborers for profit and "dropped millions of tons of bombs on unoffending Chinese women and children, causing such misery in China that Hitler's ravages in Europe are almost angelic." Rogers admitted that as young man he had admired Japan, but that by World War I he had grown concerned that it was as intent on imperialist domination as any white nation. Japan's seizure of Manchuria confirmed his suspicions, but the invasion of China in 1937 was the last straw. "Now he hope[d] to God that some strong power or powers will drop on Japan the exact same number of bombs she has dropped on China—and drop all of them at once." Rogers expected his reiteration of the "facts" of Japan's conquest to convince most readers, but the evidence would not sway "those fanatics who see in Japan some sort of racial deliverer."

Rogers also sought to dispel the widespread belief among black Americans that the Japanese did not discriminate against other nonwhite peoples. "I don't give a damn how liberal has been the reception accorded one or two Negro visitors to Japan," he snapped. He cited his own experience of being "jim crowed" in a Japanese restaurant in New York, as well as that of a group of blacks reportedly barred from a Yokohama hotel to please a white customer, to demonstrate that the Japanese both in their own country and the United States were quick to draw a color line if they could profit from it.[24]

In concluding his column on "Our Stake in the Far Eastern Question," Ralph Matthews provocatively asked, "Where do we stand on this issue?" It was a query that readers might easily have directed at Matthews and his fellow editors and columnists, all of whom regarded U.S. declarations of concern for China's welfare as cant. The *Baltimore Afro-American*, Matthews, and Prattis saw American prejudice as a key force in the current crisis. Prattis even predicted that President Roosevelt would seek war against Japan in order to enter the European conflict. It would be easier to rally Americans against Japan, he concluded, because "The element of prejudice is involved." In portraying Japan as a victim of racism, were these writers trying to justify Japanese imperialism? A closer look at their arguments suggests otherwise. Matthews, it will be recalled, likened Japan's exploitation of China to Britain's and America's. The editors of the *Afro-American* compared Tokyo's Monroe Doctrine to Washington's, but their condemnation of U.S. intervention in Latin America suggests that this was not a compliment. Prattis's callous portrayal of China as an Uncle Tom obscured his larger point that the conflict in Asia had little to do with the independence of the Chinese. Rogers, who was the most critical of Japan, agreed. Japan's greatest crime was in following the lead of the white imperialists.

In short, despite the inflammatory rhetoric, the intent of the four editorials was to awaken Americans to the dangers of their own prejudices. All four opinion pieces described the conflict in Asia as a war of rival imperialists. The white world, they asserted, was reaping the whirlwind in Asia because of its own racism. In light of its record at home, how could America justify opposition to Japan and thus ensure black support? Make this a war to spread the four freedoms to "improve the social and economic conditions of the people directly involved," Matthews urged. "Give full citizenship to colored people," was the *Afro-American*'s answer.

If that was the message the *Baltimore Afro-American*, Matthews, and Prattis wished to convey, it was muffled by their almost reflexive use of the standard images of black internationalism—Japan as conqueror of the myth of white superiority, Japan as racial victim, Japan as leader of the darker races, and China as Uncle Tom. Even Rogers, who wanted to dispel these images, felt compelled to admit that he had admired the Japanese in the days before they turned white.

For nearly two decades, black internationalists had employed the idiom of race to interpret the workings of international politics. This ideological view went far toward explaining the injustices nonwhite peoples endured at the hands of white imperialists, but when applied to the Asian crisis, it raised more questions than it answered. If Japan was leading the darker races of the world, why had it joined an alliance with Nazi Germany and Fascist Italy? One could banish Japan from the ranks of the Black Internationale and ridicule its leaders for acting white, or flay the Chinese for not identifying more closely with other nonwhite peoples, but those facile explanations still implied that factors other than race were determinant in world affairs. If nonwhite peoples were capable of shedding their racial identities in this way, what did that say about the chances for a global alliance against racism? In wrestling with this problem, black leaders found it difficult to disentangle themselves from the rhetoric of black internationalism that they had helped to propagate.

When Ralph Matthews asked his readers to ponder where they stood on the question of war with Japan, he could not have known that they would have less than twenty-four hours to provide an answer. The Japanese attack on Pearl Harbor the next day was quickly followed on 8 December by an American declaration of war on Japan, which, to the surprise of many, triggered a declaration of war on the United States by Germany. At last the remaining neutral power had joined the European and Asian conflicts, transforming them into a single global struggle. The suddenness with which the war descended placed black leaders in a difficult position. How should they respond to the crisis? The experience of the last war reinforced their unwillingness to declare a moratorium on civil rights agitation, but the knowledge that they were being watched closely by federal internal security officers made them wary of testing the government's tolerance of dissent in wartime.

Black journalists and civic leaders of all persuasions had known that Japanese efforts to recruit propagandists and fifth columnists in the black community would be only marginally successful. They worried, however, that these highly visible attempts to win black support might leave African Americans vulnerable to charges of disloyalty in the event of war. What gave substance to these fears was the seething resentment blacks felt at discrimination in the armed forces and defense industries and the widespread belief among them that racism was at the root of American opposition to Japan. Together these attitudes might undermine their patriotism to the extent that they might respond to the news of war in the Pacific with complete indifference. If black Americans were neutralized in this fashion, it would only highlight the activities of the most extreme pro-Japanese members of the African American community. The experience of World War I indicated that once federal authorities believed that they faced the danger of internal subversion, they would act without much concern for the civil liberties of black Americans.

African American leaders needed to find some way to fend off charges of sedition without abandoning their quest for equality. Over the next several weeks black editors and civic leaders fashioned a response that incorporated their continued agitation for civil rights with all-out support for the American war effort. Inspired by a letter from a young aircraft factory worker, the *Pittsburgh Courier* launched its now famous Double V campaign on 14 February 1942. Calling for victory over fascism abroad and racism at home, the paper urged black Americans to fight for their rights and the right to fight. Others soon joined the movement, causing no small amount of consternation among military officials concerned about the effects of black militancy on the army.

In his analysis of the black press, Lee Finkle has argued that African American weeklies adopted the Double V to get back in step with the black masses. According to this view, black editors and publishers first responded to the war by urging African Americans to defer their demands for equality until the danger had passed. It was only when they learned that readers refused to swallow their grievances that the editors and publishers hit upon the idea of a dual struggle. Even then, Finkle notes, they emphasized victory over the Axis powers as the first priority. Finkle attributes this caution to the political conservatism of black editors and publishers. However, evidence available to later historians suggests that the monitoring of black newspapers by the FBI and MID may have been the more immediate reason for the professions of loyalty that filled the editorial pages of black journals. Moreover, it is unclear that black American papers dropped their demands for equality for even the short period Finkle describes.

A cursory examination of the leading black weeklies suggests that African American leaders had already begun to adopt the theme of the Double V campaign even before the *Pittsburgh Courier* fixed upon the slogan to describe it. On 20 December 1941 the *Baltimore Afro-American* published a page-one editorial by Walter White under the title "War Cannot Halt Fight for Rights."[25] The *Courier* of the same day carried an article by A. Philip Randolph exhorting blacks to see that the stakes of this war were democracy at home and abroad. Although Randolph urged African Americans to rally to the colors, he reminded them that they were already engaged in another struggle at home. The fight to defeat the Axis powers, he declared, "also involves the obligation, responsibility and task for the

Negro people to fight with all their might for their constitutional, democratic rights and freedoms here in America."[26]

Writing in the same paper a week later, J. A. Rogers urged readers to "Back Our Boys." Rogers believed that black Americans should serve their country, but his column was not a paean to the patriotism of the black soldier. Rather, he acknowledged that the disillusionment of the last war left blacks with "a listless kind of loyalty, like a man who goes to a job in which he has little or no interest." To remedy this situation Rogers recommended that African Americans "enter the fight with all the zest, thrill and patriotism of every other American group, at the same time preparing ourselves mentally and otherwise, to demand, and if necessary to seize, our rights as citizens during the conflict, and especially after it."[27]

The devastation inflicted at Pearl Harbor and the military setbacks that followed created special problems for black opinion makers and leaders in light of the latent sympathy for Japan in black communities and the even more prevalent perception that U.S. opposition to Japan was motivated by racism. Black journalists dealt with this dilemma by identifying American racism as the true source of these defeats. Two weeks after Japan began its coordinated assault of Southeast Asia, a *Pittsburgh Courier* editorial titled "Underestimating Japan" observed: "Because white Americans were bitterly prejudiced against the Japanese, they liked to believe that they were an unworthy foe to be easily bulldozed and defeated. It is a fatal weakness to underestimate your opponent and we imagine from now on we shall hear less of this kind of talk." The editors concluded that a long struggle awaited Americans, "and the fact that one of our opponents is a brown nation does not lessen the danger."[28]

In similar fashion the 3 January *Afro-American* ran a page-one editorial complaining: "There has long been a tendency to hold the little yellow men lightly. . . . But two weeks after war was declared the Japs have smashed Pearl Harbor, seized Guam, beleaguered Midway Island and landed thousands of troops and tanks in the Philippines." Citing Prime Minister Winston Churchill's prediction that there would be no Allied victories for another year, the editors shifted their focus to show how this racist-inspired complacency perpetuated discrimination at home despite the nation's urgent need to mobilize all of its resources.[29]

The idea that American prejudice had been Japan's secret weapon fit perfectly the rhetorical needs of African Americans intent on agitating for their rights in the midst of a national crisis. It also allowed some to indirectly praise the Japanese by alluding to their military prowess. Predictably, it was George Schuyler who most vividly illustrated the versatility of this approach. On 10 January 1942, shortly after the fall of Manila, Schuyler's front-page column in the *Pittsburgh Courier* opened with one of the boldest leads imaginable under the circumstances: "The United States has been defeated! It has been defeated by a foe it despised because of his color." "Race prejudice and only race prejudice caused our complacence toward Japan," he added. The shock of defeat, Schuyler continued, would make Americans "more sober and realistic. They know that a warrior nation (even though colored) is not to be 'sold short' when it has the resources and manpower of Japan." After tallying up the manpower at Japan's disposal, including "37,000,000 Manchukuans," Schuyler concluded that the United States would win the war, but only if "the divisive nonsense of color discrimination and segregation" was ended.[30]

Although Schuyler's column fit the pattern of the Double V commentary, it is hard to ignore the delight he exhibited in showing his readers the price that white America was paying for its folly. His reference to "Manchukuans," the Japanese designation for the inhabitants of the conquered provinces of Manchuria, was probably also intended to rile censors. Priding himself on his familiarity with what the black man-in-the-street believed, as opposed to those who claimed to be black leaders, Schuyler dared to write what his fellow journalists feared to acknowledge. "Now in point of fact everybody knows, without holding a conference, that no matter what a large proportion of Negroes may say IN PRIVATE about Japanese aggression and the magnificent retreats, they are PUBLICLY behind the government 100 percent. What other alternative have they, except to go to jail?"[31]

As Schuyler noted, in private many black Americans were at least as pleased with the spectacle of white defeat as he was. As in 1904, the powerful emotions unleashed by Japan's humbling of whites produced similar reactions among people of color everywhere. When the Japanese routed U.S. and European forces immediately after Pearl Harbor, an Indian member of the Malayan civil service recalled that "Although my reason utterly rebelled against it, my sympathies instinctively ranged themselves with the Japanese in their fight against the Anglo-Saxons."[32] Years later, African American sociologist Horace Cayton recalled in strikingly similar fashion that as an American he did not desire a Japanese victory, but as a black man he was cheered by the spectacle of white men being humbled by the people they had derided as "little yellow bastards." J. Saunders Redding expressed the same feeling of elation before reaching the sober conclusion that life would be worse under the Axis.[33] Similar stories abound. Black workers joked about the sinking of the British warships *Prince of Wales* and *Repulse*, declared that they were having their eyes fixed like the Japanese so they could stand up to whites, and otherwise made barbed references to American and British military incompetence. Rayford Logan recalled that Laurence Reddick recorded many of these street sayings in Harlem and deposited them in the New York Public Library's Schomburg Collection on African American culture. "Leave me alone. I've got the Japs on my side," was one he recited from memory.[34]

One did not have to keep a cocked ear on an uptown street corner to glimpse the chasm separating white and black opinion in the early days of the war. Black editors assured the federal government that African Americans desired only a chance to fight, but the letters from their readers appeared to tell a different story. "The Japanese, Germans, Italians and their Axis stooges know it is futile to seek spies, saboteurs or Fifth Columnists among American Negroes," announced the *Pittsburgh Courier*. But the next week the paper printed a letter from an incensed black serviceman who doubted "that the Japs are as bad as we are made to believe." "I doubt if they would treat loyal, patriotic citizens as badly as the Negro is treated in America," he added.[35]

On 20 December the *Baltimore Afro-American* questioned five black citizens in Richmond to ascertain their views on how they would fare if Japan won the war. Three of the respondents believed that African Americans would benefit. "This would be the first step in the darker races coming back into their own," said one of the three.[36] In early January the paper carried two letters that highlighted this division. One correspondent from Boston, who alluded to the practice of white employers pitting racial minorities against each other, declared that whites were being repaid for having replaced African American bellhops with Japanese, Filipinos, and white foreigners. "This war will open their eyes," he said. Another writer from Massachusetts observed: "It seems that the object of the white races is complete segregation of all dark races. As long as Japan remains strong the other races have a champion."[37]

Several weeks later the same paper displayed a cross section of opinion in the black community. A correspondent from South Carolina wrote, "We are Americans by birth, yet we are not trusted as such, so let's stop worrying about the war and fight for our rights." Writing from Detroit, Sara P. Corbin asked if those men who defended states where they were denied the vote would be given that right after the war. "Each day the Bible is being fulfilled," she added, "and I believe that when this war is over we will live in a new world and 'Ethiopia shall stretch forth her hand.'" "The Government says 'slap the Jap.' [W]ith what," asked a Baltimorean, "our bare hands? Men must be trained to fight." New Yorker Cyril Lopez declared that fighting to defend the United States was a duty, but that fighting to "strengthen the death grip of the British and Dutch on people of Asia and Africa is something else again." Prophet Kelso Dumas of Detroit asked: "Why are colored Americans so down on Japan? The Japanese have never been known to lynch a black person."[38] Finally, "A Colored Virginian" wrote approvingly: "Unlike the rest of the colored world, the Japanese know that the only way to keep abreast of a white mob gang is to have your own mob. As a people we are not able to declare war on anyone but we can be dragged thousands of miles from home to fight someone who we never saw before for no other reason than the white man's lust for power."[39]

As this sampling of opinion suggests, in desiring to show how racism contributed to America's weakness, black leaders could not determine the uses African Americans would make of that issue. Perhaps even more important was the way in which the statements of white public figures seemed almost to invite blacks to sympathize with the Japanese. Following the attack on Pearl Harbor, the explosion of white racial hatred toward the Japanese produced a chain reaction among many African Americans. Aware of how white racism strengthened the appeal of Japanese propaganda, President Roosevelt banned references to the racial identity of the enemy over the airwaves.[40] But the practice continued, stirring up a debate over who was responsible for labeling the war against Japan a "white man's war." In April the *Crisis* angrily fixed the blame on the white media, citing radio references to "yellow bellies" and press stories that used phrases like "and for the entire white race in the Far East."[41]

The ambivalence of many African Americans toward the war and the Japanese sorely tested the ability of black leaders and journalists to reconcile the needs of their supporters with the demands of the federal government. As Robert Hill and Patrick Washburn have shown, African American leaders had reason to believe that their growing strength in the Democratic Party and the liberal views of Attorney General Francis Biddle would protect them from the worst government abuses.[42] Black editors also may have hoped that by printing letters from readers that displayed sympathy for Japan instead of editorials and featured columns, they were insulating themselves from charges of sedition.

At times they also took pains to show their disapproval of their correspondent's views. The *Baltimore Afro-American* responded to Cyril Lopez's complaint about defending the British and Dutch empires with an editorial note explaining that "Japan and Hitler are our enemies. We have to fight these enemies wherever they are or wherever they flee."[43] For his part, Ralph Matthews executed a remarkable reversal after Pearl Harbor. Gone were the references to Asian Monroe Doctrines and philosophical musings about black Americans' stake in the crisis. Instead, Matthews chided one of his readers for searching "the dark corners of America's cellar among the debris to stir up the stench of discrimination as an excuse to duck [his] responsibilities."[44]

The varied responses of many African Americans after Pearl Harbor belied the assertion of black leaders and journalists that, as the *Afro-American* put it, the "War Unites All to Crush Japs."[45] This picture of black American apathy and discontent was further underscored in January 1942, when a conference of black leaders voted 36 to 5, 15 abstaining, that African Americans were not 100 percent behind the war. The continuation of discrimination in defense industries, the infuriating decision of the Red Cross to segregate blood plasma, segregation in the armed forces, and the flaring of racial violence in the urban riots of 1943 ensured that black morale would remain a serious problem for most of the war.

In an effort to address this problem, white liberals amplified the arguments of black leaders and repeatedly stressed the ways American racism impeded domestic mobilization and alienated important allies such as India and China. Following the outbreak of the war, however, most officials charged with protecting the internal security of the United States tended to see the problem differently. Whereas they had once minimized the danger of pro-Japanese movements among black Americans, they now attributed the problem of black morale to foreign influence in the African American community. In the tumultuous aftermath of Pearl Harbor, black internationalism was gaining new converts.

[6]

Race and National Security

When news of Japan's attack reached Washington, U.S. officials were thrown into a state of near panic. Worried by the possibility of Japanese agents raiding key government offices, Assistant Secretary of War John J. McCloy promptly ordered a detachment of military guards to surround the White House.[1] Fear of Japanese suicide squads quickly passed, but FBI and military intelligence officers did not rule out the possibility that enemy operatives posed a danger to America's defense. In particular, government anxiety over the extent of Japanese influence on black Americans sharply increased over the next several months.

Several conditions accounted for this heightened concern. First, the pervasive sense of crisis lent an urgency to counterintelligence work that had been absent only weeks before. As the internment of Japanese Americans living on the West Coast indicated, many government officials were inclined to act on their worst fears and prejudices. Timing was also a factor. The continued agitation by black Americans seeking their constitutional rights had the unfortunate effect of increasing the visibility of African American protests at the precise moment when the fall of Singapore was giving Japan's claims to leadership of the darker races an even stronger aura of credibility. Finally, newly obtained evidence contributed to the heightened sense of concern on the part of intelligence officers. MAGIC intercepts and Japanese documents seized in New York detailing a program for cultivating support among black Americans imparted a sense of coherence and deliberateness to Japanese subversive activities that they previously had seemed to lack. Within weeks of the outbreak of war, the momentum of Japanese victories, the results of domestic surveillance, and the attendant publicity given to pro-Japanese sympathies in the black community by friend and foe alike converged to create a new public discourse over the relationship between race and national security.

FBI director J. Edgar Hoover viewed the connection between race and national security in mostly negative terms. In the aftermath of Japan's attack, the director's Jim Crow sensibility and his desire for favorable publicity neatly combined in a stepped-up campaign against subversion and sedition in the black community.[2] The FBI's investigation into Axis-inspired activity in New York that had begun routinely several months before the outbreak of war was suddenly transformed into a high-priority operation by the Japanese attack.

On 9 December 1941 Hoover requested a status report on the investigation into fifth-column activities in Harlem begun the previous September. On receipt of a report naming Leonard Robert Jordan and the Ethiopian Pacific League, Hoover pressed the New York office to continue the probe and to investigate possible connections between Jordan's group and the Japan Institute of New York. On 20 January, not long after the conference of black leaders had registered their lack of enthusiasm for the war effort, the director granted the New York office authority to present the Jordan case to the attorney general for prosecution for sedition.[3] Part of the FBI's evidence consisted of eyewitness testimony of a Jordan tirade denouncing the United States as a "five-headed snake" and claiming that "Japan is interested in the 150,000,000 darker races of the world and they all should wake up and start fighting for her."[4] More troubling, however, was a sheaf of documents found in the New York office of a Japanese-sponsored group called the Japan Association.

According to FBI reports, a paper apparently written by Hikida Yasuichi and titled "Interracial Understanding between the Japanese and American Negroes" asserted that "It is the general opinion of intellectual negroes in the United States that the negro's concern of Japan is not small." The author explained that the interest African Americans had developed in Japan after the Russo-Japanese War increased during the Paris Peace Conference. Further, African American newspapers denounced the Japanese Exclusion Act of 1924 and took a pro-Japanese stand during the invasion of Manchuria. The memorandum concluded with a variety of proposals for cultivating among African Americans a favorable attitude toward Japan. These included giving prominent blacks an opportunity to visit Japan and Manchukuo so they could disseminate their findings to the broader African American population through syndicated articles, sending a black press agent to the Japanese empire to establish links between the government-controlled Domei News Agency and the Associated Negro Press, creating a Japanese-Negro Interracial Committee in the United States, and supporting publication of English-language textbooks on Japan emphasizing racial themes.[5]

The Hikida memorandum reflected the author's misjudgments, as evidenced in his offer to Rayford Logan, about the extent to which black American opinion could be turned to Japan's advantage, but it contained more than enough information to impress investigators with the seriousness of the Japanese program. American code breakers intercepted diplomatic messages describing Japan's propaganda as "cultural enlightenment" and referring to Japanese contacts among influential African Americans.[6] The trips of black American dignitaries to Japan were a matter of record, W. E. B. Du Bois's being the most controversial. Editorials in black newspapers, particularly those appearing to defend the idea of an Asian Monroe Doctrine, seemed to confirm the success of Japanese propaganda. Finally, as the FBI soon learned, the goal of funneling Japanese press releases to black newspapers seemed to have been implemented through the creation of an agency called the Negro News Syndicate.

It would take weeks for FBI and military intelligence officers to sift through the material they were collecting, evaluate its importance, and pursue further leads. Meanwhile, to those monitoring Japanese documents the campaign targeting African Americans appeared to be succeeding. Information available to the reading public reinforced the impression of widespread support for Japan among black Americans. Black leaders had responded to the outbreak of hostilities with a campaign to win their rights at home while demonstrating how racism threatened American security. But black public figures were also sensitive to the way in which the hatred of American racism manifested itself in sympathy, if not actual support, for Japan among many African Africans. The numerous letters to the editors and the not-so-secret glee expressed on the streets of black neighborhoods made it difficult to ignore the existence of that sentiment among some of their constituents.

Rather than deny the appeal of Japan to black Americans, some writers tried to tackle the issue head on by disabusing their readers of the idea that Japanese armies were fighting for people of color everywhere. "Strange as it may seem," wrote the *Chicago Defender*'s executive editor Lucius C. Harper, "there are many among us who actually believe a Japanese victory over the United States will be of great value to the Negro in solving his color problem within this country." Harper ridiculed the idea of Japanese solidarity with other nonwhite peoples by describing the exploitation of Japanese workers and other Asians in the empire. "In fact," he added, "we would just change masters—from white to yellow—and in the transfer would suffer immeasurably."[7] Harper's message was unmistakable— Japan was the enemy of black Americans. Yet an unintended consequence of his editorial was to reinforce the idea that "Strange as it may seem, there are many among us" who hoped for a Japanese victory.

White liberals may have found it strange that black Americans viewed Japan as a racial deliverer, but they took the matter seriously. In November 1941 Nobel and Pulitzer prize-winning novelist Pearl Buck addressed a letter to the *New York Times* warning of the perils inherent in the perpetuation of America's caste system. "For in many colored Americans," she wrote, "hopelessness results not in simple crime but in a rejection of patriotism. There are those, and some of them leaders, who favor Japan in the present crisis, seeing in Japan the future leader of all colored peoples of the world." Buck returned to this theme in February 1942 in a speech titled "Tinder for Tomorrow" given at a New York luncheon and published in *Asia* magazine. At a time when news reports carried daily reminders of Japan's sweeping successes in Southeast Asia, Buck warned: "The Japanese weapon of racial propaganda in Asia is beginning to show signs of effectiveness. . . . 'The colored peoples,' Japanese propaganda says over and over again in a thousand forms, have no hope of justice and equality from the white peoples because of their unalterable race prejudice against us."[8]

In case they missed Buck's point, white liberals received a second dose of the same message from the magazine *PM*. In a letter titled "The Negro and the War," writer Marguerite L. Martin vividly illustrated how American racism benefited Japan. Martin dreaded a Nazi victory but she nevertheless found "ironic humor in the fact that Negroes are expected to go all-out for this war." Citing the continuation of discrimination in the armed services, the war industries, and the Red Cross's handling of blood plasma, she asked if white Americans "really think that in the face of all this prejudice we can possibly feel disposed to buy Defense Bonds and stamps, contribute blood, or even feel any great antipathy toward the Japanese, who after all, have faced the same color restrictions we have?"[9]

The attention that Pearl Buck and liberal journals like *PM* gave to the security implications of America's racism suggests that black American leaders and journalists were succeeding in their efforts to educate white liberals and win support for the Double V campaign. For the next several months these opinion shapers lost no opportunity to highlight the domestic and international dangers inherent in America's racial policies. In this way they managed to convey to a white audience made attentive by the war the increasingly militant spirit of black Americans and their nonwhite brethren around the world.

At the end of February the British surrender of Singapore provided black leaders with a glaring example of the costs of racial prejudice. Under the heading of "Why Singapore Fell to the Japs," the *Baltimore Afro-American* editorialized that British insistence "on the observance of all the racial distinctions which have characterized the Orient" had doomed the island fortress. Drawing on the previous week's press dispatches, the editors accurately noted that the British minority failed to make use of the more than four hundred thousand Chinese in Singapore and evacuated white women and children first, leaving the Chinese to fend for themselves.[10] Another story in the same issue, this one culled from a report by the Associated Negro Press, blamed British racial policies for the loss of Malaya, Singapore, and the impending defeat in Burma. "Japan is capitalizing upon resentment toward white supremacy to pave the way for absolute victory," the article explained.[11]

Once again it was Pearl Buck, this time in a "Plea to Colored Americans," who helped to underscore the connection between racism at home and abroad. Writing at the behest of a "group of very intelligent colored friends," Buck acknowledged that "there are those among you who in natural bitterness think, if they do not say, that it might be as well if Japan should win this war so that the white man would be forced out of the lands of the colored people." "It may well be," she observed, "that in the future now very close the people of Asia and Africa will look to you more than to any other Americans to see to it that the world does not divide as Japan would have it on the false lines of color, but solely on the single issue of freedom for all."[12]

The *Baltimore Afro-American*, among other papers, praised Buck's wisdom and emphasized the international dimensions of racism by citing Chiang Kai-shek's warning to Winston Churchill that unless Britain granted India real political power, another vital ally would go over to Japan. The editors added that the British treated Indians like the United States treated blacks, but, they noted bitterly, "Frankly we do not expect this Congress to pay any attention to Chiang Kai-shek or Pearl Buck."[13]

The image of racism as a double-edged sword in the hands of the Japanese had become a constant theme in black journals. "Race and Color Are Now a Chief Issue in the War," declared a page-one editorial in the *Afro-American*.[14] But black American commentators found that their success in linking domestic discrimination with the international crisis had its drawbacks. For as whites learned of the growing appeal of Japanese racial propaganda, they also feared that African Americans might be as susceptible to these blandishments as the subject peoples of Asia. To a certain extent this was an inescapable consequence of the civil rights movement in the United States. To shake white Americans out of their complacency that the nation was united in the war effort, black leaders had to awaken them to the dismal state of African American morale. In doing so, however, they helped to give the threat of black American subversion an even higher profile in the white media. This was a risky undertaking. Black leaders wanted the government to address their grievances, but the possibility existed that federal officials might treat the symptoms, seditious speech, rather than the disease, racial discrimination. In the first year of the war it was by no means clear which approach the government would choose.

The FBI and the army's MID preferred to clamp down on all signs of what they deemed as unpatriotic activities. Attorney General Francis Biddle and the Office of Facts and Figures (OFF), later reorganized as the Office of War Information, the chief government agency responsible for civilian morale, inclined toward a more understanding treatment of black complaints. This dichotomy in approach was evident in the government's divided response to the black American press and to the activities of Leonard Robert Jordan.

In late January J. Edgar Hoover appeared ready to move against the *Baltimore Afro-American* on the ground that its 20 December report on the pro-Japanese views of several African Americans constituted sedition. To his disappointment, the attorney general's office found no violation of federal statutes, but it did approve an investigation of the paper's ownership.[15] Hoover's efforts to arrest Jordan for sedition also stalled. The FBI director continued to press for an indictment against Jordan and for permission to seize the papers of the Ethiopian Pacific League, but Biddle, wary of triggering another witch-hunt like the Red Scare that followed World War I, preferred to move slowly. Hoover finally prevailed, but not until August, a half year after his initial request.[16]

The disagreement between Biddle and Hoover over how best to respond to the mounting black protest campaign was further illustrated in their reactions to the first lynching to occur after Pearl Harbor. On 25 January Cleo Wright, a black man accused of assaulting a white woman, was taken from his cell in Sikeston, Missouri, by a white mob, dragged through the streets behind an automobile, and burned to death in front of an African American church. Wright's murder was hotly denounced in the black press, and the call to "Remember Pearl Harbor and Sikeston, MO" became a new battle cry in African Americans' two-front war. As might be expected, the Japanese immediately seized upon the story of Wright's lynching to remind the peoples of Asia what white justice meant for nonwhites. Alarmed by the domestic and international ramifications of the Sikeston murder, Attorney General Biddle opened an investigation into the killing only to have a grand jury conclude that no federal offense had been committed by the mob.[17]

Meanwhile, the local office of the FBI seemed at least as interested in the swelling black protest as in the murder of Wright. Alleging that "Japanese elements" were using the Sikeston lynching as propaganda to foment rioting among African Americans, FBI field officers called for a grand jury investigation of the St. Louis chapter of the Pacific Movement of the Eastern World.[18] Ironically, a black business leader may have contributed to the FBI's call for the investigation. In mid-March an Associated Negro Press (ANP) report on the Pacific Movement described the organization as a "fifth column activity promoted here in St. Louis in the 1930's by Japanese agents." The report also quoted U. S. Falls, the regional vice president of the National Negro Business League, who called the Pacific Movement a "nightmare" to area leaders for years. "We stamped it as a scheme to swindle innocent colored persons and discouraged it," he said. Falls noted that his league had planned to counter the work of Axis agents in his community but the Sikeston lynching derailed those plans.[19]

As the ANP report revealed, local black leaders had been aware of the shady activities of the Filipino Policarpio Manansala and his cronies for almost a decade. But it is unclear why they thought agents of the Japanese government would be involved in a small-time confidence game. Nevertheless, Falls and other black public figures seemed to have accepted the charge that the Pacific Movement was both a racket and a Japanese-controlled subversive organization. Although Falls and other African American leaders wanted the federal government to respond to the murder of Cleo Wright, Falls's statements connecting the propaganda work of Japanese agents, the Pacific Movement, and black outrage over the Sikeston murder probably reinforced the tendency of the FBI to characterize all black protests as subversive.

The FBI was not alone in perceiving the Pacific Movement as a Japanese-led organization. In the early months of the war the army's MID began to see the work of Manansala and his confederates in a new light. In mid-April MID's Counter Intelligence Group (CIG) distributed a report on "Japanese Racial Agitation among American Negroes" to a broad range of staff offices, army commands, the FBI, and the ONI.

This influential report began by explicitly making a connection between Japanese agitation among African Americans and similar activities in Asia.

The authors identified three categories of propaganda—religious, political, and racial—and traced their development over the previous decade. Under the heading of religion, it gave special attention to Japanese efforts to garner support throughout Asia from adherents to various non-Western religions, especially Islam. CIG worried that Japanese influence was especially strong among India's Moslem population. Political propaganda focused on the theme of national liberation, but here the army found that the transparency of Tokyo's avarice in areas like Manchuria and China reduced the effectiveness of this approach.

Nevertheless, the authors could not ignore the reality of Asian collaboration with Japan's advancing armies, the most recent example being the newly formed Indian National Army (INA) consisting of twenty-five thousand Indian soldiers recruited from the troops who surrendered during the Malayan-Singapore campaign.[20] In addition, the report pointed to the growing restiveness among the inhabitants of India to show that the appeal of Japan's nationalist propaganda increased when combined with religious themes. Concerning race, the CIG noted the success of Japanese agitation in arousing groups in Thailand and Burma against white rule. "It would appear certain," the authors concluded, "that it [Japan's racial propaganda] has made more than a small contribution to the white man's supposed loss of that 'face' so essential to success in the East."[21]

Turning to Japanese activities in the United States, the CIG report found the enemy seeking to "foster race riots and organized revolt." "The American Negro," it added, "is to be convinced that he is the object of racial discrimination and contempt, to be removed only by Japanese victory and the subsequent liberation and triumph of the dark-skinned elements of our population." The authors obviously believed that Japan's propaganda was taking hold in black America. For evidence they cited a study furnished by "a sometimes over-emphatic" source estimating that of those African Americans who had any views on the subject, between 80 and 90 percent were pro-Japanese. The army concluded that, even after revising this estimate to take into account the "occasional alarmist tendencies" of its source, Japanese propaganda "has had a considerable effect." The authors found confirmation for this conclusion in the recent statement of the conference of National Negro Associations declaring that African Americans were not 100 percent behind the war.

CIG warned that the Japanese were recruiting agents and saboteurs and otherwise seeking to encourage subversion and draft evasion among black Americans in the armed forces. It also accused the black press "of directing the subversion among colored troops," but in a curiously indirect way.

Actual Japanese participation was doubtful, but the "propaganda" concerning discrimination in the armed forces issuing from papers "of suspected Communist Party affiliation lends itself very well to exploitation by the Japanese."

As the preceding passages demonstrate, the army counterintelligence officers based their study on the premise that black American protest served Japanese interests. According to this formulation, even papers influenced by Communists aided the enemy's cause. This conclusion shows that the army still did not understand one of the most basic political divisions in the black community, the schism between black Communists and pro-Japanese black internationalists. It also reflects the authors' predisposition to picture the black press as under the sway of subversive organizations despite evidence contradicting that assumption. Following the German invasion of Russia, nearly a year before the CIG report was written, the Communist Party urged black leaders to suspend their civil rights protests and give their all to the antifascist coalition.[22] The authors of the CIG report seemed unaware that the Double V campaign, which bedeviled the army, was an explicit rejection of the CPUSA's plea for unity. Instead, the army continued to find ways to link pro-Japanese black Americans, Communists, and the black press in some concerted effort to cripple the war effort.

The prejudice reflected in CIG's classification of nearly all black American protest groups as unpatriotic was exacerbated by a more valid concern over the possibility of enemy sabotage and subversion. More than a year before Japan's attack on Pearl Harbor, the success of Nazi subversion in Austria, Czechoslovakia, and Holland had prompted President Roosevelt to alert the nation to the danger of fifth-column movements. "A group," the president warned, "not too large—a group that may be sectional or racial or political—is encouraged to exploit its prejudices through false slogans and emotional appeals. The aim of those who deliberately egg on these groups is to create confusion of counsel, public indecision, political paralysis and, eventually, a state of panic."[23] FBI, MID, and ONI officers had already found Nazi agents at work in the United States. They had also collected evidence that Japanese representatives were attempting to recruit agents and distribute propaganda throughout the country.

The startling success of Japan's attack on Pearl Harbor and the rapid advance of imperial troops into Southeast Asia gave a new sense of urgency to fears of subversion in the United States. But Japan's conquests also created an environment where racial prejudice could masquerade as a concern for national security. Operating in the charged atmosphere after the attack on Pearl Harbor, officials on the West Coast actually convinced themselves that the absence of fifth-column activity in their area proved that the enemy was really planning to strike at a more opportune moment. Compounding this sense of alarm was the attitude of Brigadier General Sherman Miles, the head of army intelligence, who admitted that he was "almost a fanatic on morale and the possibilities of disintegration in the rear."[24]

Miles's preoccupation with fifth-column movements helps account for the attention given to "Japanese-Negro Front Organizations" in the CIC report. But even taking into account all of the contextual variables (Japanese victories, black agitation, the prejudices and predilections of individual officers), one is still left wondering how the CIC could reach the conclusion it did concerning the notorious Dr. Ashima Takis (Policarpio Manansala) and the Pacific Movement of the Eastern World. Whatever the reason, sometime between 1939 and the drafting of its report, CIC replaced its previous assessment of Takis as a confidence man with the more sinister portrait of a Japanese agent fomenting rebellion throughout the Midwest. The report described Takis and Major Takahashi Satakata as Japanese agents, noting with some understatement that Takis "operated under various names" in the United States. Also named were Robert O. Jordan and Nakane Naka as well as the Ethiopian Pacific Movement, the Nation of Islam, and several lesser organizations. The authors traced the lineage of these various organizations to the West Indian–dominated UNIA and described their doctrines as a combination of non-Western religion, racial chauvinism, and nationalism. They also noted that the UNIA was itself undergoing a resurgence and was reportedly trying to win jobs for black workers in the defense industries.

An assessment of these various movements led CIC to conclude that "Certain Japanese-sponsored agents and organizations are active among the Negroes of the United States, successfully promoting sedition and espionage." Although CIC conceded that the number of African Americans involved in these groups was small, their influence was magnified by the general discontent of the black population as a whole. The tendency of the authors to favor the worst-case scenario was also evident in their assessment that the activities of Manansala, Nakane, and Jordan were "closely inter-linked" under Japanese supervision.

To combat these activities and foil Japanese propaganda, CIC recommended a course of action, which, not surprisingly, focused on investigating any disruptions within the army including a sudden rise in African American claims for draft exemptions. Perhaps even more important for its impact on black Americans was CIG's recommendation that members of those organizations found to be under foreign influence "should be denied employment on work of a confidential nature in plants engaged in production for the armed forces." Ironically, given CIG's belief that Manansala was actually a Japanese named Takis, the authors suggested using Korean or Philippine agents in investigations since they might be "readily mistaken by the members of Negro groups as Japanese."[25]

In retrospect, it is clear that the CIG's report on "Japanese Racial Agitation among American Negroes" combined astuteness and ineptitude in roughly equal measures to create an analysis of black unrest that obscured more than it clarified. The authors properly recognized the international dimensions of antiwhite feeling, yet despite their awareness of the role played by West Indians in the American movements, they seemed genuinely bemused that black Americans might identify more closely with colonial subjects than white Americans.[26] In attributing black unrest and low morale to Japanese agents and propaganda, they fell back on a timeworn tradition of defenders of the racial status quo by blaming outside agitators for stirring up the masses. This is not to suggest that CIG should not have been concerned about black sympathy for Japan, whatever its origins. Moreover, in a very narrow sense CIG was right: Manansala, Nakane, and Jordan were outside agitators of a sort. There was, however, little evidence that they were actually Japanese agents except for their own public assertions. Inasmuch as one expects agents of a foreign government to exhibit a modicum of secretiveness in their undertakings, such public candor on the part of all three men might reasonably have been expected to create some doubts in CIG about their authenticity.

Again, it needs to be repeated that African American sympathy for Japan, even though it was a self-generated movement with little connection to Tokyo, did pose a potential problem for the military. But by fixing on the supposed Japanese origins of the various movements listed in their report, the officers in CIG ignored the true sources of black American discontent while raising unnecessary concerns about espionage and sabotage. This, in turn, led CIG to recommend closer scrutiny of black Americans seeking work in defense industries. The authors were careful to confine their concern to members of subversive groups who were applying for security sensitive jobs, but one can easily imagine that plant security officers would wish to err on the side of caution. Depending on who made the decisions, the definition of subversive groups might include subscribers to African American newspapers or members of the many organizations that voted to withhold their unconditional support for the war. After all, CIG regarded the former as subversive and the latter as evidence of the effectiveness of Japanese propaganda. For employers who were already reluctant to hire black workers in skilled positions for reasons of simple prejudice, the guidelines recommended by CIC might well have given their defiance of Executive Order 8802 a veneer of patriotism.[27]

This was precisely the sort of broad-brush approach that Attorney General Biddle hoped to prevent. Nevertheless, government officials continued to perceive black American unrest and apathy toward the war as the result of enemy propaganda. In late March the secretary at the British embassy in Washington informed his government that "members of Administration and others are a good deal perturbed by development of Negro problem under influence of colour propaganda by Japanese."[28] Surprisingly, at times the black press seemed to go out of its way to encourage this perception. On 28 March the *Pittsburgh Courier*, which was leading the Double V campaign, printed a guest column by Ira F. Lewis, the paper's president and general manager, which touched on the sensitive issue of black American relations with the Japanese and Chinese. Lewis began by declaring that the Japanese were the enemies of the United States "and are necessarily the enemies of all Negro Americans." He then undercut that statement with the observation that "between the Japanese and the Chinese, the Negroes much prefer the Japanese. The Chinese are the worst 'Uncle Toms' and stooges that the white man has ever had." Although the Chinese were discriminated against in their own country, the minute they opened a restaurant in the United States they raised the color bar. "That's the reason the Japanese hates him," concluded Lewis. "He is a such a stooge."[29]

Lewis's criticisms of the Chinese, which were a small part of his opinion piece on the war, resembled the accusations made by Japanese propagandists concerning Chinese subservience to white rule. Nevertheless, black leaders and publishers were outraged when white syndicated columnist Westbrook Pegler condemned the black press for spreading Japanese propaganda and undermining black morale. Pegler's attack, which appeared in the *New York World Telegram*, was based on a reading of one issue each of the *Baltimore Afro-American* and the *Pittsburgh Courier*. Based on that small sampling he criticized the quality of the black press in general, finding it guilty of sensationalism and hucksterism. But most worrisome to black leaders were his charges that the black press spread Axis propaganda.[30] The NAACP immediately dared Pegler to "Find a single disloyal or subversive line in any colored paper. We challenge him to find any assertion that the Japanese were provoked into this war. We challenge him to find any praise of Hitler or the Axis powers. . . . We challenge him to find any reflection in the colored press of the Axis propaganda line."[31] Fortunately for the NAACP, Pegler did not directly answer its challenge. Since Pearl Harbor, the main thrust of the black press had been to identify the ways in which discrimination at home and racism abroad created conflict and weakened America. Lewis's salvo at the Chinese broke with that trend by criticizing America's ally in the same terms employed by the enemy.

The legacy of Japanese influence on black internationalism threatened to obscure the new approach to foreign affairs embodied in the Double V campaign. African Americans leaders were finding it difficult to make a clean break between the old black internationalism and the new. Concerned that Pegler's attack might be a harbinger of government action against them, black American editors took more direct measures to distance themselves from the Japanese. On 16 May, the same day the *Pittsburgh Courier* published its readers' responses to Pegler, P. L. Prattis declared that the Japanese were wasting their time "Sugar Talking American Negroes by Short Wave."[32] Prattis admitted that "there might be some dumb clucks who would waste time listening to Hirohito and the Japanese. They're colored and we're colored, you know. So we colored folks ought to get along together." But he ridiculed such thinking and, in a not-so-subtle slap at Lewis, asserted that the Japanese he had met in the United States were so filled with prejudice toward the black man that they could teach the most rabid white racists a lesson about discrimination. Prattis, who only months earlier had denounced the Chinese as Uncle Toms who would "rather flunky for the whites" than allow the Japanese to set up an Asian Monroe Doctrine, now displayed an unexpected sympathy for the Chinese. Japanese exploitation was "a horrible blot on the pages of history," he declared. "I know the record of white imperialism in China and other parts of Asia," Prattis wrote, but "The Japanese have been just as cruel, just as merciless."[33]

A week later the *Baltimore Afro-American* printed a guest editorial by the *Chicago Defender*'s executive editor, Lucius Harper. Titled "How Do We Get That Way about Japan?" Harper essentially repeated the criticisms of Japan he had made in his own paper in December. As in that earlier article, he affirmed that some black Americans looked to Japan for salvation. "Some colored Americans seem stupid enough to believe that Japan is actually fighting in this war to bring world wide freedom and happiness to the black man." Of course, Harper scoffed at the idea. "How the colored American imagines he has something in common with the victories of Japan, and that his status of manhood rights will be fully attained

"Hitler's Troubles Have Only Begun," *Baltimore Afro-American*,
20 June 1942. Following American entry into the war, the black press sought
to refute allegations that Japanese propaganda had made inroads among
African Americans. (Afro-American Newspapers)

through a Japanese conqueror offers quite a puzzle in the channel of clear
thinking." A quick look at how the Japanese, "the most clannish people
on earth," treated blacks in America would disabuse African Americans of
any illusions about Japan's solidarity with the darker races. The Japanese
regarded black Americans and Africans as too "docile and subservient" to
be anything but a "servant or hireling."[34]

Like the recently converted Prattis, Harper turned from Japan, "the
warrior of Asia," to China, "the gentleman of Asia," and found the latter
more to his liking. He traced this fundamental difference in national char-
acter to the philosophy of Confucius, who tried to turn the Chinese into
"a race of aristocrats; not a superior race of snobs, but a civilized race

of courteous gentlemen." In contrast to the Japanese, Confucius taught that one should treat "the prince and the pauper with equal courtesy—the prince for the majesty of his rank, the pauper for the nobility of his suffering." Harper's comparison of the Japanese and the Chinese was, of course, highly debatable. Nevertheless, his portrayal of China as more worthy of respect than Japan, as well as Prattis's newfound sympathy for the Chinese, indicated that under the pressure of war, black internationalists were revising two of the most important themes in their approach to world affairs.

These changes, coming as they did amid growing concern over African American morale, went unnoticed by U.S. officials concerned with mobilizing the home front for war. For Secretary of War Henry Stimson, the problems of black morale in the army, the recruitment and deployment of troops, black and white, and the question of Japanese influence among black Americans all came under the same heading. On 12 May Stimson met with Assistant Secretary of War John J. McCloy and Army Chief of Staff General George C. Marshall to discuss the "colored problem which is very serious and explosive." McCloy recommended deploying black troops to North Africa, but Marshall vetoed the idea for unspecified reasons. The conversation on the deployment of black troops led Stimson to record his concern that the army's literacy requirement, which was designed "mainly in order to keep down the number of colored troops," was making it difficult to draft "some very good but illiterate recruits from the southern mountain states." He also confided to his diary that southern whites were hostile to the stationing of black units in their states. The situation was "getting very serious and feeling is very tense. We have direct evidence through MAGIC," he continued, "that the Japanese and Germans are conducting a systematic campaign among the American Negroes stirring up their demands for equal representation and showing that a good many of their leaders have actually been receiving pay from the Japanese ambassador to Mexico."[35]

Stimson's accusation notwithstanding, MAGIC did not reveal that "a good many" black leaders were in the pay of the Japanese. Deciphered messages had shown the Japanese to be interested in recruiting black Americans, but a report by the ONI in January 1942 had found "no indication of Japanese penetration or infiltration" of major black organizations.[36] Evidence from Japanese Foreign Ministry (Gaimushō) files supports that conclusion. Gaimushō records indicate that Japanese officials remained interested in racial conditions in the United States for the duration of the war, but that they were mainly concerned with the effects of racial strife on black American morale and with the ways that episodes of racial violence could be used for propaganda purposes elsewhere in Asia.[37]

Not long after meeting with McCloy and Marshall, Stimson replied to a letter from Walter White concerning the status of black American troops. His grim fears about a problem that "was very serious and explosive" had miraculously vanished. Instead, Stimson was "encouraged to believe" that conditions were "already far more satisfactory than is generally realized." He also pointedly told White that many "reports of racial clashes" were "quite unfounded or exaggerated in ways which can be helpful only to our national enemies."[38] As his exchange with White suggests, the prejudices of a patrician like Stimson may have been less virulent than the racism of most southern segregationists, but this did not lead him to a more thoughtful appreciation of the conditions faced by black Americans.[39] Indeed, if anything, it seemed that the secretary's "outside agitator" response to black militancy produced an inverted view of reality. According to the secretary, reports of racial conflict in the army were gross exaggerations; on the other hand, he had no difficulty believing that black leaders were agitating at the behest of Japan.

Several days later Stimson shared his concerns about the effectiveness of Japanese propaganda with other members of the president's cabinet. Following that meeting, Secretary of the Interior Harold Ickes wrote in his official diary that "There seems to be a feeling that the Japanese, particularly, are doing a good deal of disturbing undercover work among the Negroes."[40] To fully ascertain the extent of this problem, the FBI began an extensive nationwide investigation under the heading of "Foreign-Inspired Agitation among the American Negroes." The bureau's report, which was influenced by CIG's study of the same subject, would not be completed for another year.

In the meantime, while the FBI quietly investigated black America, administration officials and concerned public figures explored other means of coping with the domestic and international dimensions of American racism. In June, the same month the FBI launched its investigation, a British embassy report observed that Washington was "seriously concerned about feeling among the colored population, which according to every survey is apathetic to the war which it considers a white man's conflict." According to Isaiah Berlin, the official charged with producing the embassy's weekly dispatches, the Roosevelt administration was increasing its public appeals on behalf of civil rights, condemning labor for excluding black workers, and generally trying to create a "strong pro-Negro attitude wherever it is possible." Berlin also noted that the Phelps-Stokes Committee, an influential philanthropic organization concerned with African American life, "has been stimulated to prepare a report on [the] future of Africa, which will shortly appear as part of a campaign to arouse favorable interest in [the] Negro problem among [the] general public."[41]

It appears that June 1942 marked a new phase in the administration's response to what it perceived as the related problems of black morale and Japanese influence among African Americans. The ad hoc investigations into black subversives were now institutionalized into a comprehensive survey while the administration concurrently prepared a large-scale campaign to awaken all Americans to the perils of racism. J. Edgar Hoover could proceed with his investigation, but liberals in the administration would have time to show that discrimination rather than disloyalty was the reason for black Americans' apathy.

[7]

Black Internationalism and White Liberals

In the first months of World War II Pearl Buck's highly publicized speeches and letters helped focus attention on the international dimensions of American racism and sparked a series of sympathetic editorials in the white press. On 10 April the liberal magazine *PM* warned of the international ramifications of American racism. After referring to Buck's reminder that most of America's allies were not white, the editors criticized Americans for smugly thinking that the British had a race problem in India while failing to realize that "we have a problem more dangerous than the problem of India, more useful to our enemies, and far more easy to handle." Fearful that Allied racism, British and American, would push the nonwhite nations into the enemy camp, the editors declared: "If we lose our colored allies, our most numerous allies, we shall lose Asia. If we lose Asia we shall probably lose the war. Our past sins and present hypocrisies have become a mortal danger."[1]

Several major metropolitan newspapers trumpeted the same message. "If Britain has thus failed to solve her India problem," commented the *Philadelphia Inquirer*, "it can be said with equal justice that we in America have failed to solve our Negro problem." The *New York Times* agreed, adding: "If the United Nations win this war the principle of the world-wide equality of races will have to be recognized . . . the Chinese, the East Indians, the numerous African peoples and many other groups are on our side, or would be if they were completely convinced that we mean what we say by equality just as unreservedly as the Nazis mean what they say by inequality."[2]

Various left-liberal groups, including the previously mentioned Phelps-Stokes Committee, also moved to address the international implications of American racial attitudes. In February Edwin R. Embree, president of the Julius Rosenwald Fund, sent the White House a memorandum, titled "Race and Color in the Present World Struggle," that called for a presidential commission to devise a program for combating the effects of racism on the morale of African Americans and America's nonwhite allies. Embree hoped that the commission would be useful "in clarifying issues, raising morale, and pointing ways toward more workable democracy in the United States and in the united nations [sic]." But he also emphasized the importance of implementing policies that would lead to the genuine liberation of China and colonial territories after the war. If the Allies failed to deal with their nonwhite subjects as equals, Embree warned, they would face "a new and still more terrible world struggle, in which Asia and colonial peoples generally . . . will try to throw off once and for all the domination of the 'Imperial West.' "[3]

Several months later, in May, the socialist League for Industrial Democracy organized a conference on "The Role of the Races in Our Future Civilization," which featured panels of prominent journalists and academics discussing such subjects as "The Race Problem in the Far and Near East" and "What Is the Significance of Color?" Speakers included Walter White; Dr. T. T. Lew, a member of China's Legislative Yuan; Lawrence Cramer, executive secretary of the President's Commission on Fair Employment; and Dr. Anup Singh, author of India Today. As one of the conference organizers explained in a letter to the White House, the Allies needed to address the problem of racial discrimination in order to win the current war and "avoid racial wars in the future."[4]

These and similar signs of an awakening in the white press and among liberals received full play in the black media. African American editors were obviously pleased that the white press was beginning to respond to their arguments. In the same issue in which it excerpted recent editorials from the white press warning of the dangers of American racism, the Baltimore Afro-American weighed in with its own editorial emphasizing the necessity of immediate action on the part of the United States and Britain. "It's What You Have to Do in Order to Win: Britain Gives in to Indian Demands of Race Equality Because She Must: The United States, Allied to Red and Yellow Nations, Can't Hope for Leadership Unless She Gives Freedom to Colored People Now," read the editorial subtitle.

Given the looming danger of Japanese advances into India and the level of prewar black American interest in Gandhi and the independence movement, the paper's pairing of Indian and black concerns was not surprising.

Somewhat more noteworthy, however, was the boost the editors gave to the refurbishing of China's image as an ally worthy of black Americans' support. "Two of our great allies are colored races, the Chinese and Indians," they declared. "We shall not be able to convince them that we are for race equality abroad unless we practice it at home."[5] Quoting Dr. Stanley E. Jones, a Methodist missionary to India, on the reasons behind Japan's appeal to Asians, the *Baltimore Afro-American* noted that "China is cutting the nerve of that appeal—a yellow race has attacked a yellow race." "It is not a racial war," insisted the editors, "But it could very easily become one. Suppose China would drop out. The appeal to the colored races, including the Africans in Africa, would be terrific."[6]

Although black American sympathy for India remained stronger, China's standing in the black press was clearly improving. Chiang Kai-shek's February visit to India and his public plea to Churchill to grant India real political power impressed black journalists.[7] It remained to be seen if the Chinese could generate among the black American public the same level of admiration once reserved for Japan.

Meanwhile, liberal efforts to focus attention on American racism as the cause of African American agitation, as opposed to subversion, found a sympathetic audience in the Office of Facts and Figures (OFF). OFF and its successor, the Office of War Information (OWI), were not, as their conservative critics charged, New Deal propaganda ministries, but their staffs did take a more liberal approach to race relations than one was likely to find elsewhere in the government. For example, whereas the army's MID continued to fret over the conduct of the black press, OFF cautioned against confusing criticism of discrimination with support for the enemy and dismissed any suggestion that the black press was pro-Axis.[8]

OFF displayed the same tolerance when assessing the significance of pro-Japanese sentiment among black citizens. Reporting on a survey in May, the office acknowledged that there was a widespread desire on the part of African Americans to "see white supremacy toppled by people with darker skins." In this respect, Japanese victories provided blacks a "measure of satisfaction." This identification with the Japanese, the report noted, was stimulated by white references to "'little yellow men' or by other aspersions on their color." Nevertheless, OFF concluded, even the most violent pronouncements in support of Japan "do not necessarily denote a desire to see the United States defeated in the war." Rather, they were "expressions of hostility to the mores of a white civilization." Black Americans wanted to see America transformed, not destroyed. The restrictions placed in the way of full participation convinced them, however, that change was unlikely. This, in turn, led to the popular belief that this was a white person's war. According to the report, here was the real cause for concern.[9]

In addition, OFF underscored the serious consequences of discrimination for black morale. "The striking fact revealed by these figures," it noted, "is that one-half of the Negroes interviewed in New York city expressed to interviewers of their own race a belief that they would be better off, or at least no worse off, under Japanese rule." Interestingly, the survey found that better-educated black Americans were "more kindly disposed to Japanese rule" than less-educated. But here, too, OFF put the best face on these otherwise depressing findings. Some better-educated African Americans might actually prefer Japan, the report conceded, but for the most part these expressions of support for the enemy "may also arise out of a deeper bitterness and defiance among the Negroes exposed to intellectual influences who are more keenly aware of the discriminations against their race."

Compared to the army's survey on Japanese influence among African Americans, OFF's report was demonstrably more sophisticated and nuanced. Whereas CIG shied away from commenting on the validity of black complaints, OFF began with the assumption that African Americans did not need outside provocation to demand an end to discrimination. Liberals like Pearl Buck and the editors of *PM* and the *New York Times* did not believe that black citizens were attracted to Japan so much as they were frustrated with America. This meant that apathy among African Americans was a serious problem, but subversion and sabotage were not. Liberals defined the problem as one that was better treated by publicity than by policing.

In assessing the international crisis, liberals also downplayed the importance of Japan's attractiveness as a leader of the darker races and emphasized instead the ways that Allied racism demoralized America's Asian allies. Liberals worried that Indians and Chinese would conclude that they had little to gain from an Allied victory except a return to the prewar status quo. In that instance, the peoples of both countries might become little more than bystanders in the war. This seemed increasingly likely in the case of India. Nationalists in the Congress Party did not desire a Japanese victory so much as they sought an end to British imperialism, but they might be willing to accept the former in order to achieve the latter. In China, it was less likely that the Nationalist government would reverse a decade-long policy and accept Japanese domination of its most vital regions in order to be free of European imperialism. It was possible that large sections of the Chinese population might conclude that an Allied victory offered them so little that it was not worth the struggle.

These arguments seemed so persuasive, especially concerning India, that members of the U.S. Senate adopted them as a basis for criticizing American policy toward Britain. In late February members of the Foreign Relations Committee from both parties urged the administration to demand autonomy for India. Assistant Secretary of State Breckinridge Long summarized the committee's views as "The only way to get the people of India to fight was to get them to fight for India." He also reported that the senators believed that renunciation of extraterritorial privileges by England and the United States would lift morale in China.[10]

The senators and liberal advocates of racial equality agreed on the importance of eliminating the formal trappings of imperialism in Asia, but they parted company on how they viewed the role that racism played in weakening the Allied effort. For the most part, senators like Tom Connally (D-Tex.) were willing to see Britain and even the United States forfeit some of their imperialist privileges abroad, but they were not prepared to admit that American racism toward its own citizens was a factor in international politics. By the spring of 1942, however, liberals were beginning to affirm the salience of race as a factor in international affairs in ways that were similar to the ideas expressed by black internationalists.

What Pearl Buck and others were suggesting when they warned that the Chinese and Indians might go over to the enemy side was that these nations would make their most important political decisions on the basis of color. How would this happen? One possibility was that America's Asian allies would conclude that a racist America would never deal with any nonwhite nation as an equal. Liberals insisted that the United States could not preach racial equality abroad without practicing it at home.

The idea that American racism would undermine any alliance with an Asian power seemed plausible enough. One could argue, as many black leaders did, that American racism had prevented the United States from developing better relations with Japan in the 1920s despite the administration's insistence that cooperation with Tokyo was in the national interest. Like black internationalists, liberals held that racism was indivisible. The problems of black American apathy and Asian passivity or outright support for Japan could not be treated separately because the same forces that defended America's caste system would insist on white supremacy abroad. America's allies understood this, liberals contended, which is why they watched closely how the United States dealt with its racial minorities. American racism had been a cause of the war, liberals argued, now it might be a cause of the nation's defeat. This line of argument served so well the high ideals of black civil rights leaders and their white liberal allies that it became an article of faith that they often repeated and rarely questioned.

Unfortunately for the champions of reform, the efforts to demonstrate the centrality of racial equality to American national security failed to elicit an unequivocal endorsement from the president. In the absence of a clear signal from the White House, investigators from the FBI and CIG continued their search for black subversives even as the more sympathetic officials in the attorney general's office and OWI emphasized the loyalty of African Americans. The tension between the two approaches became readily apparent in September, when the Department of Justice finally moved against the leaders of the Black Internationale.

On 14 September U.S. attorney Matthias Correa announced the arrest of Leonard Robert Jordan and several associates for sedition. The attorney's statement, which pointedly omitted mention of FBI involvement, stressed Jordan's failure to recruit supporters in Harlem. "The colored people have been as quick as any group within our population to repudiate all efforts to win them over to the Axis line by propaganda. . . . Responsible leaders have expressed the indignation of all loyal Negro citizens at this attempt to identify Jap propaganda with the legitimate campaign against racial discrimination." Reporting on the arrests, the *New York Times* described Jordan's efforts as "diligent but almost entirely fruitless" and as a racket preying on a small number of gullible citizens.[11]

As an aside, the *New York Times* noted that other branches of the Pacific Movement existed, citing the FBI's arrest of one Mimo De Guzman, "a Filipino who has spent ten years trying to get members for a militant organization that would link the 'dark races' of the world." De Guzman, who had been arrested in New York on 30 July for draft evasion, was subsequently sent to St. Louis to answer charges of having violated federal postal laws by forging a money order. The career of Policarpio Manansala, alias Mimo De Guzman, alias Dr. Ashima Takis, alias, Dr. Koo was rapidly coming to an end.

A week after Jordan's arrest, federal authorities in Chicago cracked down on the leaders of several other pro-Japanese organizations. Once again the attorney general's office and FBI field officers differed over how to interpret the movements they uncovered. On 21 September Chicago FBI chief Albert Johnson announced the arrest of more than eighty-four African Americans and one white woman who were members of either the Temple of Islam, the Brotherhood of Liberty for Black People of America, or the Peace Movement of Ethiopia. According to the FBI, all three groups were an outgrowth of Japan's Black Dragon Society and had been organized in 1930 by "Major Satakata Takahashi of Japanese Imperial Intelligence." Most prominent among those arrested were Mittie Maud Lena Gordon and Elijah Mohammed (Poole), leaders of the Temple of Islam who along with ten others were charged with sedition. The remainder allegedly violated the Selective Service Act.

Johnson acknowledged that his agents had not found any direct connection between these groups and the Japanese, but the following day an unnamed federal official said, "It seems certain that Japanese money has been going to these organizations." Other statements by him suggest that the unnamed official was either Johnson or another member of his office. The same source told reporters that the three organizations had been under surveillance for three months and that "We have been waiting only on the go-ahead from Washington." Other arrests were expected in St. Louis, he added. In contrast to the unnamed official's intimation of a Japanese connection, the U.S. district attorney chose to emphasize that black Americans in general were not suspected of disloyalty; indeed, the majority were "fervently patriotic."[12]

Also caught in the FBI's net that September was Joseph Hilton Smyth, the white founder of the Negro News Syndicate and publisher of the magazines *Living Age, Foreign Observer, North American Review, Current History*, and *World Detective*. A "cadaverous" vagabond intellectual "of 'lost generation' vintage,"[13] Smyth achieved some success as a writer of popular fiction in the interwar years. He spent most of his time, however, in an alcoholic haze, engaging in various shady escapades and bouncing from one marriage to another. In 1938 he surfaced as the owner of *Living Age*, a venerable journal with a minuscule readership.

In his autobiography, *To Nowhere and Back*, Smyth claimed that he purchased the magazine with money he had saved from his writing. On his arrest, the FBI revealed that the $15,000 actually came from Fukushima Shintaro, Japanese vice counsel in New York, who had hired Smyth to propagandize for Japan. It was a bad bargain. As journalist Richard Rovere noted, *Living Age* was a "ponderously highbrow journal" that never claimed more than three thousand subscribers.[14] This suited Smyth, who was content to take Fukushima's money while devoting only a small portion of *Living Age* to the defense of Japanese imperialism. During the next three years Smyth used the rest of the $125,000 he eventually obtained from the Japanese to buy his other publications and indulge his taste for the good life.

Although the hapless Fukushima subsidized Smyth's publishing efforts, the Japanese did not hold exclusive rights on his loyalty. According to Rovere, while Fukushima was funding *Living Age*, the enterprising Smyth served as a ghostwriter for a virulently anti-Japanese book published by a prominent American journalist.[15] The Japanese evidently remained oblivious to how their money was being misused. In 1940 they backed Smyth's new venture, the Negro News Syndicate, with the intention of cultivating pro-Japanese sentiment among black readers, a plan similar to the one described in Hikida's captured papers. For his part, Smyth could claim some influence in the African American community by way of his recent marriage to Annastean Haines, a black nightclub singer, and his residence in the expensive Roger Morris Apartments in Harlem's Sugar Hill. Beginning in 1940, the Negro News Syndicate offered black weeklies assorted news items that purported, among other things, to provide the real story behind white opposition to Japan's role in Asia. As with Smyth's other efforts, Japan got less than it paid for. Despite Smyth's offer to provide this material without charge, he found few takers.[16]

By the late summer of 1942, what were thought to be the most serious cases of Japanese influence in the black community had been investigated by the FBI. Indictments had been brought and arrests made, some for sedition but the majority for violation of the Selective Service laws. Evidence of direct Japanese influence remained elusive. Nevertheless, the arrests and the allegations made by unnamed sources kept the specter of foreign influence alive for a little while longer.

Even the black press helped prolong the misperception of a Japanese-organized fifth-column movement among African Americans. The *Amsterdam-Star News* described Jordan as the leader of a countrywide movement allied to the right-wing Christian Front and funded by "foreign capital." The *Pittsburgh Courier*'s own investigators reported that the movement had grown so strong in the Midwest that black leaders were "becoming anxious over the growing attitude that the race would be better off if Japan won the war."[17] Writing in the *Chicago Defender*, A. Philip Randolph also saw the movement as Japanese directed. The following year Roi Ottley's *New World A-Coming*, a study of African American society during the war, added to the confusion about the true nature of the Black Internationale. Ottley, a black social worker and journalist, seemed uncertain whether Manansala was a shifty confidence man who had a "suit for every day of the week" or an agent "linked to Japan's militaristic Black Dragon Society," so he described him as both.[18]

By the time Ottley's book appeared, the FBI had obtained enough information through interrogations to reach a verdict on the extent of Japanese direction and influence over the various movements under investigation. Drawing on the individual reports from its field offices, the bureau's Internal Security Office compiled a summary report on "Japanese Influence and Activity among the American Negroes" as part of its larger file on "Racial Conditions in the United States."[19]

According to the FBI's analysts, "Japanese racial propaganda ... was attractive to certain classes of unscrupulous and pseudo-intellectual negro leaders who found the more ignorant class of colored people receptive to any scheme or philosophy which offered to relieve their economic condition and real or imagined discriminations practiced against them." These groups, including the Moslems that had concerned CIG, had "only an abstract connection with the Japanese government or Japanese aims." "Few of these organizations," the report concluded, "had Japanese affiliations or contacts of any consequence even with them as individuals. These societies appear to be chiefly devices used by racketeering negroes to solicit funds and to enhance their position with their followers." The various groups investigated, however, did serve Japanese interests by *furthering the propaganda efforts of the Japanese government without cost and leaving its imprint on negro thinking.*"

The FBI found that the "ringleaders" of the Black Internationale were actually confidence men with only an "abstract" connection to Japan. The CIG's nefarious Major Takahashi, founder of Development of Our Own and self-proclaimed member of the Black Dragon Society, was rediscovered to be Nakane Naka, an immigrant to Canada in 1903, who practiced "special doctoring" in Washington State before vanishing in 1926 because of financial problems. And the elusive Dr. Ashima Takis, alias Dr. Koo, also known as Mimo De Guzman, founder of the Pacific Movement of the Eastern World, once again became Policarpio Manansala, a well-traveled swindler who helped establish branches of his organization in St. Louis, Pittsburgh, New York, and Kansas City, where it counted approximately twenty members in 1938.

By 1942 only three branches were active: East St. Louis, St. Louis, and Boynton, Oklahoma. David B. Erwin, national president of the organization and leader of "Triumph, the Church of the New Age," admitted to FBI officers that the international-sounding names on the group's letterhead (Okamura, Sukiyaki, and Buena Comida) had been copied from the outdoor signs of Japanese businesses in California. The authors of the report accepted Erwin's explanation, noting that the names, which were translated as a proper name (Okamura), a Japanese meal (Sukiyaki), and a good dish (Buena Comida), "were probably taken from the sign of a Japanese restaurant."

Manansala, who had begun as an associate of Nakane, recruited Jordan into the movement in New York in 1935. After a falling out with Manansala, Jordan brought several Japanese to a meeting and exposed "Dr. Takis" as an impostor. The former Garveyite subsequently played up his connections to the Japanese, but it appears that he did little more than visit such organizations as the Japan Institute to obtain literature. Jordan also attempted to convince several Japanese in New York to attend his meeting to speak about racism, but they declined after concluding that he was using them for his own purposes.[20] In 1943 Jordan was convicted on charges of sedition, fined $5,000, and sentenced to ten years in prison. Manansala pleaded nolo contendere to charges of forgery and was sentenced to three years imprisonment in October 1942. In 1939 the hapless Nakane had been fined $4,500 and sentenced to three years for illegal entry and attempting to bribe an immigration official. He was subsequently transferred to a mental hospital for federal prisoners from which he was released in February 1942. Two months later he was once again apprehended as a "dangerous enemy alien" and interned.[21] By 1943, after ten years of rapid growth and even faster contraction, the Black Internationale had ceased to exist.

After a brief flurry of excitement, the handful of arrests made during the summer of 1942 worked to dissipate any fears of large-scale betrayal by black Americans. But the demise of the Black Internationale did not mean that American racism ceased to be a matter of international significance. What remained was the inescapable fact of black American apathy and widespread demoralization among the Asian allies of America and Britain. It was on these issues that black American leaders and the black press sought to focus the attention of the government and white press. Thus, although the FBI's crackdown on Jordan and the others briefly made news, in the long run it aided the cause of black internationalists by removing any taint of disloyalty from their efforts. Indeed, even as the arrests were making news, the message that racism was an international scourge was gaining new adherents.

In early September Wendell Willkie, the Republican Party's presidential nominee in 1940, sounded that theme at the NAACP's annual convention in Los Angeles. Citing America's alignment with India and China, Willkie denied that the war in the Pacific was a "clash between races." Rather, it was more accurately seen as a "clash between concepts of government and life." But this did not mean that the war was not affecting American attitudes about race. "Even Japan, our enemy, has been able to shake our racial complacency," he conceded. "Our ally, China, has by the same token taught us a new and healthy humility." Willkie added that these lessons were beginning to sink in at home as well. Comparing the treatment of African Americans in the United States to an "alien imperialism" complete with "a smug racial superiority" and a willingness to exploit the unprotected, he declared that "today it is becoming increasingly apparent to thoughtful Americans that we cannot fight the forces and ideas of imperialism abroad, and maintain a form of imperialism at home." [22]

As might be expected, Willkie's speech was especially well received in the African American community. [23] But the white press and journals of opinion with a predominantly white readership also continued to call attention to the interconnectedness of American racism and imperialism in Asia. In September the progressive journal *Nation* carried an analysis of the sources of low morale among African Americans by prominent black sociologist Horace Cayton. Provocatively titled "Fighting for White Folks?" Cayton's report began with the obvious. Black Americans could not identify with the goals of a larger society from which they had always been isolated. Moreover, few thought that their status would improve with the war, and thus their morale was low. Segregation in the armed forces, the segregation of blood plasma by the Red Cross, the killing of black GIs in uniform by white citizens, and the continued discrimination against black workers in defense industries all contributed to an overwhelming sense of apathy toward the American war effort.

But this did not mean that black Americans were uninterested in the war. Cayton explained that as a result of continued isolation from white society, African Americans identified with the cause of nonwhite peoples elsewhere in the world. "It may seem odd to hear India discussed in poolrooms in South State Street in Chicago," he added, "but India and the possibility of the Indians obtaining their freedom from England by any means have captured the imagination of the American Negro." [24] African Americans had begun to think that the war was going to change the status of nonwhite peoples throughout the world, according to Cayton, "and there is little fear that the change could be for the worse." This sense of impending seismic changes in relations between white and nonwhite peoples the world over was particularly exhilarating to black Americans. "Whereas for years Negroes have felt that their position was isolated and unalterable," Cayton explained, "some of them are now beginning to feel that dark people throughout the world will soon be on the march."

Cayton's article had begun gently, almost as if he were writing for an audience that would be surprised to learn that there was racism in America, but his tone had become more ominous as he progressed. Real and fundamental change was needed, he warned. Simple propaganda campaigns and superficial solutions would do more harm than good. Referring to an OFF film that showed black labor battalions singing at their work, he said the movie only infuriated black Americans who demanded the right to fight for their country but instead found themselves relegated to unskilled tasks in segregated units. Time was running out, Cayton insisted. The position of African Americans in American society was now a matter of "global importance." "There is a close relationship between the interracial tensions within the United Nations and the course of international events." "The present crisis in India," he continued, "is raising the expectations of American Negroes." On the other hand, Japan's victories and the demands of nonwhite members of the United Nations for equality were making whites evermore fearful and insistent on keeping down the "dark races."

Cayton acknowledged that "in the daily press and on the air the Negro is getting more attention than he has enjoyed since the Abolitionist days." But more was needed. Cayton urged the government to adopt a comprehensive plan to alter the position of black Americans in society. Inasmuch as Americans would not voluntarily undertake those changes, there was really no other solution. Either way, he concluded, "The shape of things to come—the new pattern of race relations—will be worked out on a global basis and will necessitate tremendous internal changes in many countries." [25]

The issue-oriented journal *Survey Graphic* followed Cayton's sobering analysis of American race relations in November with an entire issue devoted to "Color: The Unfinished Business of Democracy." Edited by Alain Locke, Howard University philosophy professor and "liaison officer of the Negro Renaissance," the special issue also contained articles by Assistant Secretary of State Adolf A. Berle Jr. and Syud Hossain, a Moslem and former editor of the *Bombay Chronicle*. The following month, the same magazine published an essay by Chinese author and scholar Lin Yutang titled "East and West Must Meet." In March *Survey Graphic* returned to the issue of race again with an exploration of the "Racial Roots of War" by George Edmund Haynes, the secretary for race relations of the Federal Council of Churches of Christ in America. These and other articles in similar journals made Americans increasingly aware of the ways in which the nation's dismal record on race relations undermined the war effort, but greater publicity still did not ensure agreement on how best to respond to the problem.

Editor Locke introduced the special issue on color with the observation that each month race issues stood "higher on the War Docket" and predicted that "Later on we shall confront them high up on the more constructive Ledger of Peace."[26] Nevertheless, the one contributor who could speak authoritatively on the government's plans to deal with racism, Assistant Secretary Berle, offered only vague encouragement for those who sought to confront the problem. Berle denounced Nazi "Master Race" thinking and claimed that Japan's ideas on race were an imitation of Germany's, but he did not, as many social scientists were already doing, challenge the idea of race itself as a natural means of distinguishing groups. Moreover, he concluded that since race was such an emotional subject, certain social taboos, such as intermarriage, could not be exorcised by federal legislation or treaty.[27]

On the other hand, Berle believed that there was more than enough for nations to do in dealing with political and economic issues. Questions of "social intimacy" could be left to individuals once a policy of coexistence based on nondiscrimination was enacted. Berle described this as President Abraham Lincoln's policy. "We have made some slight progress toward realizing that conception," he conceded. "The progress is not satisfactory. Yet the job can be done."

Lincoln's policy could also serve as a model for international relations. Here Berle cited Haiti as an example of the "co-existence of a Negro group, developing its own national institutions; learning through its own mistakes; fulfilling its own capacity and destiny." Certain general principles suggested themselves to Berle. Barriers to economic success needed to be removed, and stronger groups needed to maintain a self-imposed sense of restraint. Dominance of one group over another only weakened both, he believed.

"International civilization," he explained, "like national life, depends on acceptance by the strong of self-imposed, self-denying ordinances, protecting the less strong from oppression." American policy in the Philippines seemed to provide the best example of this behavior on the international level. To make this point Berle cited the example of a Filipino who gave his only shoes to an American prisoner who was being herded through Manila after the capture of Bataan. That act of kindness was the result of a long-term commitment to cooperation, equality, and independence on the part of Americans and Filipinos. "Let it be remembered by

"THE SAVIOR OF THE DARKER RACES"

"The Savior of the Darker Races," *Survey Graphic*, November 1942.
(Charles H. Alston for the Office of War Information, National Archives)

skeptics," Berle added, "that white men were cooperating in the freedom
of a race of a different color, at the time when Japanese were enslaving all
races within their reach, save their own."

This last point—that the Japanese would bring only misery to the countries they entered—was made more explicit by a cartoon contained in the
same issue in which Berle's article appeared. Produced by the Office of
War Information, the cartoonist tackled head-on the idea that Japan was
the leader of nonwhite peoples. Titled "The Savior of the Darker Races,"
the image depicted a Goliath of a Japanese soldier squinting through
glasses, teeth protruding, clasping chains in one hand and a bloody dagger
in the other. Perched above his head was a mock halo. Beneath his feet
lay the smoldering wreckage of Manchuria, China, and Korea. His work
in Asia accomplished, the emperor's soldier stomped out to sea in search
of fresh conquests.[28]

Berle's article and the owi's cartoon indicated that U.S. government officials were still concerned about Japan's appeal to the subject peoples of Asia and that they recognized that racism weakened the Allied cause. But the assistant secretary did not offer a concrete plan for dealing with that problem. Behind the scenes, the president's special representative to India was urging the British to grant greater autonomy to India, but alliance politics necessitated that Roosevelt say little publicly on the matter. Even if we make allowances for the demands of the alliance, there was little in Berle's article to comfort internationally minded African Americans and much to concern them.[29] Most would have been appalled by his assertion that Haiti had been left to make its own mistakes. Indeed, black Americans had forcefully condemned their government's occupation of Haiti during the Wilson administration as naked imperialism.

The example of the Philippines was hardly more encouraging. Leaving aside the question of how Berle learned about the anonymous Filipino's act of kindness, we can only wonder at his belief that Philippine-U.S. relations were a model of interracial cooperation. The American occupation of the islands at the turn of the century had touched off a rancid debate in the Senate about accepting "mongrel races" into the republic, and the islands had been governed as colonies at least in part to prevent Filipinos from enjoying the full rights of citizenship. Although it was true that the islands were headed for independence when Japan attacked, it was hardly the case that the two peoples interacted as equals.

Berle's rosy depiction of America's record in international race relations was matched by similarly troubling optimism about domestic race relations. Although it was not within his purview to discuss in any detail the issue of discrimination and segregation at home, let alone offer a comprehensive government plan such as Cayton desired, the assistant secretary's boilerplate assurances that America had room for improvement would have struck African American readers as nothing short of banal. Moreover, his belief that the taboos against intermarriage and "social intimacy" could not be lifted by legislation or treaty failed to acknowledge that state coercion was regularly employed to prevent closer contact between the races. More than three-fourths of the states enforced laws against intermarriage, and other forms of social intimacy were likewise restricted in the South by the elaborate system of segregation.

As an administration official, Berle was not free to publicly criticize America's diplomatic record in anything but the mildest terms. The assistant secretary was also certainly aware that any attempt to challenge the social taboos in American race relations would provoke a firestorm of criticism from the southern Democrats who controlled the most important positions in Congress. Given these circumstances, Berle probably had no other recourse but to take refuge in the hope that removing the economic and political barriers to success—no small task—would eventually lead to changes in social relations as well. But in taking such a mild evolutionary position, Berle demonstrated that although the issue of race had, as Locke put it, moved "higher on the War Docket," administration officials had yet to accept the idea that bold action was needed to solve this most vexing problem. In one sense Berle's essay did seem to prove the point made by black internationalists that American racism was unalterably linked to the broader problem of global race relations. In Berle's case, his remedies for racial discrimination at home seemed an accurate barometer of his pallid solutions for the international dilemma of racism.

In fact, Berle's views were indicative of policies being worked out in the State Department as the first year of the Pacific war drew to a close. After months of meetings, research, and consultations with scholars, the legal subcommittee of the Postwar Advisory Committee produced a draft for an international bill of human rights. Starting from the premise that any guarantee of basic human rights would promote international peace, the subcommittee's final draft contained a clause declaring that the enumerated rights would "constitute a part of the supreme law of each state and shall be observed and enforced by its administrative and judicial authorities, without discrimination on the basis of nationality, language, race, political opinion, or religious belief, any law or constitutional provision notwithstanding." [30]

The subcommittee members recognized, however, that the mere mention of enforcement would alarm all those who dreaded surrendering their sovereign rights to a future replacement for the League of Nations. The task of winning support for U.S. participation in a postwar international organization would be hard enough without raising the prospect of some international body tampering with the nation's laboriously crafted system of institutional racism. Like Berle, the legal subcommittee found its solution to this problem in a broad declaration of human rights that would be short on specifics insofar as enforcement was concerned. In effect, the State Department's team decided that the only satisfactory solution was to rely on the good faith of the member nations. As the drafters noted, just getting the member nations to agree to something as radical as the principle of basic human rights would not be easy. [31] This prediction proved accurate. In the months to come, the members of the legal subcommittee would have their hands full trying to get their own government to support the inclusion of a racial equality clause in the charter of the proposed international organization.

After nearly a year of calling attention to the interconnected dangers of American racism and white supremacy in Asia, African American leaders had succeeded in placing racism on the war docket. But although most federal officials recognized that racism posed a threat to national security, they showed little inclination to tackle the problem head-on. The Department of State had responded with only an endorsement of general principles and a reliance on social evolution and world opinion to achieve racial justice in the world. The Congress, as represented by the Senate Foreign Relations Committee, had approached the matter in a way that suggested that its members believed that America's race relations and the problem of white rule in Asia were discrete issues. The latter could be resolved if Britain granted India greater autonomy and if Britain and America surrendered their claims to extraterritoriality in China.

As for the Congress, clearly many senators did not regard America's race relations as a problem in need of government action. From the perspective of black leaders who were trying to convince U.S. officials that America's race relations were an international problem, it was difficult to know which approach was more discouraging. One promised only rhetorical support coupled with the deferral of meaningful solutions until, in all probability, much later. The other ignored domestic discrimination entirely while urging others to act. If this was as far as the government was willing to go when Japan was on the march, what would happen when the tide of battle turned in favor of the Allies?

As if the government's reaction were not discouraging enough, the start of the second year of the war found black leaders once more under public attack. This time their adversary was not a bombastic political gossip writer like Westbrook Pegler, but a putative ally who employed the tenets of black internationalism to impugn the loyalty of black civil rights advocates. In the January *Atlantic*, Viginius Dabney, editor of the *Richmond Times-Dispatch*, lashed out at black leaders for what he called their "rule-or-ruin" radicalism on the issues of political and social equality. Dabney, who had supported the antilynching bill in Congress and otherwise urged a "fairer and saner treatment of our Negro citizens," warned that black American demands for a complete end to segregation would provoke "an interracial explosion that would make the race riots of the First World War and its aftermath seem mild by comparison." Unless saner heads prevailed on both sides, Dabney feared, internal clashes could leave thousands dead and turn back the clock on amicable race relations by decades. If "extremist" black leaders did not change tactics, he added, the resulting violence could also have "far-reaching and heavily adverse effects upon the colored peoples of China, India, and the Middle East—peoples whose attitude can be of crucial importance to the Allies in the war."[32]

Dabney did not spare southern bigots like Governor Eugene Tallmadge of Georgia, but he directed most of his fire at black public figures like NAACP assistant secretary Roy Wilkins for declaring that African Americans were "determined to be forever through with the status quo." In particular, Dabney blamed what he described as radical black newspapers, citing the *Pittsburgh Courier* as one example, for their unrelenting attacks on anyone, white or black, who counseled patience and caution. Although admitting that black Americans were "overwhelmingly patriotic," he vitiated that assertion by adding that "too many of them have been indoctrinated with the belief that since the Japanese are a colored race the blacks might be more equitably treated by Tokyo than by Washington. . . . Like the natives of Malaya and Burma, the American Negroes are sometimes imbued with the notion that a victory for the yellow race over the white race might also be a victory for them. These ideas may or may not be planted by Axis agents. Certainly they are seriously disruptive of morale."

Finally, to those who argued that the cause of the allies in Asia would be weakened unless the United States ceased discriminating against black Americans, Dabney countered that to launch a social revolution against majority opposition in the midst of global war would be "the height of folly." The ensuing turmoil would "plunge us into the bitterest and most disastrous fratricidal strife in eighty years, and fatally weaken us in our battle for survival."

Dabney's answer to the problem of black and white extremism was to hope that "the disturbing elements on both sides can somehow be muzzled for the duration." Having narrowly avoided federal sanctions earlier in the war, the black press would manage to survive this latest call for censorship. More troubling, however, was Dabney's use of black internationalist themes to blunt African American demands for equality and, worse, to revive the question of black American loyalty. His references to black American sympathy for the Japanese and his intimation that it had been planted by enemy agents forcefully demonstrated how hard it would be for African Americans to escape the lingering effects of their ideological attachment to Japan. But his other arguments indicated that even if one accepted the essential premise of black internationalism, the interconnectedness of domestic and international racism, it was possible to arrive at a completely different conclusion from the one desired by black leaders. This is what

Dabney did when he argued that because Asians were watching how the United States handled its own race relations, it was imperative that African Americans cease agitating for dramatic changes in the status quo.

Black internationalists had, of course, maintained the opposite. It was precisely because all of Asia looked toward America for some indication that racism would no longer poison relations between white and nonwhite peoples that the United States needed to provide full equality for its black citizens. But Dabney seemed to say that if black Americans abandoned the Double V campaign, it would be easier to persuade Asians that the United States was capable of conducting relations with nonwhite peoples in a way that was harmonious and mutually beneficial. In his view, it was not racism so much as it was the strident calls to end the effects of racism that posed the real threat to American security.

As Lee Finkle has noted, Dabney's salvo against the Double V campaign with its predictions of a racial cataclysm was itself written in the inflammatory style he decried. Although his article outraged black editors and journalists and briefly rekindled fears of censorship, the Virginian's attack on black extremism actually proved to be one of the last significant attempts to muffle the black press. In the months that followed, liberal journals such as the *New Republic* came to the defense of the African American press, giving it high marks for candor and patriotism.[33]

The failure of this latest effort to depict the black press as disloyal once again cleared the way for civil rights leaders to define American racism as part of an international problem in need of immediate attention. In mid-January the *Nation* published an article by Charles Williams that accepted some of Dabney's premises but identified white racism rather than black extremism as the source of trouble in America's African American communities. Williams reported that in Harlem the war "doesn't seem to matter much." Black Americans still wanted the United States to win, "but only casually." Williams found expressions of apathy pervading newspapers, pulpits, and street corners. A sense of disinterestedness about the outcome of the war was commonly held by Harlem's intellectuals and cleaning women alike.[34]

Like Dabney, Williams believed that Japanese propagandists, "with customary thoroughness," had invaded Harlem years before the outbreak of the war. It was a credit to Harlem's "basic loyalty" that individuals like Leonard Robert Jordan had failed to win much of a following. Admittedly some members of the community cheered at the early success of the " 'brown man's' success over the 'white.' " But unlike Dabney, Williams concluded that this was a "race consciousness, which the country by every device of wrongheadedness has brought to a new pitch; it is not sedition." Williams also differed from Dabney in his assessment of the international implications of black militancy. "Harlem's heightened race consciousness has taken a turn that is constructive and immensely interesting," he calmly observed. "Partly as a result of the insistent hammering of its newspapers and many of its leaders, Harlem is acquiring a sense of oneness with India, China, the West Indies and, of course, Africa."

The "sense of oneness" with Africa and India that Williams observed had been building over previous decades. African American identification with the Chinese was, however, a more recent development in black internationalism. Following the outbreak of war, despite their previous disagreements concerning China and Japan, black leaders began to reach a new consensus on the importance of China as a symbol and potential ally in their own struggle against racism. Within a year after Pearl Harbor, African American leaders seemed poised to anoint China, the only non-white member of the Big Four, as the new champion of the darker races. The quickness with which black leaders moved to forge an alliance with China demonstrated the extraordinary adaptability of black internationalism that was at once its greatest strength and its biggest weakness.

[8]

The Rediscovery of China

Early in the war, after years of condemnation as a nation of Uncle Toms, the Chinese had begun to take on a new, more favorable appearance in the black press. In an attempt to align black Americans' crusade for civil rights with the crusade for liberation in the colonial world, the NAACP and many prominent black editors and commentators launched a press campaign to recruit Nationalist China as an ally in the struggle for racial equality. At the same time that black internationalists sought to distance themselves from Japan, their relationship with China underwent a conversion. The "rediscovery" of China served complimentary purposes for black Americans. It allowed them to stress on the role of race and racism in the Pacific war while immunizing them from charges of sedition stemming from their previous sympathy with Japan. More concretely, making common cause with China, the only nonwhite member of the Big Four, might also help advance the cause of civil rights at home.

The refurbishment of China's image by black American opinion makers was facilitated by writer-activist Pearl Buck. Raised in China by missionary parents, Buck had become a devoted evangelist for universally humane values. By 1941, a decade after her Pulitzer Prize–winning novel *The Good Earth* appeared, she was already America's most important interpreter of Chinese life. But Buck, who had returned to America in 1934, was also justly renowned for her ardent advocacy of racial equality. According to Walter White, Pearl Buck was one of two white Americans who understood the conditions that African Americans faced on a daily basis; the other was First Lady Eleanor Roosevelt. Scholars have emphasized Buck's roles as "the most influential Westerner to write about China since the thirteenth-century Marco Polo" and as a civil rights activist, but during World War II she also performed the more specialized task of introducing black Americans to China.[1]

Buck's efforts on behalf of better understanding between Chinese and African Americans were the natural result of her attempts to warn white Americans of the dangers created by their own prejudices. In her famous letter to the *New York Times* in November 1941 and in a well-publicized speech at the Book and Author Luncheon in March the next year, she described how oppressed colonial subjects and despairing black Americans were beginning to look to Japan as a savior. In her "Plea to Colored Americans," also published in March, Buck tried to disabuse black Americans of their illusions about Japan. "Japan's whole culture, ancient and modern," she insisted, "is based on a stern subjugation of the individual." If black Americans were looking for a true friend in Asia, they needed to look to the mainland. Buck reminded her readers that "We have as our great ally the old democracy of China . . . China will be deeply concerned with the peace, but there are concerned [*sic*] also the peoples of India and Malaysia, the Philippines, Europe and Africa." All of those peoples, she concluded, were looking to black Americans to see if the world would divide on "the false lines of color" or unite behind the idea of freedom for all.[2]

As might be expected, Buck's letters, which were widely published in the black press and subsequently collected and issued under the title *American Unity and Asia*, were warmly received by black Americans. "If we had more like Pearl Buck what a better world it would be to live in," was a typical reader's response.[3] The editors of the *Baltimore Afro-American* agreed, titling one of their editorials "The Wisdom of Pearl Buck."[4] To some extent, Buck's stature among black Americans was enhanced by the company she kept on the pages of the black press. Her letter to the *New York Times* appeared on the same day as the announcement of the Red Cross's decision to segregate blood plasma. And her calls for racial equality drew a rebuke from Mississippi congressman John Rankin, who charged that she advocated the intermarriage of whites and Chinese.[5] The juxtaposition of Buck's letter and the Red Cross story, as well as Rankin's attack, vividly dramatized Buck's role as the voice of sanity in a world of irrational bigotry.

The extent to which her decency and honesty influenced white America to rethink its racial policies is a subject for another study. For our purposes, however, it is important to note that Buck's notoriety facilitated the rehabilitation of China's image in the black community. The names of Pearl Buck and Chiang Kai-shek regularly appeared together in the black press, with the former adding luster to the latter. During the war Buck's

Pearl Buck delivers her "10 Points" at the Howard University
commencement, June 1942. (Moorland-Spingarn
Research Center, Howard University)

work on behalf of racial equality and her role as the champion of free
China merged in a way that made the two causes indistinguishable. In
late March she appeared with world-famous black actor, vocalist, and civil
rights activist Paul Robeson on a radio salute to China. Several weeks later
she and Robeson spoke to an audience of four thousand gathered in New
York. In May she addressed a conference at Lincoln University, a black
college in Pennsylvania, on the perils of racism. Also speaking were Walter White; Judge William Hastie, special assistant to the secretary of war
on racial affairs; Krishnatal Shreedharam of the All-India Congress; and
Liu Liang-Mo, a Chinese representative for United China Relief, an um-
brella group for American agencies providing relief to China, organized
by Henry Luce, publisher of *Time* and *Life* magazines.

In June 1942 the *Baltimore Afro-American* published a front-page story
on her commencement address at Howard University. Blocked and titled
in bold print, "Pearl Buck's 10 Points for Victory and Peace" was described by the editors as "the most remarkable address ever delivered at
Howard." The list, which combined self-help formulas and a summons to
battle racism in all its forms, called for black Americans to urge repeal
of the Chinese immigration act, support more aid to China, and push for

India's freedom. The editors were especially pleased to single out that aspect of Buck's message because of the way it explicitly linked the problems of racism at home and abroad. "If granting equality to colored Americans, Chinese and Indians is the price we must pay for victory," they vowed, "the nation will override the obstructionists of 1942 as completely as it did the secesns of 1863."[6]

After years of neglect a new China seemed to be emerging on the pages of the black press. According to Joseph Bibb of the *Pittsburgh Courier*, China's alliance with the United States and Britain could provide "the means by which the darker races of the earth may be able to win a place in the sun." Bibb admitted that many thought Japan would play that role, but the current war was bound to leave it defeated and confined to its home islands. Formerly a land of "docile Celestials," China, the "slumbering giant," was about to take Japan's place in the world. With the help of white aviators and military strategists "the sons of Confucius" were avenging their earlier humiliations at the hands of the Japanese. Once the war was over, the "inherently smart and intellectual" Chinese would repulse the other imperialists and declare an Asian Monroe Doctrine. "Thus the 'Rising Tide of Color' will be made evident," Bibb predicted. Apart from revealing an addiction to journalistic clichés, Bibb's column was noteworthy for its emphasis on white agency in the process of China's redemption. Like Japan, China would borrow from the West to achieve its independence. China's alignment with the West, previously perceived as the mark of an Uncle Tom, was now viewed favorably as the sign of a revitalized nation liberating itself from oppression.[7]

As one of the "leaders of the colored world," to borrow Walter White's description, Chiang Kai-shek as well as China benefited from being linked to other causes of significance to black Americans. According to the *Baltimore Afro-American*, China was "astonished by our weakness." Having fought Japan to a standstill with borrowed planes and a poorly equipped army, the Chinese, one of America's "great allies," was appalled by the disorder in the Allied camp as evidenced most glaringly by Britain's unwillingness to deal fairly with India. Chiang was doing all he could to remedy this situation, the editors explained, by conferring with India's leaders and imploring Britain to grant autonomy to that country.[8] Impressed by Chiang's support for Indian nationalism, Walter White went a step further than the *Afro-American* and requested that the president assemble a conference of Indian Nationalists, British leaders, and Chiang Kai-shek to seek a solution to the colonial issue.[9]

The work of Pearl Buck, China's determined resistance to invasion, and

Chiang's efforts on behalf of India provided black journalists and public figures with useful materials for remaking China's image in the African American community. More was needed, however, to overcome the widespread feeling among African Americans that the Chinese were a clannish, secretive people who would eagerly discriminate against blacks to curry favor with whites. P. L. Prattis's description of the Chinese as Uncle Toms and Ira Lewis's blistering criticism of the Chinese in America were only the most recent manifestations of this perception. Although similar comments had been made about the Japanese in America, most recently by J. A. Rogers, they were less frequent and outweighed by the image Japan had created as an opponent of the racial status quo in world politics. The infrequent contacts between African Americans, Chinese, and Japanese in America only added to the highly impressionistic flavor of these attitudes.

Initially some attempts to acquaint black Americans with their new allies may have actually reinforced negative perceptions of the Chinese. Reporting from the West Coast immediately after the attack on Pearl Harbor, the *Baltimore Afro-American*'s Ralph Matthews provided his readers with a cultural guide to differentiating between Japanese, Chinese, and other Asians. According to Matthews, "Chinese while having slanting eyes, are taller than Japs and darker—a real yellow—while the Japs are nearer white than yellow." For some unexplained reason, he added, the Japanese were more prone to weak eyes, had flatter faces, and squarer chins. Despite these physical differences, the real distinction between the peoples was mental. The Japanese were "thorough, progressive and open to modern ideas," whereas the Chinese were "lackadaisical, dreamy and prefer to live in the past rather than the future." Japanese operated "exclusive hotels and stores" but the Chinese ran "shadier enterprises like gambling houses and cabarets." In general, the Chinese managed family businesses rather than large concerns. Family loyalty made it hard for the Chinese to enter into partnerships. "He does not mean to be dishonest," Matthews explained, "but the Chinese mentality makes it hard for him to pay dividends on stocks and bonds while any member of his family is in need of either funds or a job." In contrast, the Japanese who had "no family obligations to fulfill," knew "but two loyalties—the emperor and efficiency."[10]

Intended to make the Chinese seem more familiar, Matthews's first effort as an orientalist produced an unflattering portrait that probably made his subject appear even more exotic. In his hands, such usually positive traits as family loyalty became a constraining force for the seemingly backward Chinese. His depiction of the more progressive Japanese as almost white was also telling. Despite this awkward start, however, Matthews began to warm to his subject. Two weeks later he presented a second report on the Chinese that, although containing stereotypes, presented America's ally in a far more favorable light. After visiting the shop of Suey Chee, a Chinese herbalist in San Francisco, Matthews told readers of China's newfound unity in the face of Japanese aggression. Chinese scientific knowledge, as exemplified by the venerable "Dr. Chee," was presented as the equal of Western medical science, although it was discovered through "devious and sundry ways." Matthews also helped readers sympathize with Chee by providing a detailed description of Japanese atrocities as displayed in the photographs on the shop walls. In all, his positive portrait of Chee conveyed an image of a dignified people united in defense of their homeland.[11]

Readers of the *Pittsburgh Courier* did not have to rely on the observations of outsiders to learn about the Chinese. For insights into Chinese society, they could turn to the regular columns of Liu Liang-Mo. Liu became a regular contributor to the editorial page not long after appearing with Pearl Buck at Lincoln University. At the time he spoke at Lincoln, Liu worked as a spokesman for United China Relief. A graduate of Shanghai College with a bachelor's degree in sociology, he had gained fame in China when he started a YMCA program to teach Chinese workers "mass singing" to lift morale. The movement became a huge success, with other Y's taking it up.[12]

According to author Lin Yutang, when Japan invaded China, Chiang Kai-shek called on Liu to teach mass singing to troops at the front lines. A one-man United Service Organization, in one instance Liu had ten thousand soldiers singing together. Madame Chiang said that he had "taught a nation of soldiers, guerrillas, farmers, and road builders to sing while they toil and fight." The Japanese placed a price on his head. When Paul Robeson recorded a collection of Chinese folk songs for United China Relief, he included "Ch'i Lai: The March of the Volunteers," a song Liu popularized in China. After arriving in the United States in 1941 to work for United China Relief, Liu logged nearly 100,000 miles speaking to groups on behalf of his country.

His appearance before the students at Lincoln University was one such occasion. In his address to the gathering, Liu compared Jim Crowism and anti-Semitism in the United States to fascism. "If we lick fascism and Japanese imperialism we lick jim crow and anti-Semitism at the same time," he declared. Liu's call "to colored people all over the world to join our fight" was a common theme sounded repeatedly at the meeting, but at least one member of the audience was unaccustomed to associating that message with the Chinese. *Pittsburgh Courier* editor P. L. Prattis was evidently so

Liu Liang-Mo, ca. 1941–45. (Princeton University Library)

impressed by Liu that he hired the representative of United China Relief to provide a Chinese perspective to *Courier* readers.[13]

Over the next three years Liu used his coveted space in the nation's largest black weekly, with a reported circulation of two hundred thousand, to try to create a more positive image of China in the African American community. In his first column for the *Pittsburgh Courier*, he wrote of attending a rally for India with such prominent black leaders as Max Yergan of the Council on African Affairs, Adam Clayton Powell Jr., and Paul Robeson. Referring to the latter's recording of Chinese folk songs, Liu declared that Robeson's "singing of these songs is a strong token of the solidarity between the Chinese and Negro people."[14]

Others also attempted to dispel black perceptions of the Chinese as prejudiced toward African Americans. Pearl Buck told listeners at Lincoln that China, "more than any country I know, practices human equality." On another occasion she declared that "the Chinese have fewer prejudices than any people I know. They have no race prejudices against black or white."[15] Of course, Buck's depiction of China as a land of equality hardly squared with reality. But her praise for Chinese egalitarianism might be better understood as an expression of her hopes following the formation of a united front by Communists and Nationalists and American entry into the war. Moreover, when Buck spoke of China, she meant the mass of peasants, with whom she sympathized, not the elite.[16] By idealizing China in this way she presented a sympathetic and positive portrayal of the Chinese people, but she also unintentionally misled black Americans about the Nationalists' interest in their cause.

The belief that the Chinese held no race prejudices was so widely held in some circles that U.S. military planners counted on it in making troop deployments. In drawing up plans for overseas assignments, officers on the general staff included China among the countries where they could post black GIs without fear of provoking racial hostility.[17] Editor Lucius Harper was also convinced that the Chinese did not harbor any prejudice toward black Americans. Having previously described China as the "gentleman of Asia," Harper wrote a second article expounding on the admirable qualities of its people. He found the Chinese "friendly, gregarious folk, who like to talk, will discuss anything, and are devoid of what we call 'race prejudice.'"[18]

According to Harper, the Chinese were so secure in their identity that they did not fear combination with other races, nor did they practice discrimination against races "darker or less advanced than their own." As Harper knew, this statement directly contradicted the experience of African Americans who complained of being discriminated against by Chinese businesses. To resolve this discrepancy, he relied on an explanation that had previously been offered in mitigation of Japanese aloofness toward black Americans in the United States. The Chinese, or Japanese, depending on who one spoke to, were not prejudiced in their own country, but they were encouraged or even compelled to adopt those attitudes by the overbearing white majority in the United States. Those Chinese "who have not been misled by their association with the white man have shown a total disregard for jim crow and miscegenation laws in this country."

Harper's assessment of Chinese racial attitudes appeared to be confirmed by no less an authority on Chinese civilization than critic Lin Yutang, whose books were published by the John Day Company, a firm owned by Pearl Buck's husband. In an article for *Survey Graphic* that appeared in the issue after Alain Locke's special edition on race, Lin explained that the Chinese were committed to racial equality as a wartime goal. On the other hand, Lin criticized the Americans and British for acting as though only the Nazis suffered from a master race psychology. He related that when traveling across the United States he had been shocked to find the existence of caste in a country dedicated to freedom. Americans might laugh at the Hindus with their untouchables, he said, "but if white treatment of Negroes in America is not caste, I do not know what caste is."[19]

As a policy-oriented journal, *Survey Graphic* did not have the mass audience of the more popular black weeklies. Thus, although Lin's criticism of American racism was bound to be well received by educated readers, the articles by Pearl Buck, Liu Liang-Mo, Ralph Matthews, and Lucius Harper were likely to reach a broader audience in the black community. All of these would be unproductive, however, if their message of Chinese devotion to racial equality contradicted the daily experience of black Americans, whose contact with Chinese in the United States was limited. According to Roi Ottley, approximately two thousand Chinese lived in Harlem. Since most Chinese on the West Coast resided in San Francisco, a city with a small black population, interaction there was also minimal. The limited scope of Chinese activities in black communities meant that anecdotal evidence and occasional episodes of contact formed the basis on which black Americans judged the validity of the press's representation of China. Here the auguries for China replacing Japan in the affections of average black citizens appeared mixed.

Ottley reported that the small number of Chinese in Harlem were highly integrated into the life of the community. "Uniformly they make the best adjustment to the Negro community," he wrote, "even to stomping the lindy hop at the Savoy Ballroom." Chinese restaurants were popular with black Harlemites and Chinese merchants frequently intermarried with African Americans. On the death of a prominent Chinese businessman, more than five hundred African Americans attended his funeral. Ottley noted that the community's residents also seemed sensitive to Chinese concerns. On one occasion, a black quartet dropped the song "Minnie the Moocher" from its repertoire at the request of the Chinese consul, who had unsuccessfully sought to have the offending song banned from the airwaves.[20] On the West Coast, contact was more casual, most of it associated with the illegal Chinese lottery. At a bazaar for China relief in 1941, black sponsors raised three thousand dollars. An observer noted, however, that the recipients of the aid seemed ill at ease, "much as white persons might be." Ottley concluded, "At best Negroes and Chinese are not hostile to each other, nor are they neighborly—actually, they are strangers."[21]

Black leaders hoped to rectify that situation in the coming months and to transform the casual contact between African Americans and Chinese into a mutually beneficial relationship. The arrival of Madame Chiang Kai-shek, the former Soong Meiling, in the United States at the end of 1942 provided an opportunity to inaugurate the alliance desired by black leaders. Although she was in the country for medical reasons, Madame Chiang was expected to use her considerable political skills to advance her country's cause with the American public and to campaign for additional federal and private aid for China.[22]

In December 1942 Walter White sought to enlist China's first lady in the Double V campaign. Specifically, White wanted Madame Chiang to appear at a Madison Square Garden rally to publicize the "Global Aspect of [the] Race Question." White also hoped to enlist the support of Congresswoman Clare Booth Luce, Wendell Willkie, and Eleanor Roosevelt at the rally. Mrs. Roosevelt notified him, however, that Madame Chiang did "not want to appear for special organizations but for the Red Cross or War Bonds." The American first lady conjectured that Madame Chiang had been asked by so many groups that she could not possibly satisfy them all. She advised White that Madame Chiang would be making a series of radio addresses and suggested that he ask her to devote one of them to "a subject of interest" to the NAACP.

Undeterred, White wrote directly to Madame Chiang asking for a brief conference with her as her schedule permitted. White assured her of the affection that African Americans held for China and reminded her that this "admiration had been concretized in funds raised for Chinese relief through American artists like Miss [Marian] Anderson and through funds raised by branches of this Association." He proposed a small gathering to discuss "further ways in which we can help and, also, some implications of the world-wide problem of color which are inherent in the situation in the Pacific as well as in race relations in the United States." White noted that Marian Anderson, W. E. B. Du Bois, and Judge William H. Hastie would also be present and that Eleanor Roosevelt, Wendell Willkie, and Pearl Buck were expected to participate.[23]

White's conference never took place. Madame Chiang did speak at a

Walter White, June 1942. (Library of Congress)

rally at Madison Square Garden on 2 March 1943, but it was not the event White envisioned. Preceding her on the podium were the chief of the U.S. Army Air Force, Lieutenant General Henry A. Arnold; the president of the Union Theological Seminary, Dr. Henry Sloane Coffin; and the governors of New York and several neighboring states. Madame Chiang then spoke about China's needs in the war against Japan. Her presentation contained several references to the equality of nations, and she observed that the Roman empire lasted as long as it did because all of its inhabitants were citizens, "there was no racial discrimination as we have today." But apart from those few comments, she did not address the issues that concerned White.[24] After the rally White settled for a perfunctory meeting with China's first lady at a reception at the Chinese consulate in New York. According to his press release, he assured her of the "deep interest" African Americans had in China's struggle. Madame Chiang thanked "the NAACP official for the expression of interest in her country on the part of American Negroes." The announcement made no mention of the "world-wide problem of color."[25]

Despite Madame Chiang's reluctance to speak more forcefully on the issue of discrimination in America, the black press continued to burnish China's image. In mid-March a *Pittsburgh Courier* poll showed that although 54 percent of respondents thought that the United States was doing all it could to aid China, 29 percent did not. Another 16 percent was undecided. The editors treated both the survey results and the question "Do you believe our government has done what it should have to furnish China with materials of War?" as an opportunity to comment on the racial aspects of American alliance politics.

Although 70 percent of the respondents answered yes or could not make up their minds, the *Courier* titled the story "Aid to China Not What It Should Be." A large graph, approximately twenty lines high and one-half page wide, actually reversed the results by incorrectly showing that 54 percent had answered no to the question. Even if this mistake was unintentional, the bias of the editors was evident in the amount of attention devoted to those who answered no. One participant, a social worker in Chicago, was quoted as representative of the negative responses. According to the story, she said: "I have no way of knowing all that has been done for China. But I do know that China is a yellow race and having observed a number of our public men's utterances in regards to China's needs I have drawn the conclusion that some of them are not doing what they could to expedite materials of war to that nation."[26]

As Madame Chiang traveled across the country, China continued to receive coverage in the *Pittsburgh Courier*. A story titled "Race Active in Honoring China's First Lady" carried a photograph of the "Gracious Visitor from Brave China" and a subheading announcing Madame's abhorrence of all bias. Readers were informed that black Americans had played a prominent role in arranging the rally for the distinguished guest at New York's Madison Square Garden and that she insisted on meeting with all members of the press together rather than holding a separate conference for black reporters. China's first lady reportedly believed that all races should be given equal opportunity to develop. She added that there was no discrimination in the Chinese Republic.

Courier correspondent Llewellyn Ransom reintroduced the subject of aid to China by referring to Chinese sources who contended that Ameri-

Madame Chiang Kai-shek and Speaker of the House of Representatives
Sam Rayburn (D-Tex.), 1943. (Photograph by Associated Press;
Library of Congress)

can assistance was flagging because China had offended Britain by supporting Indian autonomy. Thus readers were assured that Madame Chiang
supported two positions of greatest concern to black Americans, racial
equality and Indian independence. The story could not have been more
favorable to Madame Chiang and the Chinese.[27]

A week later, however, the tone of black press coverage of her tour
began to change as journalists became frustrated by her unwillingness to
appeal directly to African Americans. Reporting from Chicago on her visit
to that city, the *Pittsburgh Courier* informed readers that because Madame
did not wish to distinguish between groups of Americans, she "declined
to issue a special greeting to the Negro people of America through the

Negro press." According to the *Courier's* page-one story, similar attempts by black journalists in Washington and New York had been unavailing. Madame's statements on equality were now considered pro forma generalities of little significance. Her refusal to speak directly to black Americans through their own representatives indicated that "either she could not see that American Negroes were fighting for their own freedom here at home as well as the freedom of all other peoples, or that she hesitated to make a statement publicly that might be held to have some bearing on America's race problem." [28]

The remainder of the story made it clear that the *Courier* believed it was the latter. As Soong Meiling had been educated at Wesleyan College in Georgia and Wellesley College in Massachusetts, she could hardly expect people to believe that she did not understand the special circumstances of black Americans. If anything, her own experience should have made her more attuned to black concerns. According to this account, she was almost forced out of Wesleyan because she was Chinese. Nevertheless, she continued to snub the black press.

The *Baltimore Afro-American* also made much of Madame Chiang's alleged description of herself as a southerner during her college years. Black Americans had a special name to describe people of color who curried favor with whites by turning their backs on their own. The editors of the *Afro-American* and the *Pittsburgh Courier* did not call Madame an Uncle Tom, a label they had pinned on China before, but they came very close. [29]

As James C. Thomson has noted, Madame Chiang's tour of the United States was enormously successful. Some observers even suggested that if she had been an American citizen, she could be elected president. [30] It is doubtful, however, that China's first lady would have run well in Harlem or America's other predominantly black communities. Despite her diplomatic skill, she could not continue to finesse the requests from African Americans without raising doubts about China's intentions. Her smooth replies to Walter White and the black press provided little succor for blacks seeking a dynamic ally in the international war against racism. As the *Pittsburgh Courier* quickly concluded, Madame Chiang was not going to enlist in the Double V campaign. She was in America to appeal for increased aid to her beleaguered country and was unlikely to antagonize powerful southern congressmen while lobbying for that objective. Calculations about China's national interest did not preclude broad statements on behalf of humankind, but where national survival conflicted with specific issues of human rights, Chinese nationalism prevailed over inter-nationalism.[31]

Black leaders understood the reasoning behind Madame's refusal to ad-dress African Americans separately, but they disagreed with its premise. Without true racial equality in the world, they argued, peace would be impossible. And without solidarity between the members of the darker races, racial equality could not be achieved. Columnist Horace Cayton took Madame Chiang to task for failing to understand this central proposi-tion of black internationalism. China's first lady was "no Wendell Willkie," he wrote. Indeed, she appeared incapable of recognizing "any similarity between the Chinese fight for liberation and that of the American Negro." In contrast, Cayton offered the example of a small black church he had recently visited. Despite their own obvious needs, the members of the con-gregation had taken up a collection for United China Relief. This was proof that "These Negro Baptists saw a relationship between their prob-lem and non-white people and that of the Chinese that escaped Madame Chiang."[32]

In a similar vein, Rayford Logan reminded an audience in June 1943 that the problem of "inter-minority repression" kept all minorities in a position of subservience. Although he included the much-admired Indians among the exploiters, his description of Chinese racial attitudes may have seemed the most troubling in light of Madame Chiang's visit. Referring to the notorious sign at the entrance to a park in the International Settle-ment in Shanghai that allegedly read "Chinese and Dogs not allowed," Logan sadly told his listeners, "Imagine our dismay then when Miss Pearl Buck told a Washington audience recently that the Chinese had put over a swimming pool in Singapore: 'For Chinese Only.'"[33]

Logan's use of this anecdote was intended as a warning about the perils of racism everywhere. In linking the two signs in the same parable, how-ever, he could not help reminding his listeners of China's dubious standing as an ally. For black Americans, the sign in the Shanghai park had too many disturbing parallels to the signs they encountered throughout much of the United States. That the Chinese tolerated such humiliation in their own country was bad enough, but for Chinese to inflict similar treatment on others was an even greater sin.

Although black American leaders were disturbed by Madame Chiang's refusal to speak on behalf of their cause, NAACP officials soon found reason to hope that China might still become a worthy ally. In July 1943 Wal-ter White received a solicitation for donations to the China Blood Bank, which was operated by the American Bureau for Medical Aid to China, an affiliate of United China Relief. (The American Bureau's letterhead listed Madame Chiang as honorary chair and the Chinese ambassador and consul general in New York as honorary president and vice president.) In appealing for contributions, Helen Kennedy Stevens, the bureau's executive director, noted the NAACP's interest in breaking down racial barriers, adding, "Needless to say, no distinction is made at the Blood Bank as to race or color."[34] This oblique reference to the Red Cross's segregation of blood plasma did not fail to catch White's attention.

Perhaps no issue more clearly illustrated the virulence of American racism than the refusal of the American Red Cross to mingle the blood of African Americans and whites in its blood bank. Although the medical community knew that there was no difference between the blood of black and white donors, it bowed to segregationist political pressure and established separate banks. In acting as if some real difference did exist, the Red Cross strengthened one of the pillars on which racist theories stood. To say that this was a matter of great symbolic importance to civil rights leaders would be an understatement. Indeed, it would be hard to exaggerate the anger and resentment in the black community produced by the Red Cross's decision.[35]

Not surprisingly, White responded enthusiastically to the American Bureau's invitation. Copies of Stevens's letter were sent to the NAACP's branch offices in New York. White's cover letter explained that the NAACP was doing everything possible to aid the blood drive and emphasized that "there is to be no segregation of blood plasma because of the race or color of the donor." Branch offices were advised to "Organize Donor Parties and go in groups to make blood contributions, doing so, with appropriate publicity, which will show the contrast between the China Blood Bank and the American Red Cross."[36] In refusing to countenance discrimination in this highly symbolic manner, the China Blood Bank, and by implication China itself, seemed to stand once again on the side of racial equality.

In the final months of 1943, African Americans continued to hope that China would become an international leader in the Double V campaign, but doubts about its fitness as an ally continued to plague the relationship. During 1943 the debate over repeal of the Chinese Exclusion Act, first introduced in February, provided further grounds for skepticism about China. If passed, the bill would establish a quota allowing a maximum of 105 Chinese to enter the country each year. Despite the largely token nature of the measure, when hearings began in May it became clear that southerners on the House Immigration and Naturalization Committee feared that the proposed legislation might be a prelude to other attacks on America's race codes.[37]

Black Americans, of course, hoped to use the hearings as a forum for a broader attack on racist legislation. After the bill died in committee that summer, two new versions were quickly introduced in the House. To overcome congressional resistance, Liu Liang-Mo urged *Pittsburgh Courier* readers to start a mail-in campaign to their representative in favor of repeal and to tell their friends to do the same. He believed that "With this method we can repeal the Chinese Exclusion Act, but also pass the Anti-Poll Tax Bill and the Anti-Lynching Bill."[38] Despite this by now familiar practice of encouraging nonwhite solidarity by portraying Chinese and black Americans as allies in the same struggle against racism at home and abroad, Liu's readers were less likely to accept his assurances that China and black Americans were fighting for the same goals.

Testimony before the House of Representatives on the earlier bill in May had seemed to confirm the perception that even the strongest opponents of discrimination in America were willing to abandon, at least temporarily, their advocacy of black civil rights to gain passage of the immigration bill. In her statement before the House committee, no less an ally than Pearl Buck retreated from her public pronouncements on the interconnectedness of the domestic and international manifestations of racism. Buck repeatedly emphasized the military necessity of repeal, but she added that it need not apply to other Asians to be helpful. When asked by Representative A. Leonard Allen (D-La.) if she believed in social equality between "Negroes and whites," Buck declined to answer, stating that she did not think the question was relevant and that she had come only to speak about the legislation under review.[39]

In contrast, Dr. Taraknath Das, a history professor at the College of the City of New York and an activist in the Indian nationalist movement, chided the United States for practicing "double standards of international morality." Asked by Allen if he believed that whites and members of the "Ethiopian race" should dine together, Das replied that it would be an honor for a person to dine with someone like Booker T. Washington.[40]

As the debate over the legislation intensified, black leaders attacked Chinese exclusion as an example of racism. W. E. B. Du Bois welcomed the possible passage of the bill to repeal the prohibition against immigration because it would show that "the attack on Pearl Harbor forced America to acknowledge the equality of the white and yellow races" and that war with Japan was unnecessary, "since a similar yielding to Japan would have avoided the chief cause of war."[41] But African American support for repeal was tempered by the perception that the federal government seemed more solicitous of Chinese feeling than that of its own African American citizens.

Franklin Roosevelt's intervention on behalf of the endangered legislation in mid-October prompted the *Pittsburgh Courier* to editorialize in favor of repeal, but not without registering its dissatisfaction with his silence on matters of even greater importance to blacks. Although applauding his message to Congress, the editors declared: "Here the president lives up to the highest traditions of great statesmanship. . . . But it irritates colored Americans for the President to consistently refuse to come to grips in the same forthright and statesmanlike manner with a much greater problem than that of a handful of Chinese: i.e. the problem of color discrimination." Roosevelt, as commander-in-chief, could end discrimination in the armed services. As president and leader of his party he could ask Congress to pass laws enforcing the Fourteenth Amendment and end discrimination in labor unions and factories receiving war contracts. Admitting 105 Chinese into the country was clearly a gesture born of necessity and could have little effect on the Chinese or as a propaganda measure, the editors observed. Adoption of their recommendations, however, would not only lift black morale but also "completely kill the Japanese charge of white supremacy prejudice and practices." [42]

During the prolonged debate over repeal of the exclusion law, Chinese officials had remained silent for fear that their involvement would provoke charges of foreign interference in domestic legislation. The friends of China, most notably Pearl Buck and her husband Richard Walsh, had taken the lead in publicizing the need for repeal. But despite the opportunity presented by this debate, they had declined to reiterate Buck's earlier arguments on the need to end racism at home as well as abroad. On this issue, the silence emanating from the hearing room was disturbing, but the sin was one of omission. Whatever frustration black leaders may have felt by being let down in this way was soon overshadowed by a more serious threat to the idea of nonwhite solidarity.

In mid-December a front-page story in the *Pittsburgh Courier* told of allegations of widespread discrimination against African Americans on the West Coast by "Chinese cafes and pleasure emporiums." Complaints had been lodged in Los Angeles, San Francisco, Seattle, and Walla Walla, Washington, where black members of the U.S. Women's Army Corps had been refused service at a café. The Chinese consul in Los Angeles, T. K. Chang, held a conference to address the complaints and sought to assure black Americans that the vast majority of Chinese bitterly opposed discrimination. Peter SooHoo, a prominent member of the Chinese community, noted that many of the rumors had been unfounded, but his subsequent comment implied that at least some of the complaints were valid.[43]

Readers who followed the editorial note directing them to Horace Cayton's column of that day soon learned that Chang's and SooHoo's efforts were not enough to dispel the outrage of black Americans. Writing under the heading "NON-WHITES: Chinese Have Shown More Prejudice Than Any Other Group," Cayton opened his article by relating how the previous spring a group of students at Fisk University, a black college, had called the Chinese "'Yellow Uncle Toms.'" The students believed, Cayton explained, that Chinese in America had received better treatment than any other nonwhite group and as a result they had developed a "superiority complex toward the Negroes, Filipinos, Japanese, Indians, etc."

Cayton, whose father had opposed discrimination against Chinese immigrants in the Pacific Northwest, admitted that he shared the same feelings as the students and proceeded to cite examples of Chinese behavior that riled him. He complained that Madame Chiang, "Aristocrat that she was," when asked if she favored repeal of the poll tax answered that she would want to know how blacks would vote first. Black Americans might vote to aid the "slaving millions of China," Cayton wrote, but "they would not vote for what the Madame represents after that crack."

Cayton cited the recent convention of the Congress of Industrial Organizations (CIO) as another instance where Chinese had slighted African Americans. During the conference Willard Townsend, head of the United Transport Service Employees of America, a predominantly black union, introduced a resolution calling for repeal of the Chinese Exclusion Act. According to Cayton, "This was a carefully thought-out plan to show to the public and to the members of the conference that an American Negro was mindful of the problems of the Chinese people."

Although Townsend introduced the resolution, on its favorable reception by the convention H. T. Liu, the overseas representative of the Chinese Association of Labor, thanked the secretary of the CIO for its passage. The secretary directed Mr. Liu to Townsend as the person most responsible for the resolution. But instead of seeking out Townsend, Liu reportedly left only a scribbled note of thanks in Townsend's hotel mailbox. The significance of that gesture was plain to Cayton. "If that Chinese gentleman had really felt the brotherhood of man and recognized the similarity of the problem of non-white people throughout the world, he would have thrown his arms around Townsend rather than slipping up to the white man first."

Despite this evident bitterness, Cayton, who also recalled being refused service in Chinese restaurants, claimed that most black Americans were deeply sympathetic to China's problems. He reminded readers that several months earlier he had written of the members of a small black church who collected money for Chinese relief "because they saw an affinity between their condition and that of the Chinese." If the Chinese wished to show their appreciation for the friendship of black Americans, Cayton advised, they could start by having their officials attend black affairs when invited instead of avoiding them "for fear that someone in the diplomatic service will detect that they are non-white themselves." Chinese could also eliminate any signs of discrimination from their businesses. "There are thirteen million of us here," he concluded, "and we could be a strong ally to the Chinese people in their fight for liberation and they'd better begin to understand it." [44]

In light of Cayton's story on Chinese ingratitude for black support of repeal of the Chinese Exclusion Act, Liu Liang-Mo's column of the same day celebrating passage of the bill probably did not engender warm feelings in readers of the *Pittsburgh Courier*. Liu thanked the measure's white and black supporters and hoped that the next step would be abolition of segregation in America, "as there is no question that it is a political and military necessity for winning the war." But his elation on recognition of Chinese equality by the U.S. government seemed to underscore the difference in treatment accorded blacks and Chinese portrayed by Cayton. [45]

In his response to Cayton's column two weeks later, Liu called on oppressed peoples, especially Chinese, African Americans, and Jews, to unite in defeat of their common enemies. He admitted that some Chinese were prejudiced against black Americans, as were some Jews, but he reminded readers that there were African Americans who were also anti-Chinese and anti-Semitic. In an obvious reference to Cayton's article, he asked: "Would it be fair for me to accuse the Negro people as the most anti-Chinese and anti-Semitic people among the colored people? You will protest and say, 'No!' So I shall also protest when we, the Chinese people, are being accused as the most anti-Negro people among the colored. It is most unfair." Liu conceded that all Chinese were not angels, but he advised his readers not to form opinions on the basis of a few Fascists or officials who were unrepresentative of a whole people. Like Roi Ottley, Liu believed that black Americans and Chinese needed to get to know each other better. In closing, he offered the prayers of the season for better understanding between the two peoples. [46]

Despite the friction between Chinese and African Americans at the end of 1943, there were signs that the relationship might still be salvaged. Madame Chiang's refusal to speak to black reporters on the issues that mattered most to black Americans was only slightly less of an affront than her alleged quip concerning the poll tax. Liu evidently recognized Madame as a liability and had appeared to distance himself from her by his reference to certain officials not being representative of China.

The treatment accorded Liu Liang-Mo's column by the *Pittsburgh Courier* may have provided the best indication that reconciliation was possible. This time the paper carried a front-page story describing the measures that consul Chang was taking to eliminate Chinese discrimination against black patrons. The paper's correspondent described Chang and his associates as bitterly opposed to any and all forms of discrimination. According to the report, Chang was asking any black Americans who encountered discrimination to notify him immediately. Moreover, investigations into the "alleged case" of discrimination in Walla Walla and Seattle were already under way. Finally, in the same issue the editors directed readers to Liu's plea for unity.[47]

As the year ended, black American leaders still hoped to ally with China in the fight against racism. But their relations with China were still in a probationary period. African Americans viewed their contributions to forging a new relationship with the Chinese as significant. On the other hand, they felt that the Chinese had not reciprocated. The Chinese, it seemed, did not appreciate the warm greeting given to Madame Chiang, the improved image of China in the black press, support for repeal of Chinese exclusion, or even African American contributions to China's relief. Instead, the "yellow Uncle Toms" were still "slipping up to the white man," unaware of who were their real friends. As Cayton's heated reaction to the perceived slight at the CIO convention suggests, black Americans had not abandoned their previous skepticism about the Chinese.

The *Pittsburgh Courier* regarded the quick response of Chinese consular officials to the alleged cases of discrimination as a favorable sign. But the Chinese would have to do more to erase the bad feeling created during the last year. Liu Liang-Mo admitted as much when he wrote of the Chinese desire to learn more about black Americans. In particular, he recommended that the American Christian student movement send a black representative to China in the coming year. Liu noted that the organization was reluctant to do so because the gesture might antagonize other whites in China, especially since, as everyone knew, there was no discrimination in China. He dismissed white apprehensions as irrelevant, since the student would be an ambassador to the youth of China, not to Americans who worked there.

The message was clear. White prejudice would not be permitted to prevent Chinese and black Americans from knowing each other better. Fortunately, Liu added, closer contacts between the two peoples were already taking place in India and Burma. There, African American and Chinese soldiers labored, side by side, to build a new road into China. Facing hardship and even death together, these men, he wrote, "know that all are comrades and brothers."[48]

[9]

The Loss of China

By early 1944 the Allies had halted the Axis advances and begun to drive the enemy back with a series of counteroffensives. Russian victories at Stalingrad and Kursk, the successful American and British campaigns in North Africa, and Japanese reverses in the Solomon Islands and New Guinea persuaded observers that although the war was far from won, the greatest moment of peril had passed. China remained the lone exception to this otherwise brightening picture. For the Chinese, 1944, America's third year of war but China's seventh, would be the most devastating. During the previous year China's victories had been mainly political. The Western powers had relinquished their extraterritorial privileges in China, and the United States had grudgingly eliminated the Chinese exclusion provision in its immigration law. More significant, Chiang Kai-shek had gained Allied support for the restoration of Manchuria and Taiwan to Chinese sovereignty after the war. But these accomplishments would provide cold comfort to the Chinese unless they could continue their resistance to Japan until the war ended.

Stalin's promise the previous year to enter the Pacific war soon after Germany's defeat reduced but did not eliminate China's military importance to the Allies. If China collapsed, the Japanese would threaten India once again or be free to reinforce their defenses in the Pacific. China also held political significance for the Americans. In early 1944 China still retained its image as a valiant opponent of fascist aggression. If the United States failed to rescue its Asian ally, the administration would undoubtedly face an unwelcome political inquest during an election year. China's survival was also important to Roosevelt's postwar plans. Early in the war FDR had hoped that China would act as a junior partner in policing Asia.

By 1944, however, the possibility of China performing that role, even with U.S. assistance, began to diminish. Nevertheless, Roosevelt hoped that continued support for China would help ease the American public into accepting a more active role in world affairs after the war. Finally, administration officials worried that China's collapse would raise questions about America's fidelity to its major nonwhite ally and weaken the nation's appeal to the peoples of Asia and Africa.[1]

The administration's policy toward China remained a concern for black Americans. Black leaders and commentators continued to perceive the U.S. policy as a barometer for the broader issues of racial equality and colonialism. But they also continued to hope that China would use its special position as one of the Big Four to champion the causes of greatest concern to nonwhite peoples everywhere. These hopes, and by implication the tenets of black internationalism, were sorely tested in the final year of the war.

The public debate over the significance of race and racism in the war intensified during 1944 as the Allies began preparations for the postwar world. The domestic side of the Double V campaign continued unabated, with black Americans scolding and petitioning the government for fairer treatment in the armed forces and war industries. African Americans persisted in dramatizing the connection between the treatment of racial minorities at home and the future of the world's colonial peoples, but they also strove to highlight their commitment to victory over Japan.

At times, however, the continuing political and economic vulnerability of black Americans during the war led to behavior that undercut calls for racial solidarity with other minorities. The NAACP and black newspapers condemned the relocation and imprisonment of Japanese and Japanese Americans on the West Coast as an act of racism. But despite general agreement on the injustice of the relocation, blacks faced with overcrowding in Los Angeles and San Francisco moved into the abandoned houses of the cities' "Little Tokyos" and worried about the original inhabitants' return.[2]

The war against Japan also posed a special challenge for black Americans who viewed the Pacific war as a race war. On the one hand black journalists sought to highlight the contributions of black GIs in the war, while on the other they attacked the racism in American society. The problems latent in this approach were illustrated by a laudatory front-page account in the *Baltimore Afro-American* of a black sergeant who kept "two Japanese gold teeth as souvenirs." Slightly more than a year later, a *Life* magazine story on white soldiers making trophies of enemy bones provoked the *Afro-American* to see racial implications in the hideous practice. "Our own mobs who lynch colored men and women in Dixie have frequently brought home a finger, a toe, a tooth or an ear as a souvenir," wrote the editors. "We hope," they added, "that our colored soldiers never sink to that level."[3] On other occasions black journalists told of the Japanese soldier's allegedly superior night vision and his indifference to death. One editor mused that "Even insect powder, it appears, does not serve to abate the ferocious Japs."[4] Another caption read, "Killing Japs Like Stepping on a Cockroach." After the bloody victory on Tarawa, the *Afro-American* concluded that the only way to defeat the Japanese was "to exterminate" them.[5]

The readiness with which some members of the black press succumbed to the temptation to deny the enemy its humanity testified to the coarsening effect of the war on all concerned. Compared to the white press, such instances were relatively few. But they raised disturbing questions about the possibility of attaining a more enlightened society in the midst of war. Black internationalists hoped that the conflict would change American society, but it appeared that even some black Americans were yielding to the crushing conformity demanded by the war. Despite these occasional lapses, however, African American leaders and the black press remained hopeful that the nation's need for manpower at home and allies abroad would enable them to achieve equality and liberation for themselves and colonial peoples.

For those seeking to influence government policy on race issues, the last half of 1944 loomed as an especially critical period. Both major political parties would hold their conventions during the summer.[6] In September and October the Big Four would convene the first meetings to draft an outline for the international organization that would replace the League of Nations. Although much fighting continued in the current struggle, many leading figures on race issues warned that failure to deal justly with the world's nonwhite peoples would lead to yet another war.

In June 1944 Edwin Embree, head of the Rosenwald Fund, told the National Conference of Social Workers that whites were being given their last chance for equality in the world. During the first year of the war, it will be recalled, Embree had asked President Roosevelt to create a special commission on "Race and Color in the Present World Struggle." Embree believed that the commission would contribute to the war effort by improving morale at home and planning for a workable world order after the war. At the time FDR demurred, saying that various agencies were already working on the morale problem and that planning for postwar issues would distract Americans from the more pressing struggle at hand. Two years of delay and seeming indifference from the government convinced Embree that the administration did not understand the severity of the problem. Time was running out. If the West refused to abandon the dogma of white superiority after this war, he warned, the "500,000,000 non whites may in surging rebellion smash them into a nonentity."[7]

The same month, the *Baltimore Afro-American* published a "Message to the Republican and Democratic Conventions from the Negroes of America" calling for an end to colonial exploitation in Africa, India, and Asia, and demanding a place for black Americans at the peace conference. "We insist," the document read, "that all parties and candidates formulate a foreign policy that will recognize China as an equal partner with America, England, and Soviet Russia, and which will resolutely and unequivocally oppose either perpetuation or extension of exploitation based upon white superiority or political advantage to 'white' nations."[8] The broadside was endorsed by the NAACP, the Brotherhood of Sleeping Car Porters, the AME Church, Max Yergan's Council on African Affairs, and Adam Clayton Powell Jr.'s Peoples Movement. Also supporting the petition were several prominent professional and fraternal organizations including the National Association of Colored Graduate Nurses and Alpha Phi Alpha, the prestigious academic fraternity, which included among its members W. E. B. Du Bois, Rayford Logan, Paul Robeson, and future Supreme Court justice Thurgood Marshall.

Following the conventions, John Robert Badger identified the Republican nominee, New York governor Thomas Dewey, as the greater obstacle to racial justice. Despite ample grounds for disappointment with Roosevelt, Badger maintained that Dewey's connection to former president Herbert Hoover disqualified him for high office. Hoover, Badger reminded his readers, had made millions as a mining engineer from the toil of Chinese miners, "And that is the specter which today haunts the colonial peoples when they think of the November elections."[9]

The numerous articles, public forums, petitions, and resolutions urging the U.S. government and, by extension, the Western allies to end imperialism and white supremacy set the stage for the planning conference for the new postwar organization that convened at Dumbarton Oaks in Washington, D.C., in September 1944. As was the case in the summit conferences at Cairo and Tehran the previous year, the meetings were arranged to avoid undermining Russia's official position of neutrality in the Pacific war. In the first phase of the Dumbarton Oaks conference, Russian delegates met with their American and British counterparts. During the second phase, beginning in October, China was scheduled to take Russia's place. For some black observers, this relegation of China to the second seating, especially when China was reeling under the force of Japan's latest offensive, smacked of discrimination. Sizing up the arrangements, J. Saunders Redding told *Baltimore Afro-American* readers that "China needs security from its 'friends' as much as enemies, as do all Asiatics."

News from the British-American military conference in Quebec in September fueled Redding's worst suspicions. "China and Kai-shek [*sic*] are not even mentioned in the latest dispatches as belonging to the United Nations," he complained. China faced its gravest challenge of the war, yet Britain and the United States appeared willing to let it be defeated because "A beaten China . . . is a weak China, too weak to have equality with the nations that will eventually rescue her."[10] The story of Y. Chan, a successful Chinese American businessman denied burial in a whites-only cemetery, seemed to offer vivid proof that nonwhite peoples could not hope for justice until they forced the great powers to treat them as equal members in the family of nations. "Not only the Chinese," wrote Joseph Bibb, "but all the dark folks on earth are insulted and infuriated by such notions." Bibb concluded that, despite the enormous blood sacrifices made by Chinese in the struggle for democracy, "The story of Mr. Chan leads us to believe that they and other colored allied soldiers perhaps fight in vain."[11] The *Philadelphia Tribune* argued in a similar fashion that China's treatment at Dumbarton Oaks would be watched by "millions of other dark people the world over." "To rebuff China," the editors warned, "will be tantamount to telling the darker people of India, Africa and other sections of Asia, 'You are still not ready for equality.' "[12]

There was little new in the way black commentators used China's mistreatment to draw attention to the broader implications of Anglo-American racial and colonial policies. But these stories seemed especially pointed in light of the revelation that of the four nations meeting at Dumbarton Oaks, only China had proposed including a clause on racial equality in the charter of the new organization. Black readers first learned of the proposal in late August, when the *New York Times* published a series of highly detailed articles on the supposedly secret American, British, Chinese, and Russian draft plans for the new organization. The leak to the *Times* was almost certainly a calculated move on the part of the Chinese delegation to make its influence felt during the first phase of the conference. As reporter James Reston later revealed, the leak came courtesy of a member of the Chinese delegation who, having once worked as an intern for the *Times*, generously deposited the classified materials on

Reston's desk during what appeared to be a friendly visit with his former colleagues. As Reston later remembered, he and editor Arthur Krock decided that "it would be cruel to dump the whole load" on their competitor, the *New York Herald Tribune*. Instead, they opted for "the Chinese torture treatment" by stretching out their coverage over a period of days. The outraged delegates failed to halt publication, and by the end of August the public knew most of the details of the Big Four's plans.[13]

In relating the *Times*'s scoop to their own readers, black journalists were quick to point out that only the Chinese draft contained a clause recognizing the equality of the races. Once again, a Pearl Buck letter to the *Times* served as the voice of reason linking China's cause with the interest of black Americans. Under the heading "Pearl Buck Recalls," the *Pittsburgh Courier* told readers how the famous author "and foremost champion of race equality" sought to remind the American and British delegations that the inclusion of a racial equality clause in the league's charter had been the only issue that China and Japan had agreed on at Versailles. Noting that press reports indicated British and U.S. opposition to China's draft, Buck urged Americans to contemplate the cost of denying nonwhite peoples racial justice. "Again there will be new bitterness and again it will be against the United States." "What," she asked, "will be the fruit of this new attitude, say, in 20 years?"[14] The *Crisis* also anxiously awaited the outcome. "[I]t remains to be seen," read its lead editorial, "whether [China's proposal] will not be bypassed once more and whether the seeds of another more terrible war along racial lines will not be sown."[15]

The report of China's proposed clause on racial equality once again raised Walter White's hopes that some collaboration between black Americans and Chinese officialdom was possible. Early in October, as the Chinese phase of the conference began, White asked W. E. B. Du Bois, now the NAACP's research specialist on postwar affairs, to prepare a memorandum for submission to the conference dealing with the Chinese proposal. White reasoned that further publicity would strengthen support for the proposal "and force thinking on the necessity of such a stand." Du Bois agreed, but the moment for action had already passed.[16]

As Pearl Buck feared, the U.S. delegation was not prepared to accept the Chinese proposal. A year earlier, State Department planners had identified racial equality as one of several "Basic Human Rights" that the postwar organization should promote. An early tentative draft of the U.S. proposal for a new organization cited the defeat of the racial equality clause at Versailles and wartime pronouncements by Under Secretary of State Sumner Welles and Chiang Kai-shek to justify inclusion of such a clause in the new charter.[17] But by the time such a proposal appeared in the Chinese draft a year later, American attitudes had changed. Sometime before the conference, U.S. planners decided to postpone discussion of a possible bill of rights, which would have included a racial equality clause, in favor of dealing with what they viewed as the more important and less troublesome constitutional provisions of the organization.[18] Thus, on reviewing China's tentative proposal, the American delegates noted with concern that, "unlike other plans," the Chinese draft "would be based explicitly on the principle of equality of the races."[19]

The Americans responded immediately. On 30 August Lawrence Pruess, a legal adviser to one of the State Department's planning committees, informally conveyed his uneasiness with the Chinese proposal to Liang Yuen-li, a delegate of the Nationalist government. The Chinese, it appears, had anticipated U.S. opposition to their proposal. In all likelihood at least some of the delegates hoped to put the Americans on the defensive by leaking their proposal to the press. They had also planned to make their plan more acceptable by explaining to the conferees that the clause would "not necessarily entail obligations of any kind." Rather, it represented an "ideal" that member nations should strive toward.[20] Thus, despite early indications of American disapproval, several members of the Chinese delegation urged their colleagues "to put forward China's views even though they might not be welcomed by other powers."[21]

This attitude did not prevail for long. Dr. H. H. Kung, China's vice premier and finance minister, then in Washington, told his colleagues that he believed it "inadvisable to press the question of racial equality — Internationally it might be desirable, but [the] U.S. had its own negro problem." "China had already regained its equality," he continued. "To ask for it now implied we ourselves did not consider we had equality." Kung's explanation did not sit well with other members of the delegation. One of them, Dr. Victor Hoo, China's vice minister of foreign affairs, countered that the offending clause was aimed at Japanese "master race" ideas and the German persecution of the Jews. Hoo wanted the Chinese to state their views on the subject at the conference, but Kung disagreed.

At this point, Wellington Koo, ambassador to Great Britain and the head of the Chinese delegation, took Kung's side. Koo recommended that if the subject came up at the conference or appeared in the conclusions of the first phase of the Dumbarton Oaks meetings, they could state their views. Otherwise, he explained, "we had better not start a discussion because it was bound to lead to no result."[22] Koo's was the voice of experience in the delegation. Twenty-five years earlier, as China's representative on the committee that drafted the League of Nations covenant at Paris, Koo had tangled with the Americans and British on this very subject. Neither he nor Kung felt disposed to try again.

As Kung made clear during the subsequent discussion, Chinese interest in securing the symbolic victory of a racial equality clause in the new charter was outweighed by a more pressing concern for the overall health of U.S.-Chinese relations. Only days before, the worsening situation on the Chinese front had led Roosevelt to urgently request that Chiang turn over control of his armed forces to Chiang's American adviser, General Joseph Stilwell. Chiang, fearing that he would lose control of his government and appalled at the prospect of U.S. arms going to his communist enemies, refused.[23] The Generalissimo ultimately prevailed, forcing Stilwell's recall, but China's military setbacks and the concurrent controversy surrounding Stilwell's dismissal left the ambassador in too weak a position to publicly challenge the United States on the racial equality clause.[24]

If black Americans had been privy to the discussions within the Chinese delegation, they would probably have felt their worst suspicions confirmed. Chinese empathy for what Kung described as the Americans' "own negro problem" would have been damning enough, but perhaps worse was Hoo's explanation that the racial equality clause was offered only as a way of contrasting Allied war aims with Japanese and German racial policies.[25] Black internationalists had spent nearly three years arguing that the problem of racism was indivisible and universal, a sin of the Allies as well as the Axis. The Chinese, in their own private conversations, clearly thought otherwise.

Following the conference black Americans blamed their own government and Britain for suppressing the racial equality clause. And by refusing to press the issue, the Chinese lost much of the sympathy they had gained before the conference began. The *Chicago Defender* noted that the Chinese "did not even bring up the subject, in spite of the fact that it was a part of their original plan."[26] In early December political gossip columnist Charlie Cherokee reported that the Chinese "were shushed, and didn't press the matter." The same day the *Defender* offered a stronger verdict. Referring to the racial equality clause, the editors chided "[s]ome of our more unrealistic brothers" for hoping that "Soviet Russia or China would throw the problem into the international arena. They have been disillusioned in a hurry."[27]

"Disillusioned" was probably too strong a word to describe the reactions of those black Americans who previously had hoped that China's membership in the Big Four might help to overturn Allied racial policies. Like most Americans, the unidentified black leaders referred to by the *Defender* had their confidence in China shaken. News reports from the China theater following Stilwell's recall cast doubt on Chiang's leadership and highlighted the inefficiency and corruption in Chungking. China's retreat at Dumbarton Oaks added to the general uneasiness they felt about China but did not force them to abandon all hope.

On the other hand, those, like Du Bois, who had been skeptical of the Chinese government, had their views confirmed. Du Bois's opinions appeared early in 1945 in a brief monograph titled *Color and Democracy*. Writing in his new capacity as the NAACP's researcher for postwar colonial affairs, Du Bois returned to familiar themes in discussing conditions in Asia. Although he blamed the Allies for the suppression of the racial equality proposal, he still managed to convey the impression that the Chinese government was comfortable in the role of lackey to the West. Du Bois made his point by recalling for his readers an interview with Chinese educators, journalists, and officials during his visit to Shanghai in 1936. At that time, he related, he assured the Chinese that he could "well understand the Chinese attitude toward Japan, its bitterness and determined opposition to the substitution of Asiatic for an European imperialism; but what I could not quite understand was the seemingly placid attitude of the Chinese toward Britain." His Chinese hosts talked "long and informingly" but "they did not really answer my question." [28] In truth, it is difficult to see how they could have done so. For Du Bois, in 1945 as well as in 1936, the test of any Chinese government's worthiness was its willingness to confront the West, no matter what the circumstances.

Not surprisingly, one of the strongest defenses of the Chinese government came from Du Bois's nominal boss, Walter White. Seizing on a report of American bigotry toward Japanese Americans in Oregon, White warned that the "white *uber alles*" policies were driving the Chinese and other Asians into the arms of the Russians and Japanese. The pernicious effects of American racism were especially evident in China, he observed. The Chinese, "despairing of any real change in America's and Britain's condescension towards colored people, are in some instances resuming trade relations with the Japanese as the lesser of two evils." Chiang "had made his mistakes," White conceded, but the Chinese had fought "almost literally with bare hands" for four years, while America sold war materials to Japan and Britain held Hong Kong. Given these circumstances, White could well understand why the Chinese resented being told to turn over their troops to an American commander. Now, as if conditions were not already demoralizing enough, the "battle weary Chinese" would be treated to Japanese propaganda broadcasts telling of the "stupidity" of "cheap little bigots" like those in Oregon. For White, China on the verge of defeat remained at the very least an important symbolic ally in the cause of racial justice.[29]

John Badger, writing in the same paper, continued to take the united front position by lauding the efforts of the Chinese and the Russians in supporting racial equality. Badger claimed that the Russians had been sympathetic to the Chinese position and predicted that at the next meeting to plan for the United Nations, Russia, China, and the Latin American countries would press the issue harder.[30] Badger was concerned, however, lest China collapse before it could make its influence felt on the world stage. Until now, he wrote, Chiang had only reshuffled his cabinet without making necessary reforms. The Generalissimo, Badger warned, had one last chance "to straighten up and fly right." If he succeeded in restoring the common front with the Communists, the benefits to black Americans would be great. A united and democratic China would contribute to economic prosperity, which would mean jobs for American workers; equally important, a strong China would "help break the shackles of colonialism that today fetter the great populations of Asia" and "speak against racialism in the policies of powerful states."[31]

Despite their differences, Du Bois, Badger, and White all saw special significance in China's status as the only nonwhite nation in the Big Four. Although they disagreed about whether China under the Nationalists would ever take a firm stand against racial inequality, they concurred that China's true interest lay in finding solidarity with the oppressed peoples of the world. China's disappointing performance on racial issues up to this point of the war challenged the assumptions of black internationalists, who believed that race and color remained determining factors in international relations. Nevertheless, in the aftermath of the Dumbarton Oaks conference, most African American commentators continued to hope that China would play an active part in the global struggle for equality. It was perhaps with China in mind that Walter White wrote in early 1945 that "the Negro soldier is convinced that as time proceeds that identification of interests will spread even among brown and yellow peoples who today refuse to see the connection between their exploitation by white nations and discrimination against the Negro in the United States."[32]

As interest in the postwar settlement increased as a result of the Dumbarton Oaks conference, one of the most important books on African American war aims began receiving attention in the white and black press. *What the Negro Wants*, a collection of essays written by fourteen prominent black Americans and edited by Rayford Logan, stunned southern liberals with its near unanimous demands for full citizenship and an immediate end to segregation. The contributors' insistence on social equality, including several references to interracial marriage, shocked the publisher and almost led him to reject the book.[33]

William T. Couch, director of the University of North Carolina Press (1932–45), finally agreed to publish the book after Logan threatened him with legal action. *What the Negro Wants* became a Book-of-the-Month Club selection, quickly went through three printings, and sold nearly nine thousand copies in the first year. The book was widely reviewed in the white-owned press, including the *New York Times*, *New Republic*, and *Nation*. The black press, of course, gave it special attention. *What the Negro Wants* is rightly viewed by historians as a harbinger of the civil rights activism of the postwar decade. What has been less noted, and what the manuscript's critics seemed to overlook in their hurry to condemn the authors' claims to full citizenship, was the extent to which most of the contributors, regardless of political affiliation, linked the cause of black Americans to the emerging power of the world's nonwhite peoples.

Mary McLeod Bethune, former director of the Division of Negro Work in the National Youth Administration and founder of the National Council of Colored Women, saw black women lifted by "the surge of all women of China and India and of Africa who see the same light and look to us to march with them."[34] Leslie Pinckney Hill, former president of Cheyney State Teachers College in Pennsylvania and a member of the YMCA's Committee of Colored Work and of the Peace Section of the American Friends Service Committee, declared that "In Chiang Kai-shek Negroes can recognize a great spiritual ally." Emphasizing Chiang's conversion to Christianity, his patience, and his country's struggle against great odds, Hill saw similarities between the plight of the Chinese and black Americans. "Chiang Kai-shek and the whole structure of his accomplishment may topple," he concluded, "but the record of his exalted adventure will remain for our chastening and profit."[35] Sterling A. Brown, writer, poet, and professor of English at Howard University, asserted: "Negroes know they have allies. There are the numerous colored peoples of the world, the millions of yellow, brown, and black men in China, India, the Philippines, Malaysia, Africa, South America, the Caribbean, all over the globe, where hope for democracy is stirring a mighty ferment."[36] Roy Wilkins of the NAACP also remained hopeful that pressure from abroad would force a change in American racial practices.[37]

Others were less optimistic that the Allies were getting the message. Poet

Langston Hughes found it necessary to remind readers of the effects of Jim Crow policies on the morale of America's nonwhite allies.[38] A. Philip Randolph condemned the Allies for continuing to fight a war for imperialism and warned that "The colored people of Asia, Africa, and Latin America will measure the genuineness of our declarations about a free world to the extent that we create a free world within our borders."[39] Noting the new assertiveness of colonial peoples, George Schuyler nevertheless remained pessimistic that the Allies would solve the "Caucasian problem." He noted that Allied interest in racial justice never seemed greater than when the "Afrika Corps was pounding toward Alexandria, when the panzers were on the outskirts of Moscow and half our fleet lay at the bottom of Pearl Harbor." Now that victory seemed assured, white interest in racial justice was evaporating. Unless that trend was reversed, he warned, "The alternative is to drift toward an international color war."[40]

The publication of *What the Negro Wants* had a time capsule quality about it, reminding black readers of their earlier hopes and the extent to which they remained unfulfilled. The essays, which were submitted to the editor in late 1943, reflected the growing sense that a turning point had been reached in the war. As the essays by Bethune, Hill, and Wilkins indicate, in 1943 it was still possible to hope that the emerging solidarity of nonwhite peoples would help make the victory over the Axis a victory for racial justice as well. But it was also possible to argue, as Schuyler did, that if the British and American governments had not significantly altered their racial policies in the bleakest moments of the war, there was little reason to expect them to do so when victory drew closer. By late 1944, when the book was published, it seemed more likely that Schuyler had gotten the better of the argument.

The contributors' almost obligatory inclusion of China among the nations concerned with the cause of racial justice probably struck many readers as a relic from an earlier era. In the aftermath of Stilwell's recall and China's disappointing showing at Dumbarton Oaks, it was unlikely that black readers would take inspiration from Chiang's wise leadership. Nor did it seem certain, as Hughes claimed, that China judged U.S. intentions by the way black Americans were treated. Until now black leaders had found that support for China was useful as a way of deflecting government suspicions of pro-Japanese sentiment among African Americans while highlighting American prejudice and dramatizing the role of nonwhite peoples in the Allied war effort. But in the absence of strong Chinese support for racial equality, black Americans could only continue to speculate about what role China might play in the battle for racial justice. After nearly three years of war, Roi Ottley's observation that black Americans and Chinese were strangers to each other remained valid.

Yet parties on both sides continued to close the gap that separated them. Early in 1945 Lin Yutang was invited to speak at a forum on "A World View of the Negro Situation," held at the New York Public Library's Schomburg Collection of Negro Literature, the special collection named for the late Arthur Schomburg. Speaking on "The People of China and the Negro Problem," Lin declared that "Racial equality is a necessary foundation stone of a world peace." He concluded by urging the darker races to continue striving to make that principle a reality.[41] That Lin would be invited to speak at an institution named for a black American who had defended Japan's invasion of China was a promising sign of the distance that some black intellectuals had moved from their earlier fascination with Japan. Lin's reassurance that the Chinese saw racial equality as a necessary precondition for peace also sounded the right note. But the author's awkwardly phrased observation that the Chinese "had never had a Negro problem as such," because of their lack of contact with people of African descent, served as a reminder of how much the mutual perceptions of black Americans and Chinese had been formed in the absence of actual contact. Apparently that situation was about to change, however, for earlier that month American and Chinese engineers had helped reopen the land route from India to China. Dubbed the Stilwell Road, the newly constructed supply line began in northeastern India, traversed the rugged mountains of northern Burma, and ended in the southwestern Chinese city of Kunming. For the first time in the war, China was opened to overland truck convoys.

In 1943 and 1944 African American newspapers followed the progress of the road-building project through the Burmese jungle with interest, owing to the large number of black engineer and quartermaster truck companies involved in the project. Deton Brooks of the *Chicago Defender* and Frank Bolden of the National Negro Publishers' Association reported on the activities of black troops in the theater. Both men were surprised in mid-January 1945 when the first convoy shoved off for China without any black drivers. The absence of black troops in the convoy appeared to confirm persistent rumors that African American GIs were barred from entering China. Almost immediately, the two correspondents and *Newsweek*'s Harold Isaacs began pressing U.S. authorities at the convoy's stop in Myitkyina, Burma, for an explanation. In response to these queries ten black drivers were added to the first convoy, and Bolden, Brooks, and Isaacs proceeded with it to Kunming, the road's terminus.[42] On 5 Febru-

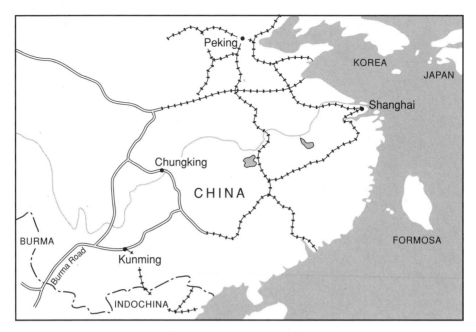

China during World War II

ary Isaacs met with Major General Gilbert Cheves, commanding general of the Services of Supply, China theater, and Brigadier General Lewis Pick, who had similar responsibilities for the India-Burma theater, and asked if the Chinese government had banned black troops in the China theater. Cheves deflected Isaacs's question with a request that he "go above me for that answer." Isaacs continued to press for more concrete answers, but to no avail.

The next day Cheves and Major General Frank Merrill met with Bolden and Brooks in separate interviews. Brooks began by declaring: "It is no secret that there are no colored troops in China nor are they wanted here. This is a hot potato. . . . We want facts and the truth." The officers responded defensively, asking why the issue had suddenly become so important. "It is not coming up all of a sudden," Brooks replied, "it is just coming to a head all of a sudden." Additional queries about whether the Generalissimo had formally banned black troops from the China theater met with evasions, but a subsequent interview ended with the categorical statement by Major General Robert McClure, head of an American liaison mission to the Chinese army, that "the Gimo has never indicated that negroes could not come into China at any time."[43]

Despite these assurances, Bolden and Isaacs surmised that restrictions had been placed on the movement of black soldiers into China. Brooks apparently reached the same conclusion, but in reporting from China he chose not to challenge the censors.[44] His first story on the opening of the road emphasized the satisfaction of black GIs in being represented in the first convoy. Told that he was the first black soldier over the road, one GI replied that it was an honor. "We have worked with the Chinese and they are fine fellows to work with. For some 15 months they have treated us like brothers." Another soldier expressed his gratitude that "when this gesture of friendship between China and America is being symbolized, our racial group has not been forgotten."[45]

The following week Brooks's dispatch dealt with the alleged ban. Referring to "unconfirmed but persistent rumors that Generalissimo Chiang Kai-shek's government is barring Negro troops from the Chinese theater of operations," Brooks quoted Cheves as saying: "to the best of my knowledge no such order existed and no commitment between the Chinese and American governments on this issue has been made." Chinese authorities, Brooks added, had also denied the rumor. Brooks told readers that the rumors began because of the absence of black troops in the theater throughout the war, and he alluded to an unconfirmed story that General Stilwell and Chiang had reached an agreement on a ban early in the conflict. Using language that hinted at his own nagging suspicions, Brooks declared: "This correspondent is certain that any color bar in this theater does not reflect the feeling of the Chinese masses." " 'We are colored people too,' " one official told Brooks. " 'We certainly could not condone any racial bar in our country against other dark-skinned races. That would be an international scandal.' "[46]

In fact, during the last two months Chiang and General Albert Wedemeyer, the commanding general of U.S. forces in China, had twice confirmed an agreement to limit the entry of black GIs into China. On 31 December Wedemeyer raised the issue in a way that suggested that a previous understanding existed. Referring to a memorandum he had submitted on the use of black troops in China, he said that "there should not be a hard and fast rule against the use of negro troops in China." Wedemeyer was concerned that as the road moved closer to China, restrictions on black soldiers, who made up approximately 60 percent of the construction troops on the project, would hamper completion of the work. According to the minutes, Chiang stated that "he would reconsider the matter," but he "advanced the explanation that the Chinese people are not accustomed to mixing with Negroes, and that they might excite undue sensation." In response, Wedemeyer said that he would limit the use of African American troops to the west of Kunming.[47]

A week later he told his subordinates, including Cheves and McClure, that Chiang "did not favor the use of colored troops in China and that the Commanding General (China Theater) did not wish to ask for any dispensation from the Gimo in that regard except in the greatest emergency." The group agreed that black drivers would be used "the shortest possible distance into China, it being preferable to stop them at the China-Burma border." Cheves thought that it might be possible to use black drivers for part of the run and then have white drivers make the final push into Kunming. McClure, who told American correspondents that no restrictions had been imposed by Chiang, said that the "ultimate goal [was] driver turnover at the border."[48]

On 17 January General Pick's headquarters asked Wedemeyer to obtain Chiang's approval to employ black troops in the China theater. According to Pick's office, black GIs would be needed to construct the oil pipeline along the road and to drive the trucks bringing supplies into China.[49] Wedemeyer's office replied with a copy of an order from Chiang dated 14 January confirming his understanding that black troops could be used in China but were "not permitted in territories east of Kunming." In the letter of transmittal, however, Wedemeyer added a stipulation prohibiting black troops from entering Kunming as well.[50]

There the matter rested until the three war correspondents became involved, forcing Pick to add the black drivers. At the end of the month, as the first convoy began making its way along the road, Cheves's office learned that the procession included ten black drivers and two black war correspondents (Bolden and Brooks). Cheves, who was unaware that Brooks's questions had led Pick to add the black drivers while the convoy was under way, promptly alerted Pick's headquarters to the possible violation of the understanding with Chiang.[51] The following week, the convoy arrived on the outskirts of Kunming, and Bolden, Brooks, and Isaacs entered the city looking for their story.

When Wedemeyer met with Chiang on 7 February, he raised the issue of the ban with the Generalissimo. Wedemeyer explained that a shortage of Chinese and white drivers forced him to use black drivers. He reminded Chiang of their earlier conversation on the subject and, alluding to the recent queries by Bolden, Brooks, and Isaacs, informed him that the press was "now playing up the matter" by alleging that Chiang discriminated against black Americans. The whole issue, Wedemeyer cautioned,

A black GI and a Chinese soldier place the flag of their ally on a jeep
just before it rolls into Kunming, China, with the first convoy to traverse the
Stilwell Road on 6 February 1945. This ceremony was held shortly after
war correspondents Bolden, Brooks, and Isaacs questioned authorities
about the absence of black drivers in the convoy.
(Photograph by Sergeant John Gutman; National Archives)

was "a very delicate subject." Minister of War General Chen Cheng inter-
jected that he had fielded questions on the subject during his press conference that very day. Wedemeyer identified Isaacs as the troublemaker
and urged the Generalissimo "to take precautions to preclude embarrass-
ment." Speaking more for the record than each other, Wedemeyer and
Chiang then rehearsed their own versions of the agreement. Wedemeyer
was sure nothing had been put in writing regarding the exclusion of black
troops and that it had been agreed to introduce them "gradually and not
in great numbers at any one time." Chiang recalled deciding to allow black
troops as far as Kunming and, revising the record slightly, "that if necessity dictated, they could be used east of Kunming." Satisfied, Wedemeyer
ended the conversation with a final word of caution about keeping the
story out of the press.[52]

Wartime restrictions on the press and outright prevarication by American officers made it possible to smother the story, at least for a while,
but the prodding by the three war correspondents had already forced the

Allied authorities to revise policy by adding black drivers to the first convoy. Discrimination against black troops in the U.S. Army was, of course, not news. But the possibility that Chinese authorities conducted a similar policy toward blacks would come as a bitter disappointment to those who had hoped to cement the alliance between African Americans and China. As the soldiers interviewed by Brooks had indicated, they had embraced the rhetoric and goals of the Double V campaign and saw themselves as representing black American support for other nonwhite "brothers" in a war for freedom. Chinese officials also recognized that news of a ban on black troops would be a "scandal."

Ultimately, fear of damaging publicity prompted Lieutenant General Daniel Sultan, Wedemeyer's counterpart in the India-Burma theater, to revoke the restrictions on the use of black troops. On 14 February Sultan's headquarters announced that "Any restrictions heretofore placed upon the use of negro troops within China in connection with truck operations on the Ledo-Kunming Road are hereby removed." [53] The ban on black troops, which allegedly never existed, was officially ended.

Meanwhile, the *Pittsburgh Courier* published Frank Bolden's interview with General Sun Li-jen, commander of the Chinese First Army in Burma, which had been delayed by censors. Sun, who had attended Virginia Military Institute, asked Bolden to convey "to the Negro people of America through your press channels my statement of gratitude and appreciation for the valiant work of their sons." Calling the black troops in Burma "soldiers and gentlemen second to none," he assured Bolden that the black troops had gained the respect and admiration of Chinese soldiers and that "the Chinese people will be ever grateful for your people's contributions in helping to establish world freedom for all nations loving liberty." [54] The interview, which had been given en route with the first convoy on the Stilwell Road but was not published until 10 March, had the effect of assuring readers that black Americans and Chinese were working shoulder to shoulder for the Double V.

That perception soon changed. On 21 April 1945 P. L. Prattis of the *Pittsburgh Courier* broke the story of a ban on black troops in a column titled "Chinese Are Question Mark in Common Struggle [of] Colored Peoples of the World." According to Prattis, some Chinese leaders were said to "toy around with western white supremacy notions and even in their own country curry favor with white Americans seeming to share their prejudices." Prattis quoted the *Courier*'s correspondent in the theater (Bolden) as having "serious doubts about the sincerity of certain elements in the present government.... Of course one would have to live there for a while in order to be absolutely sure; but strong evidence and some present indications (which are censorable by them), leave little doubt that James Crow lurks somewhere within the 'august body.'"[55]

Lamenting the news from China, Prattis noted "once again, with considerable regret, that Chinese leadership fails to give the aid and comfort it could to its natural allies in this world-wide struggle." In contrast, India's leaders were "all inclusive in the [sic] demands for freedom and equality." Comparing Madame Chiang's earlier stay in the United States with the current visit of Nehru's sister, Prattis complained that although Madame Vijaya Lakshmi Pandit had seized every opportunity to speak out on the subject of racism, Madame Chiang "studiously avoided the discussion of the issue of race and color in the present conflict." "One wonders," he solemnly concluded, "if the Chinese leadership can be true to its own masses if it ignores the common relationship between the problems of these masses and other masses throughout the world."

Prattis left little doubt about his own thoughts on the question. Liu Liang-Mo's column, the editor announced, would not appear in the paper "for perhaps, a long, long time."[56] In some respects, canceling Liu's column was a self-defeating gesture. During the previous months Liu had been a strong critic of the Generalissimo's government and a persistent advocate of greater American support for the Communists. Nevertheless, depriving Liu of his valued forum in one of the nation's most important black journals was a highly symbolic way of severing the partnership between the African Americans and the Chinese.

It is unclear if the Chinese government was discomfited by Prattis's accusations, but shortly after his article appeared the American ambassador in Chungking, Patrick J. Hurley, asked General Wedemeyer to investigate the whole affair. Hurley was particularly concerned with Isaacs's role in stirring up controversy over the use of black GIs in the China theater. Isaacs, who was on leave in the United States, had recently published several articles in *Newsweek* critical of the Generalissimo. In the course of the investigation, which Wedemeyer insisted be kept secret to avoid further publicity, theater officers collected a copy of Prattis's column along with the abbreviated transcripts of the Bolden, Brooks, and Isaacs interviews.

The inquiry did not move beyond this preliminary stage. When Hurley received the assembled files, he judged them too incomplete to proceed. The investigation did, however, contribute to the barring of Isaacs from the China theater. As the public relations officer for the Service of Supply explained, Isaacs's "party-line" (left-wing) views, as exemplified in the dispute over the use of black troops and other articles, made the correspondent unfit for service in China.[57]

In responding to the controversy surrounding the use of black troops in China, U.S. officials hoped that they could avoid additional complications by relying on recently trained Chinese drivers. As Cheves had explained to Isaacs earlier, it would be more efficient to use Chinese drivers. The Chinese would be fed from their own supplies in the theater, whereas American troops would need additional supplies trucked in, which would consume valuable cargo space in the convoys. Of course, reliance on Chinese drivers would have the additional advantage of reducing the number of black soldiers in the theater.

American officials soon found that these plans were unworkable. Writing to Ambassador Hurley, Wedemeyer reported that there were so many black units in the India-Burma theater that he needed to call on their services to keep the road open. The general assured Hurley, however, that although he was "compelled to accept them," he was "gradually infiltrating negro troops into this theater," which made it sound as though he was sneaking them into enemy territory instead of deploying them in an Allied country.[58]

In mid-May the all–African American 858th Engineer Aviation Battalion entered China to maintain the road from Salween, Burma, to Kunming. As the official history of the 858th notes, the unit was the only black battalion in the China theater. "All personnel knew these facts," according to the unit historian, "and were proud that of all the Engineer Battalions in the India-Burma Theater, the 858th . . . had been given the honor of going to China."[59] Perhaps, but if the men of the 858th knew that they were the only black GIs in China, it is likely that they also knew why that was the case. Given the persistent rumors circulating among the troops that the Chinese had barred the entry of black GIs into China for most of the war, and in light of the information provided in Prattis's article, it seems doubtful that the soldiers of the 858th viewed their service in China as the honor that the unit history claimed it was.

Not long after news of the ban on black GIs reached the United States, African American leaders arrived in San Francisco for the charter meeting of the United Nations Organization. Several blacks served in the U.S. delegation and a larger number attended as reporters and commentators for the leading African American newspapers and journals.[60] Developments at the conference offered these observers little cause for optimism regarding the issues of greatest concern to black internationalists. Although the member nations eventually accepted a racial equality clause in the United Nations charter, the much-desired statement won approval only after it was stripped of any enforcement provisions and so freighted with restrictions that it was deemed useless by black observers.[61] Even more disturbing was the failure of the conference to set a timetable for colonial independence in Africa and much of Asia.[62]

In this bleak setting political setbacks and personal insults were almost indistinguishable. When P. L. Prattis and Rayford Logan tried to dine at the Forbidden City, a well-known Chinese restaurant and nightclub, they were told "none too courteously," according to Logan, that there were no tables. The two men and their female companions went to the bar. Logan, convinced that they were being refused service because they were black, returned to the dining room and told the waiter, "I hope the Japanese kill every goddamned Chinese in China." The party was promptly seated and received the effusive apologies of the establishment's Chinese owner.[63]

The performance of the Chinese delegation at the conference did little to erase the bitter feelings engendered at the Forbidden City. By this time black observers were conditioned to expect little from the Chinese. Ralph Bunche, now a member of the State Department's trusteeship commission, told Logan that the Nationalist delegation "could not be counted on too strongly to present a plea for either international trusteeship or racial equality."[64] Bunche's predictions were only half correct. The Chinese delegation, led by T. V. Soong, Madame Chiang's brother, held back on proposing the addition of a racial equality clause to the organization's Bill of Human Rights, but it joined Russia to urge that "independence" rather than "self-government" be made the goal of the trusteeship program. Although that plan failed, Walter White welcomed China's support on an issue of significance to black Americans.[65] Most observers were less charitable. The *Chicago Defender*'s correspondents played up China's part in the trusteeship fight but also highlighted Soong's timidity on the racial equality question.[66]

The Chinese Communists attracted more favorable attention. In a special interview with the *Defender*, "lean tough minded" Tung Pi-wu, a member of the People's Political Council and the only communist representative from China, excoriated America's Jim Crow system and "blasted the timid stand taken by the delegates of Generalissimo Chiang Kai-shek" on racial discrimination. "In Chiang Kai-shek's area in China, minority groups are not treated as equals," explained Tung.[67] It is unlikely that black readers needed convincing on this point. Rayford Logan appeared to sum up the feelings of black Americans when he wrote shortly after the conference, "Few people still believe that the government of Chiang Kai-shek speaks for the masses of China."[68] After more than three years of effort, the African American search for racial solidarity with Nationalist China had come to a bitter end.

Epilogue: Black Internationalism
in Peace and War

In the aftermath of the San Francisco conference, black Americans scanned the political horizon and found few potential allies at home or abroad. Conservative strength in Congress seemed destined to overwhelm the government's tepid support for civil rights. Although the wartime expansion of the economy had benefited African Americans, the return of millions of soldiers into the job market and the possible elimination of the Fair Employment Practices Commission threatened to wipe out many of those hard-won gains. The rejection of the African American agenda at San Francisco cast a shadow over an already bleak situation. The imperialists, it seemed, stood ready to defend their economic and political supremacy in Asia, Africa, and the United States. Doctrines of racial supremacy might have been discredited by the war, but the system on which they rested persisted.

In the waning months of the conflict the African American press continued to trumpet the contributions of black GIs to the struggle against Japan, but the suddenness of the war's end and the means by which victory was achieved evoked a range of responses reminiscent of the conflicted feelings held by many African Americans at the start of the hostilities. Reporters following the movement of black servicemen described how black sailors kept "Big B-29's flying over Tokyo" and how "the promise of a chance to blast Japan's key cities from B-25 bombers under a Negro commander skyrocketed morale" throughout a black bombardment group.[1]

During the same period the *Baltimore Afro-American*'s Ralph Matthews noted that the enemy was "of a different race than America's ruling majority" and that "If left to our dictates, a lot of us would just as soon sit this second stanza out."[2] Earlier in the war, the *Afro-American* advertised to raise money to help "lay Tokyo in smoldering ruins!" But in July 1945 the editors concluded that it had become "convincingly clear that the war now being fought is a racial war." They doubted that white leaders would see the error of their ways any time soon. "The race wars to come," the editors warned, "are going to be the most bitter in history."[3]

News of the atomic destruction of Hiroshima and Nagasaki and Japan's subsequent surrender abruptly forced African Americans to face the uncertainties of the postwar world. The sudden end of the war accentuated the ambivalence many black Americans felt in waging war against Japan. Many commentators, including Horace Cayton and George Schuyler, denounced the use of atomic weapons as an act of racist barbarity. Langston Hughes captured much of this sentiment when he speculated that the bomb had not been used against Germany because the Germans were white.[4] Not all black Americans shared Hughes's reaction. A poll of blacks in five cities following the explosion of the second bomb showed that most continued to seek Japan's unconditional surrender.[5] The same issue of the *Chicago Defender* that carried Hughes's speculation about racist motives in the bombing of Hiroshima and Nagasaki proudly announced that "Negro Scientists Help to Split Atoms." Chicago's Southside erupted in unrestrained gaiety at the declaration of Japan's surrender. Hughes also acknowledged that despite indications of black disaffection earlier in the war, the signs of celebration after Japan's capitulation indicated that "Harlem had long since accepted the war as its own, too."[6]

Celebration quickly gave way to concern, however. Questions about postwar employment and the persistence of racism at home were summed up by a *Chicago Defender* illustration showing a black sergeant on "The Road Back," staring at road signs marked "Insecurity," "Fear," "Discord," and "Native Fascism." Once again it appeared that blacks would be deprived of the fruits of the victory for which they had sacrificed so much.

As the artist of "The Road Back," indicated, black Americans would have to battle discrimination on their own. A defeated and occupied Japan made a poor champion. Early in September the USS *Mississippi* steamed into Tokyo Bay flying the flag of the Confederacy while on deck a band played "Dixie." Once again a *Chicago Defender* cartoon captured the ambivalent feelings of many African Americans. Titled "Asiatics Are Colored Too," it showed a rugged black soldier debarking from a ramp on the *Mississippi* marked "colored" and slapping a startled bespectacled Japanese on the back as he offered the following words of sympathy: "I know just how you're going to feel, Bub!" Black Americans could empathize with Japanese who would have to play host to American racism, but most ceased to admire them.

W. E. B. Du Bois did manage a eulogy for Japan's empire. "So far as Japan was fighting against color caste, and striving against the domination of Asia by Europeans, she was absolutely right," he wrote. "But," he added, "so far as she tried to substitute for Europeans an Asiatic caste system

"Asiatics Are Colored Too," *Chicago Defender*, 8 September 1945.
After Japan surrendered, black Americans could sympathize with the
Japanese as victims of racial prejudice, even if they no longer
admired them as champions of racial equality.

under a 'superior,' Japanese race, and for the domination and exploitation
of the peasants of Asia by Japanese trusts and industrialists, she was offering Asia no acceptable exchange for Western exploitation." Du Bois had
abandoned his earlier argument that Japanese imperialism was preferable
to European imperialism, but his statement was hardly an admission of
error. Significantly, he omitted from his analysis an explanation of when
Japan's purpose had changed from liberation to self-interested imperialism. In the end, he never subjected Japanese imperialism to the unflinch-
ing examination he gave to most other subjects. After Japan's surrender
the aging scholar remained optimistic. "The ideas that Japan started and
did not carry through are not dead, but growing," he asserted.[7]

The Chinese, preoccupied with their own internal conflicts, were slow
to pick up those ideas. In the midst of mounting civil strife after the war,
many Chinese resented foreign interference in their internal affairs and
came to view the presence of U.S. troops in coastal China as an unwelcome
reminder of their nation's inferior international status before the war.[8] As

incidents between off-duty GIs and Chinese civilians proliferated, Chinese of all political hues complained of the imperious conduct of the Americans. Searching for a way to make its objections understood, a progressive Shanghai newspaper settled on a disturbing comparison that revealed the gulf that separated black Americans and Chinese. *"The Chinese are not Negroes,"* proclaimed the paper, "so they cannot stand these endless wrongs." [9]

The implication of that editorial—that the Chinese refusal to tolerate American insults distinguished them from African Americans who passively suffered "endless wrongs"—shows how little understanding even educated Chinese had of the crusade mounted by black Americans during the war. Until now, historians interested in the role of race and racism in American–East Asian affairs have limited themselves to studying how white Americans' sense of racial and cultural superiority impaired their relations with Asian peoples. In the words of the late Christopher Thorne, one of the leading scholars in this area, despite their disagreements over strategy and politics, when it came to dealing with the Chinese, white Americans and their English cousins were really "Allies of a Kind." African Americans shared that perception at first, but by the end of World War II they had concluded that when it came to racial equality, the U.S. government and Nationalist China were also "Allies of a Kind." [10]

In the postwar era, the ensuing turmoil in China and the occupation of Japan all but erased both countries as areas of concern for most black internationalists. During the 1950s the continuation of American dominion in Japan even after the end of the occupation left Japan with little ability or inclination to lead an international struggle for racial equality. Moreover, its adoption by the Western camp during the Cold War seemed to accentuate its identification with the dominant powers rather than the former colonial areas.

In 1949 the victory of the Chinese Communists created a radical and potentially serious successor to Japan's prewar role as self-proclaimed liberator of the world's subject peoples. The previous year, however, the majority of black Americans able to vote had cast their ballots for President Harry S. Truman, who had run on a program of reform at home and containment of communism abroad. Some black internationalists watched with interest and, in some cases, admiration as Chinese foreign minister Zhou Enlai reached out to the representatives of the newly independent nations at the Bandung Conference of Afro-Asian countries. But opportunities for contact with the People's Republic of China were few, and the threat of government action was too great to create much grassroots interest in China. In the 1960s leaders of the Black Panther Party and other militant groups found the revolutionary thought of Mao Tse-tung helpful in shaping their worldview and frequently spoke of a revolutionary alliance of nonwhite peoples reminiscent of the most radical proponents of black internationalism. Like its predecessor, however, this later incarnation was plagued by disputes between those who sought alliances based on class interests and cultural nationalists who emphasized color as the organizing principle. In any event, the revolutionary appeal of Mao faded with the advent of détente.[11]

For a brief period after the war, the Soviet Union seemed like a potential ally. During the war the Soviet empire's image had improved among black Americans largely because of what were perceived as Moscow's enlightened racial policies. As in the case of earlier black admiration for Japan, the personal experiences of visitors and Moscow's pronouncements engendered black interest in the Soviet Union. Black newspapers reported that there was no racial discrimination in Stalin's Russia. Not only Leftists such as John Badger and Langston Hughes, but also black GIs who came into contact with the Red army in Iran, observed that "racial differences are unknown to Russians."[12] Before the San Francisco conference, the *Baltimore Afro-American* editorialized that of all the participants, "Russia seems to be the only one, so far, holding out first class citizenship to all people under its control."[13]

These expressions of hopefulness betrayed a lack of knowledge of life within the Soviet empire and recalled earlier reports asserting that Japanese imperialism differed from the Western variety in that the Japanese did not discriminate against others. African American perceptions of the Soviet Union as an enemy of colonialism suffered a setback in the immediate postwar era when it was revealed that Joseph Stalin had regained tsarist concessions in Manchuria as a result of the wartime Yalta Conference. The image of Moscow as the leader of a nonwhite alliance was further undermined by the emerging confrontation between the Soviet Union and the People's Republic of China in the late 1950s. By that time, however, U.S. Cold War policies had already made favorable comments about the Soviet Union a risky activity for black Americans.[14]

Of the few countries in a position to challenge white control of the international system after the war, India provided black Americans with the most encouragement. Public interest in India remained high during the war and, in contrast to the experience with China, African Americans' esteem for that country's nationalist leaders actually grew. Black GIs returning from the India-Burma theater probably contributed to what was already a favorable impression of Indian leaders. Surveys filed from the theater as part of an army project to study the problems of deploying segregated units overseas indicated that in most cases black troops got along well with Indians, especially those whom the reports referred to as "the wealthier and higher type Indian families."[15]

It is likely that these experiences reinforced the appeal of Indian independence leaders to black Americans, whereas China suffered by comparison.[16] As P. L. Prattis noted in the *Pittsburgh Courier*, Madame Pandit's unofficial tour of the United States, timed to correspond with the charter meeting of the United Nations, stood in stark contrast to the earlier visit by China's first lady. Instead of Madame Chiang's evasions, black audiences read of the Indian Congress leader's refusal to speak at Baltimore's Lyric Theatre until African Americans were admitted. "I feel very close to Negroes in America," she told the *Courier*, "in fact I feel like one of them and I am certainly in sympathy with their struggle for full citizenship rights." On another occasion she reportedly said, "I am colored myself and so are my people."[17]

Apart from strong moral support, however, it is difficult to measure how Indian independence materially aided the cause of racial equality in America. Intellectually black protest leaders had always found Gandhi an inspiring example, but programmatically they had ambivalent feelings about the applicability of his strategy of passive resistance to the conditions faced by African Americans. The campaigns against segregation in the South were well under way when Martin Luther King Jr. publicly endorsed Gandhi's approach.[18]

King's embrace of Gandhi's legacy furthered the program of civil rights leaders in the NAACP and other groups who had earlier decided to forsake the Left and adopt an anticommunist, anticolonial agenda. This identification with the Indian independence leader coincided with a renewed interest in India among white liberals and most likely enhanced the sense of a shared agenda between white liberals and anticommunist black civil rights leaders.[19] As in the most desperate hours of World War II, African American civil rights spokespersons and their white liberal allies argued that racial discrimination in the United States undercut the appeal of American democracy abroad. Under Secretary of State Dean Acheson made that point before Congress in 1946. This effort to make racial reform a matter of national security met with dubious success. In 1961 Secretary of State Dean Rusk still found it necessary to warn that racial discrimination in the United States was "the biggest single burden that we carry on our backs."[20]

The difficulty that civil rights activists faced during the Cold War in seeking remedies for American racism in the international arena had been foreshadowed by the earlier quest for solidarity with Japan and China. For more than four decades black internationalists had argued that race mattered most in foreign affairs. They believed that a shared experience of racial discrimination created a mutuality of interests between the world's nonwhite peoples and that other countries would base their relations with the United States on the way that America treated its minority citizens. These arguments surfaced again during the Cold War, but they had already been tested and found wanting.

In the years between the Russo-Japanese War and the attack on Pearl Harbor, black Americans of varying political views, intellectual temperaments, and economic status argued that a strong Japan would help end the international scourge of racism. As noted in this study, black Americans developed a view of world politics that drew a connection between racism in the United States and Western imperialism in Asia and Africa before Japan and Russia went to war. But Japan's victory, coming as it did in one of the bleakest moments in African American history, had a catalytic effect on the development of black internationalism by providing black Americans with an example of defiance that nicely matched their own mood. At a time when white dominance seemed almost universal, Tokyo's challenge to Western hegemony in Asia demolished the myth of white supremacy and provided black internationalists with a means of exposing the hypocrisy of white rule in the colonial world.

Japan's challenge to the West also provided black internationalists with an opportunity to embrace a nation that seemed poised to destroy the imperialist system that African Americans despised. Convinced of the connection between white imperialism in Asia and Africa and the subjugation of racial minorities in the United States, black internationalists welcomed any blow to the imperialist order. They reasoned that a powerful Japan would demand equal treatment not only for itself but for other nonwhite peoples as well. The white world would have to abandon its racist policies, black internationalists predicted, or face a worldwide racial conflict.

As Brenda Gayle Plummer has noted, Japanese defiance of the Western powers in China permitted black Americans to applaud a country that had the temerity to confront the white world. But those who spoke on Japan's behalf were not, as she suggests, African Americans of "middling education" who made little distinction between Japan and China.[21] At one time or another, important black American intellectuals and leaders like

W. E. B. Du Bois, James Weldon Johnson, Kelly Miller, George Schuyler, William Pickens, and numerous editors and publishers of black newspapers hailed Japan as a champion of the darker races.

By the 1920s the widely held belief in the emerging solidarity of nonwhite peoples and the related perception of Japan as a champion of the downtrodden had gained a strong hold on the thinking of internationally minded black Americans. Even those who vigorously opposed a racial analysis of world politics as unscientific found they had to address the ideology of black internationalism if only to rebut its claims. For many African Americans, the breakdown of the international order in the 1930s enhanced the persuasiveness of black internationalism. Western acquiescence in the Italian conquest of Ethiopia and opposition to Japanese expansion in China reinforced black internationalist perceptions of a racial double standard in world affairs. After Ethiopia, left-liberal activists acknowledged the potency of black internationalism by adapting their own programs to account for the role of race and racism in international affairs.

The historic shift of black voters into the Democratic Party made a foreign policy alliance of black and white Americans on the Left seem like a natural extension of the coalition already forming in domestic politics. This ability of black internationalism to accommodate class and racial categories of analysis when dealing with the regions of the African diaspora or India contributed to its appeal. Japan, however, remained an anomaly. Despite the growth of an antifascist popular front that assailed racism and colonialism in equal measure, many black internationalists continued to see race as the key to understanding events in East Asia.

Once the war between Japan and the United States that many black internationalists had predicted finally began, the Roosevelt administration remained largely indifferent to most issues of concern to black Americans. At home the administration did little more than offer token support for civil rights reforms.[22] Its record abroad was little better. Under pressure from Japanese advances, the United States repealed the Chinese exclusion provision in American immigration law and negotiated an end to extraterritoriality. But despite private warnings from his special representative to India that most of Asia would be lost unless Britain granted greater freedom to India, Franklin Roosevelt remained unwilling to force the issue with Winston Churchill.[23]

At times it seemed that the demands of war in all its dehumanizing savagery might overwhelm black internationalists' calls for a new era in race relations. Nevertheless, black leaders and commentators kept alive the message of black internationalism despite the many setbacks they encountered. The first of those, of course, was being deprived of Japan as a model. Black internationalists adroitly responded to this blow by raising up China as a potential ally in the international struggle against racism.

The abrupt transformation of China's image in the black press testified to the malleability of black internationalism, but it also demonstrated its limitations. China served as a useful symbol for black editors and commentators, yet the campaign in the black press produced little enthusiasm for America's Asian ally among the larger black public.[24] Although there were moments when it appeared that China had embraced the black internationalist agenda, for the most part the campaign to recruit Nationalist China as an ally was the political equivalent of one hand clapping.[25]

Chinese intellectuals living in the United States such as writer-philosopher Lin Yutang and United China Relief's Liu Liang-Mo were sincere in their opposition to discrimination. But the evidence of similar feeling among Chinese officials was lacking. Chinese government functionaries knew how to employ the rhetoric of black internationalism, but their actions or, in the case of Madame Chiang, inaction, revealed the relatively low priority they gave to matters of race during the war. African American sympathy for Japan in the 1930s as well as Chinese prejudice toward black Americans and Africans probably contributed to these attitudes. But in the final analysis Chinese officials simply did not share black internationalists' belief in the interconnection between colonialism in Asia and discrimination against black Americans. Chungking was more concerned with finding its place in the existing international system than with transforming it. Like FDR and most administration officials, Chinese diplomats concluded that they could achieve victory over Japan without ever confronting what they termed America's "Negro problem." That calculation on the part of Nationalist officials was painfully obvious by the time the San Francisco conference ended.

The travails of the war showed that as an interpretation of events in Asia, black internationalism left much to be desired. Neither American racism nor a Japanese devotion to missionary uplift sufficed as explanations for Japan's policies in China. Japan's early conquests did hasten the end of European imperialism, as black internationalists predicted it would, but the national liberation struggles of the postwar era never came close to merging into the global race war predicted by Du Bois, Schuyler, White, the *Crisis*, and others.

As a program for action, black internationalism in Asia fared little better. Because of their close identification with Japan, black internationalists had exposed African Americans to the possibility of increased government repression in the early stages of the war. The effort to recruit Nationalist China into an alliance against racism was a failure. Despite the efforts of black internationalists to convince others that racial injustice undercut the nation's security, reform at home proceeded at a glacial pace.

Nevertheless, after the war African American leaders continued to find in black internationalism a viable means of interpreting world politics. Perhaps black internationalism's most tangible benefit was the broad cosmopolitan outlook and interest in the non-European world that it instilled in African Americans. This global consciousness could be discouraging when one compared the sluggish pace of desegregation in the United States to the breakneck pace of decolonization in Asia and Africa. But the numerous independence celebrations in the former colonial world also reminded black Americans that others had shared their fate and prevailed. By the early 1960s that awareness was no small matter.

As Harold Isaacs observed at the time: "Negroes accustomed to always feeling the big wind blowing against them now feel a new sensation of having the wind at their backs. Suddenly, all the big facts of life and history—*they* are out there—were working for them and not, as always before, against them."[26] Given the otherwise low returns on black internationalism as an approach to foreign policy making, its real value may have been in its power to rally the disparate elements in the African American population for the long battle against discrimination that awaited it at home.

Notes

Abbreviations

In addition to the abbreviations used in the text, the following abbreviations are used in the notes.

Berle Papers   Adolf Berle Papers, Franklin D. Roosevelt Library, Hyde Park, N.Y.

FDR Papers   Franklin D. Roosevelt Papers, Franklin D. Roosevelt Library, Hyde Park, N.Y.

FRUS   U.S. Department of State, *Foreign Relations of the United States* (Washington, D.C.: GPO, 1942–44).

FSAA   *Federal Surveillance of Afro-Americans, 1917–1925: The First World War, the Red Scare, and the Garvey Movement* (Frederick, Md.: University Publications of America, 1986), microfilm.

Garvey Papers   Robert A. Hill, ed., *The Marcus Garvey and Universal Negro Improvement Association Papers*, 9 vols. (Berkeley: University of California Press, 1983–85).

Koo Papers   H. V. Wellington Koo Papers, Butler Memorial Library, Columbia University, New York, N.Y.

Logan Papers   Rayford Logan Papers, Correspondence Files, Moorland-Spingarn Research Center, Howard University, Washington, D.C.

MIRSR   *U.S. Military Intelligence Reports: Surveillance of Radicals in the United States, 1917–1941* (Frederick, Md.: University Publications of America, 1984), microfilm.

NAACP Papers   National Association for the Advancement of Colored People Papers, Library of Congress, Washington D.C.

Pasvolsky Papers   Leo Pasvolsky Papers, Library of Congress, Washington, D.C.

RACC   Records of the Allied and Combined Commands, China-Burma-India Theater of Operations, RG 493, Federal Records Center, Suitland, Md.

RG   Record Group

SCCF   Schomburg Center for Research in Black Culture,

	Schomburg Center Clipping File, 1925–1974 (Alexandria, Va.: Chadwyck-Healey, 1986), microfiche.
USC Papers	United Services to China Papers, Seeley G. Mudd Manuscript Library, Princeton University, Princeton, N.J.
Washington Papers	Louis R. Harlan and Raymond W. Smock, eds., *The Booker T. Washington Papers*, 14 vols. (Urbana: University of Illinois Press, 1972–89).
WDGS	Records of the War Department, Army General and Special Staffs, RG 165, National Archives, Washington, D.C.
Wedemeyer Papers	Albert C. Wedemeyer Papers, Hoover Institution on War, Revolution, and Peace, Stanford, Calif.
Wilson Papers	Arthur S. Link et al., eds., *The Papers of Woodrow Wilson*, 69 vols. (Princeton: Princeton University Press, 1966–94).

Introduction

1. Isaacs to Logan, 2 December 1959, box 166-14, Logan Papers.

2. At the time he wrote to Logan, Isaacs was doing research for *The New World of Negro Americans*. See also Isaacs, *No Peace for Asia* and *Images of Asia*, and Rotter, "In Retrospect."

3. Isaacs and Logan worked together to oppose South Africa's apartheid policy in the 1950s. Logan later wrote a letter recommending Isaacs for a permanent position on the MIT faculty. Logan to Professor Robert C. Wood, 14 July 1965, box 166-14, Logan Papers; Plummer, *Rising Wind*, 233.

4. This brief description is drawn from Janken, *Logan*.

5. Kapur, *Raising Up a Prophet*; Scott, *Sons of Sheba's Race*; Harris, *African-American Reactions*; Plummer, *Rising Wind*; Von Eschen, *Race against Empire*.

6. Important exceptions are Kearney, "Afro-American Views," and Ernest Allen, "When Japan Was the 'Champion of the Darker Races.'"

7. For further discussion of this idea, see Emily S. Rosenberg, "Walking the Borders."

Chapter 1

1. Russian derision of the Japanese as monkeys appears in Connaughton, *Russo-Japanese War*, 53 and illustration 1. Concise summaries of the war can be found in Boyle, *Japan*, 139–41, and Beasley, *Modern History of Japan*, 171–73.

2. Tinker, *Race*, 39.

3. Snow, *Star Raft*, 62.

4. Kearney, "Afro-American Views," 35.

5. Little, "Quest for Self-Determination."

6. For the black press in the age of imperialism, see Marks, *Black Press*, which reproduces excerpts from major papers of the period. Also valuable are Gatewood, *White Man's Burden*, and Gaines, "Pauline Hopkins on Race Imperialism," 433–55.

7. Marks, *Black Press*, 100–101, 107–8; Gatewood, *White Man's Burden*, 301; Fredrickson, *Black Liberation*, 73–80; Scott, *Sons of Sheba's Race*, 12–22.

8. Little, "Quest for Self-Determination," 197.

9. Ibid., 210–17 (quotation, p. 210); Gatewood, *White Man's Burden*, 321.

10. Little, "Quest for Self-Determination," 215.

11. Little, "Quest for Self-Determination," 228; Lewis, *Du Bois*, 250–51. Du Bois made his prediction to the historic first gathering of the Pan-African Congress in London.

12. Hunt, *Ideology and U.S. Foreign Policy*, 46–91; Emily S. Rosenberg, *Spreading the American Dream*, 43–48.

13. Snow, *Star Raft*, 65.

14. Little, "Quest for Self-Determination," 246–50.

15. Ibid., 251.

16. Gatewood, *White Man's Burden*, 228–29.

17. Logan, *Betrayal*, 130, 160; Aarim, "Chinese Immigrants"; Jung, "Influence of 'Black Peril.'"

18. Marks, *Black Press*, 188–89. The quotation is from journalist John E. Bruce, who was employed by the Republican National Committee in New York. Bruce used the pseudonym "Bruce Grit" in most of his published work.

19. Gaddis, *Russia*, 26–47.

20. Iriye, *Across the Pacific*, 104.

21. Esthus, *Theodore Roosevelt*, 64–65; Neu, *Troubled Encounter*, 44–47.

22. Little, "Quest for Self-Determination," 254.

23. "War in the Far East," *Voice of the Negro* 1 (March 1904): 79–81.

24. Kearney, "Afro-American Views," 62.

25. "The Result of the Battle," *Voice of the Negro* 2 (April 1905): 225; W. S. Scarborough, "Our Pagan Teachers," *Voice of the Negro* 2 (June 1905): 404. See also "The Effect of Togo's Victory upon the Warfare between Races," *Colored American Magazine*, July 1905, 347–48, and Isaacs, *New World of Negro Americans*, 35.

26. Washington to Naochi Masaoka, 5 December 1912, in *Washington Papers*, 12:84–85.

27. "From the Great White Nation of the West," *Colored American Magazine*, November 1905, 595–97. At a banquet for the departing Russian peace delegation, the editors of the *Colored American Magazine* reacted sharply to the characterization of Russia as "the Great White Nation of the East" by several sympathetic Americans. They also complained that the Japanese delegates had been deliberately snubbed.

28. Walter LaFeber, *The Clash*, 87–92 (quotation, p. 89); Neu, *Troubled Encounter*, 52–65.

29. "In the Sanctum," *Voice of the Negro* 2 (July 1905): 492.

30. Kearney, "Afro-American Views," 70–71.

31. Iriye, *Pacific Estrangement*, 159.

32. Washington to J. Harada, 10 November 1913, in *Washington Papers*, 12:328–29.

33. Kearney, "Afro-American Views," 76–77.

34. Franklin and Moss, *From Slavery to Freedom*, 287–88.

35. *Voice of the Negro* 2 (August 1905): 552.

36. "China," *Crisis* 3 (February 1912), reprinted in Lester, *Seventh Son*, 296–97.

37. Pauline Hopkins, "The Dark Races of the Twentieth Century, III: The Yellow Race," *Voice of the Negro* 2 (May 1905): 332 (Katsura); Gaines, "Pauline Hopkins on Race Imperialism," 444–46. In "The Yellow Race" Hopkins compared the "servile and crafty" Chinese with the more energetic and "warlike" Japanese.

38. Cohen, *America's Response to China*, 71–72; Iriye, *Across the Pacific*, 127–29.

39. On Wilson as a progressive internationalist, see Knock, *To End All Wars*.

40. Franklin and Moss, *From Slavery to Freedom*, 291–93.

41. "World War I and the Color Line," *Crisis* 9 (November 1914), reprinted in Lester, *Seventh Son*, 65–68.

42. Du Bois, "The African Roots of the War," *Atlantic*, May 1915, reprinted in Weinberg, *Du Bois*, 360–71. See also Lewis, *Du Bois*, 503–5.

43. Carrier, "Ideas," 75 (first quotation); "Fortune Calls It a 'Crazy Congress,' " *New York Age*, 4 January 1919, 7; "For Africa and the World Democracy," *New York Age*, 11 January 1919, 2; Kapur, *Raising Up a Prophet*, 11 (second quotation).

44. Padmore, *Colonial and Coloured Unity*, 13–17; Lewis, *Du Bois*, 561–64. Du Bois was also supposed to be gathering information for an NAACP-sponsored history of black Americans in the war. While in Paris, he attended the Pan-African Congress, which was being held to "impress upon the members of the Peace Congress sitting at Versailles the importance of Africa in the future of the world." Padmore, *Colonial and Coloured Unity*, 13.

45. "League of Darker Peoples Sees Light," *New York Age*, 11 January 1919, 2; Plummer, *Rising Wind*, 16.

46. See, for example, "Mongolians to Query Race Discrimination at Peace Conference in Paris," *Cleveland Advocate*, 30 November 1918, 1.

47. Lauren, *Power and Prejudice*, 77.

48: Plummer, *Rising Wind*, 16–20; Kearney, "Afro-American Views," 87–88; Skinner, *African Americans and U.S. Policy*, 395.

49. Lauren, *Power and Prejudice*, 79–81.

50. Kawamura, "Wilsonian Idealism and Japanese Claims," 515–16.

51. Diary of Edward House, 4 February 1919, and Draft of an Article for the Covenant, [5 February 1919], *Wilson Papers*, 54:484–85, 500. The emphasized clause was added by Wilson in place of the phrase "as far as it is in their legitimate power."

52. Diary of Edward House, 13 February 1919, *Wilson Papers*, 55:155–56.

53. Minutes of Two Meetings of the League of Nations Commission, 13 February 1919, *Wilson Papers*, 55:140; Lauren, *Power and Prejudice*, 86 (Ray Stannard Baker, Wilson's confidant).

54. Diary of Edward House, 13 February, 1919, *Wilson Papers*, 55:155.

55. Breckinridge Long to Wilson, with enclosure, 4 March 1919, *Wilson Papers*, 55:436–37.

56. Lauren, *Power and Prejudice*, 89.

57. "Japan Heard From," *Philadelphia Tribune*, 1 March 1919, 4.

58. "Japan Forces the Race Issue," *New York Age*, 29 March 1919, 4.

59. Kearney, "Afro-American Views," 91.

60. Lauren, *Power and Prejudice*, 90–91.

61. Ibid., 92–93.

62. Cohen, *America's Response to China*, 79–80; Kawamura, "Wilsonian Idealism and Japanese Claims," 524–25; Knock, *To End All Wars*, 249–50.

63. "The Week," *Nation*, 26 April 1919, 644.

64. "Fourteen Questions for Mr. Wilson," *Nation*, 19 July 1919, 67–70.

65. Bailey, *Great Betrayal*, 115, 161–64; Knock, *To End All Wars*, 257.

66. *New York Age*, 29 March 1919, 4.

67. "The Shantung Grant," *New York Age*, 26 July 1919, 4.

68. Bailey, *Great Betrayal*, 164.

69. "The League of Nations," *Crisis* 18 (May 1919): 10–11.

70. Lewis, *Du Bois*, 399–400, 471–72, 533, 544, 576; Steel, *Walter Lippmann*, 39, 158–63, 551–54; Padmore, *Colonial and Colored Unity*, 15. Villard and Du Bois had been feuding for some time. Although he was in Paris when the Pan-African Congress met, Villard did not attend. As his biographer explains, Lippmann's views on racism in the United States were similar to those of many other progressives in that he opposed racial violence and economic exploitation of black Americans but did not believe that the government should force integration. He rarely commented on racial issues in his publications, but he did maintain a cordial relationship with Du Bois. In 1911 he nominated Du Bois for admission in the Liberal Club in New York. Du Bois was on the *New Republic*'s editorial board, and the two men conferred on African issues while in Paris.

71. For other examples of progressive and socialist opposition to the league because of the secret treaties, see William I. Hull, "The Proposed League of Nations: Seven Fundamental Amendments," *Advocate of Peace*, November 1919, and Scott Nearing, "The League of Nations as Seen by an Economist," pamphlet in the Swarthmore College Peace Collection, both reprinted in Chambers, *The Eagle and the Dove*, 444–50, 456–57.

72. *Philadelphia Tribune*, 3 May 1919, 1; 2, 16, 30 August, 6 September 1919 — all editorials on p. 4. An exception was the strongly Republican *Philadelphia Tribune*. At first the editors welcomed Japan's fight for racial equality. When the debate over Shantung began, they denounced the betrayal of China but also noted

that the Japanese viewed senatorial use of the issue as a partisan tactic. By late summer, however, they lumped Japan with the other imperialists and referred to the "rape" of Shantung. The editors were also appalled that Wilson had not thought to exempt the Monroe Doctrine in the first draft of the league covenant.

73. On the "unholy alliance" between white progressives and Wilson's foes, see Knock, *To End All Wars*, 257.

Chapter 2

1. Gibbons, *Red Napoleon*. In 1976 the book was reissued by the Southern Illinois University Press as part of a series on "Lost American Fiction." References are to the reissued edition, which also contains an afterword by John Gardner.

2. *New York Times*, 25 August 1929, 9.

3. "Discreditable Journalism," *Nation*, 4 December 1929, 694–95.

4. Robert Ezra Park, "Negro Race Consciousness as Reflected in Race Literature," *American Review* (September–October 1923), reprinted in Park, *Race and Culture*, 284–300.

5. Neu, *Troubled Encounter*, 94–101; Iriye, *Across the Pacific*, 134–39; Knock, *To End All Wars*, 155–58.

6. Stavrianos, *Global Rift*, 513–16; Tinker, *Race*, 39–40.

7. Franklin and Moss, *From Slavery to Freedom*, 298–303.

8. Stavrianos, *Global Rift*, 513. On the impact of Wilson's ideas in China, see Schmidt, "Democracy for China."

9. Franklin and Moss, *From Slavery to Freedom*, 307–8.

10. Stavrianos, *Global Rift*, 513.

11. Harding, *Other American Revolution*, 95.

12. Gilbert, *Writings of . . . Bruce*, 151–53.

13. Higham, *Strangers in the Land*, 264–330; Divine, *American Immigration Policy*, 26–51.

14. Higham, *Strangers in the Land*, 156–57, 271.

15. Stoddard, *Rising Tide of Color*; Gossett, *Race*, 390–99.

16. Stoddard, *Rising Tide of Color*, 306–7.

17. Ibid., 97.

18. Ibid., 28–30.

19. Ibid., 232–33.

20. See Kusmer, "Toward a Comparative History of Racism."

21. Weinstein, "Fu Manchu and the Third World"; Dower, *War without Mercy*, 157–59; Oehling, "Yellow Menace," 182–206.

22. Locke, *New Negro*, 14–15.

23. Carrier, *Ideas That Shaped the West*, 108 (Senghor); Tinker, *Race*, 38. The delegates to the International Congress at Brussels included prominent figures in the European Left and representatives from China, India, Africa, and Latin America.

24. Locke, *New Negro*, 6.

25. See Holt, "African-American History," 329.

26. Toll, *Resurgence of Race*, 147, 168–69; Fredrickson, *Black Liberation*, 150.

27. "The League of Nations," *Crisis* 18 (May 1919): 11.

28. Du Bois, *Dark Princess*, 18.

29. Ibid., 296–97; Isaacs, *New World of Negro Americans*, 216–20.

30. Harding, *Other American Revolution*, 98.

31. Higham, *Strangers in the Land*, 173. In 1908 the national party succumbed to fears of the "yellow peril" and dropped its opposition to the restrictions on Asian immigration.

32. Foner, *American Socialism*, 323.

33. Gilbert, *Writings of . . . Bruce*, 156.

34. Ibid., 143.

35. Ibid., 158.

36. Miller, *Everlasting Stain*, 89.

37. Ibid., 94.

38. Ibid., 67.

39. [Summary Report of Washington, D.C., Meeting, n.d.], and Mrs. Booker T. Washington to [?], 10 November 1924, box 102-12, Mary Church Terrell Papers, Moorland-Spingarn Research Center, Howard University, Washington, D.C.

40. International Council of the Women of the Darker Races, ca. 1929, in Aptheker, *Documentary History*, 616–18; Janie Porter to Mrs. Booker T. Washington, 23 October 1924, 12 February 1925, Mary Church Terrell Papers. The council does not appear to have been very active although it paid for a study of conditions in Haiti, heard reports on India and the West Coast of Africa, and maintained approximately five hundred dollars in its treasury. The membership also encouraged educators to introduce material on foreign women of color into their curriculum. It held at least two conferences in Chicago and Washington, D.C. In 1929 the group planned to meet in New York and listed having a member at Geneva, the location of the League of Nations, as one of its goals for the coming year. It is not known if the council met in New York, but the group apparently died out as a result of the depression.

41. Conn, *Buck*, 82.

42. "Japan and the Far East," *Messenger*, July 1918, 22–23.

43. Ibid., 27. Consistent with this view, Randolph praised Oswald Garrison Villard, Du Bois's nemesis at the NAACP, for his opposition to the war and his reporting on the Versailles Treaty. Villard, according to the *Messenger*, was "a true political scientist." "Oswald Garrison Villard," ibid., August 1919, 28.

44. "Report Japan Will Fight Reds" and "China's President Rejects Tokyo's Demand," *Messenger*, March 1919, 19.

45. Williams, *Black Response to the American Left*, 88 (Briggs); Foner, *American Socialism*, 309–11, and *American Communism and Black Americans*, 16–18; Hill, *Crusader*, 1:xxv.

46. *Crusader*, December 1920, 12.

47. Kapur, *Raising Up a Prophet*, 25–40.

48. Du Bois, "African Roots of War," in Weinberg, *Du Bois*, 370; Miller, *Everlasting Stain*, 75.

49. "Report of Special Agent P-138," 20 October 1920, *Garvey Papers*, 3:49.

50. George Van Dusen to J. Edgar Hoover, 19 March 1921, transmitting extracts from Garvey's address at Bethel AME Church, Baltimore, on 18 December 1918, ibid., 3:258.

51. Report by Bureau Agent H. B. Pierce, 25 April 1921, ibid., 3:364. See also Report by Bureau Agent Adrian L. Potts, 18 January 1921, ibid., 3:136–38. According to the report, Gordon was referring to the controversy over the island of Yap.

52. Reports by Special Agent P-138, 22 October, 6 November 1920, ibid., 3:62, 65.

53. J. J. Hannigan, Commandant, 12th Naval District, to Director, ONI, transmitting "Weekly Report of Japanese Activities, UNIA," ibid., 4:233–37.

54. Hannigan to Director, ONI, 5 July 1922, ibid., 4:477.

55. Barnhart, "Driven by Domestics," 190–212. As Barnhart has noted, in the navy's case this view persisted through the 1920s despite an official posture of cooperation in Tokyo and Washington.

56. This assessment of the diplomacy leading to the Washington Conference draws on Dingman, *Power in the Pacific*; Neu, *Troubled Encounter*, 105–19; and Iriye, *After Imperialism*, especially the first chapter.

57. Address by Garvey at Olympia Theater, 13 November 1921, *Garvey Papers*, 4:174–75.

58. Ibid., 3:633 n. 2.

59. "Japan in Jeopardy," *New York Age*, 23 July 1921, 4.

60. "Japan versus China," *New York Age*, 24 December 1921, 4.

61. "The Japanese Delegation," *New York Age*, 7 January 1922, 4.

62. "The World and Us," *Crisis* 22 (January 1922): 103.

63. Address by Garvey at Olympia Theater, 13 November 1921, *Garvey Papers*, 4:187.

64. "Washington a Blaze of Color to Welcome Delegates to Disarmament Conference," *Philadelphia Tribune*, 12 November 1921, 9.

65. "Labor and Disarmament," *Messenger*, February 1922, 352.

66. Cohen, *America's Response to China*, 89.

67. Beasley, *Japanese Imperialism*, 167–69.

68. Asada, "Japan and the United States," 401–8.

69. Hellwig, "Afro-American Reactions to the Japanese," 93.

70. Ibid., 98.

71. Kearney, "Afro-American Views," 98; Taylor, *Forging of a Black Community*, 127–28.

72. Spickard, *Japanese Americans*, 68, 79–80.

73. Aarim, "Chinese Immigrants," 441 (quotation); Hellwig, "The Afro-American and the Immigrant," 13.

74. Hellwig, "The Afro-American and the Immigrant," 118.

75. Taylor, *Forging a Black Community*, 125.

76. Foner and Rosenberg, *Racism, Dissent, and Asian Americans*, 241.

77. Shankman, *Ambivalent Friends*, 16.

78. Ibid.

79. T. Thomas Fortune, "The Filipino," *Voice of the Negro* 1 (May 1904): 199–200.

80. Hellwig, "Afro-American Reactions to the Japanese," 103.

81. Daniels and Kitano, *American Racism*, 71–72.

82. Hellwig, "The Afro-American and the Immigrant," 137–38.

83. Kearney, "Afro-American Views," 109.

84. Shankman, *Ambivalent Friends*, 19; Broussard, *Black San Francisco*, 82.

85. Hellwig, "The Afro-American and the Immigrant," 117.

86. Ibid., 120; Plummer, *Rising Wind*, 67.

87. "Bamboo Inn, Harlem Night Life Center, Bars Race Patrons," *Pittsburgh Courier*, 8 January 1927, 4.

88. "China Finds a Way," *Pittsburgh Courier*, 22 January 1927, 8.

89. "Cast the Beam out of Thine Own Eye," cartoon and caption, *Pittsburgh Courier*, 9 April 1927, 8.

90. "The Significance of China," *Pittsburgh Courier*, 16 April 1927, 8.

91. Ibid.

Chapter 3

1. Stephan, *Hawaii under the Rising Sun*, 60–62; Peattie, "Forecasting a Pacific War," 118–19.

2. Jansen, *The Japanese and Sun Yat-Sen*, 35–36; Storry, *The Double Patriots*, 12–13; Morris, *Nationalism and the Right Wing in Japan*, xvii; Ernest Allen, "When Japan Was the 'Champion of the Darker Races,'" 29. The Japanese and the Chinese pronounced the name differently but wrote it with the same characters.

3. "Our Position, Racial Equality Proposition, and Anti-Japanism in the East," *Asian Review* 1 (February 1920): 27–29, 34.

4. "Coloured and Whites," *Asian Review* 1 (July 1920): 459.

5. "Treatment of Negroes in the United States: Awakening of the Negroes," *Asian Review* 1 (October 1920): 692–93; "Yellow or Dark Peril?," ibid., 2 (January 1921): 50–52; "Lynching in America," ibid., 2 (February 1921): 198; "Lynching in America," ibid., 2 (May–June 1921): 560.

6. McWilliams, *Prejudice*, 56; *Philadelphia Tribune*, 16 July 1921, as cited in Kearney, "Afro-American Views," 103. K. K. Kawakami, whom James Weldon Johnson referred to as a professional acquaintance, wrote for the *Asian Review* and met with other black American leaders before the Paris Peace Conference.

McWilliams described Kawakami as an "official apologist for the Japanese government."

7. *Asian Review* 1 (February 1920): 110–13.

8. In addition to the inaugural edition cited above, see "Foreign Propaganda Work in China," *Asian Review* 1 (May–June 1920): 384–88.

9. Dower, *War without Mercy*, 203–33; Howell, "Ethnicity and Culture." The myth of Japanese purity reached its apotheosis during the Pacific war.

10. Koshiro, "Trans-Pacific Racism," 12 (Keene).

11. Gulick, *American Japanese Problem*, 155.

12. Morikawa, *Japan and Africa*, 36–37.

13. Koshiro, "Trans-Pacific Racism,, 27–28, 33 (Abe); Ienaga, *Pacific War*, 6–9.

14. Ienaga, *Pacific War*, 38–40; Peattie, "Japanese Attitudes toward Colonialism"; Dower, *War without Mercy*, 262–90.

15. "Japanese Influence and Activity among the American Negroes," in Hill, *RACON*, 510; Kearney, "Afro-American Views," 124–27.

16. Jervis Anderson, *Randolph*, 148–49; Draper, *Roots of American Communism*, 192; Naisson, *Communists in Harlem*, 3–10.

17. The previous summary of events in China and Manchuria is drawn from Borg, *American Policy*; Cohen, *Chinese Connection* and *America's Response to China*, 97–112; Doenecke, *When the Wicked Rise*; and Neu, *Troubled Encounter*, 129–40.

18. *Crisis* (December 1931), reprinted in Lester, *Seventh Son*, 394.

19. Kearney, *Afro-American Views*, 113.

20. Ibid., 115.

21. "War in the East," *The Negro Worker*, May 1932, reprinted in Aptheker, *Documentary History*, 718–29.

22. "As the Crow Flies," *Crisis* 39 (November 1932): 342.

23. Naisson, *Communists in Harlem*, 17–19, 45–48; Draper, *Roots of American Communism*, 387; Harry Haywood, "Against Bourgeois-Liberal Distortions of Leninism on the Negro Question in the United States," *The Communist*, August 1930, reprinted in Foner and Shapiro, *American Communism and Black Americans*, 17–35; Padmore, *Pan-Africanism or Communism*, 284–86.

24. Sitkoff, *New Deal for Blacks*, 154 (quotation), 146–51; Fredrickson, *Black Liberation*, 200–202.

25. Much of this summary relies on Scott, *Sons of Sheba's Race*, and Plummer, *Rising Wind*, 47–53.

26. Harris, *African-American Reactions*, 98.

27. Scott, *Sons of Sheba's Race*, 125.

28. Ibid., 124–27; Naisson, *Communists in Harlem*, 156; Clarke, "Periphery and Crossroads." Clarke's superbly researched paper draws on Soviet, Italian, and Japanese archival sources.

29. Padmore, *Pan-Africanism or Communism*, 285–86. Padmore was vilified by American Communists for his criticism of Russia. He left the party soon afterward.

30. Naisson, *Communists in Harlem*, 127; Fredrickson, *Black Liberation*, 202–3.

31. Kapur, *Raising Up a Prophet*, 69.

32. Ibid., 51, 69.

33. Robertson, *Mussolini*, 102–3.

34. Kearney, "Afro-American Views," 115–18; Clarke, "Periphery and Cross-roads"; Robertson, *Mussolini*, 153.

35. Scott, *Sons of Sheba's Race*, 144.

36. Franklin and Moss, *From Slavery to Freedom*, 385–86, 406.

37. Clarke, "Periphery and Crossroads."

38. Du Bois, "Inter-Racial Implications," 87.

39. Ibid., 88–89.

40. Morikawa, *Japan and Africa*, 47–48. The Japanese government did not recognize the Ethiopian government in exile.

41. Scott, *Sons of Sheba's Race*, 144; Hardie, *Abyssinian Crisis*, 64, 155–57; Clarke, "Periphery and Crossroads" (quid pro quo). Another possible interpretation would have been that the Admiralty's fear of a Japanese southern advance hampered Britain's willingness to oppose Italy.

42. Rudwick, *Du Bois*, 234.

43. Bunche, *World View of Race*, 95–96.

44. Gossett, *Race*, 423–30; Sitkoff, *New Deal for Blacks*, 190–215.

45. Von Eschen, *Race against Empire*, 11–21, and "Changing Old Cold War Habits," 630–31; DeConde, *Ethnicity, Race*, 107–8.

46. "Forum of Fact and Opinion," *Pittsburgh Courier*, 20 March 1937, 10.

47. Ibid., 6, 13, 20 February, 1, 13, 20, 27 March 1937, *Pittsburgh Courier*; Marable, *Du Bois*, 156–57; Takemoto, "Du Bois and Japan."

48. "Forum of Fact and Opinion," *Pittsburgh Courier*, 13 March 1937, 15; Ienaga, *Pacific War*, 9.

49. "Forum of Fact and Opinion," *Pittsburgh Courier*, 25 September 1937, 12, and 23 October 1937, 12.

50. DuBois to Harry F. Ward, in Aptheker, *Correspondence of W. E. B. DuBois*, 2:147.

51. Kearney, "Afro-American Views," 129.

52. *New York Amsterdam News*, 30 October 1937, 14, and 26 March 1938, 12.

53. "Soap Box," *New York Amsterdam News*, 20 November 1937, 13.

54. *New York Amsterdam News*, 16 October 1937, 13.

55. "Chinese Are Not Negroes," *New York Amsterdam News*, 11 September 1937, 6.

56. "Soap Box," *New York Amsterdam News*, 13. Although Powell could not know it at the time, the NAACP was on the verge of a historic increase in membership. In 1940 the NAACP had 50,556 members, but by 1946 that number had jumped to 450,000.

57. "Japan Gets Both Cheers and Boos," *New York Amsterdam News*, 4 September 1937, 14.

58. *New York Amsterdam News*, 9 October 1937, 14.

59. "Conflict in China," *New York Amsterdam News*, 8 January 1938, 12.

60. "Soap Box," *New York Amsterdam News*, 19 February 1938, 11.

61. *New York Amsterdam News*, 16 October 1937, 13.

62. "Egging for War!," *New York Amsterdam News*, 5 March 1938, 12.

63. "Advises China to Deal with Japanese," *Pittsburgh Courier*, 18 December 1937, 14. Pickens's views on the press are reported in "Japan Gets Both Cheers and Boos," *New York Amsterdam News*, 4 September 1937, 14.

64. "That's Resolving," *New York Amsterdam News*, 15 January 1938, 12.

65. Plummer, *Rising Wind*, 70–71; Fredrickson, *Black Liberation*, 216. An exception was A. Philip Randolph. Although he denounced Japan, Randolph insisted that black Americans control their own protest organizations. But as Fredrickson notes, Randolph was not a black separatist or a nationalist. Throughout his career he remained committed to the ideal of a fully integrated society. Plummer observes that during this period Du Bois endorsed programs more in line with black nationalism.

66. "The Far East and Us," *Pittsburgh Courier*, 30 October 1937, 18.

67. "The World This Week," *Pittsburgh Courier*, 11 December 1937, 11.

68. *Pittsburgh Courier*, 18 December 1937, 11.

69. Vann's concern that black Americans were overcommitted to the Democrats is discussed in Bruni, *Vann*, 290–91.

70. "Is Japan the Champion of the Colored Races?," August 1938, in Negro Troops file, Chronology 1939–45, World War II, *SCCF*.

71. *New York Amsterdam News*, 4 June 1938, 2.

72. "Sino-Jap Dispute Explained," *New York Amsterdam News*, 5 February 1938, 4.

73. Ibid.

74. Ibid

75. Ibid.

76. *New York Amsterdam News*, 12 March 1938, 12.

77. "Discuss Japanese in Chinese Intervention" (19 March 1938, 11) and "No Decision in Borough Debate" (9 April 1938, 11), *New York Amsterdam News*.

Chapter 4

1. Hill and Rasmussen, *Black Empire*, 279.

2. Schuyler to P. L. Prattis, 4 April 1937, Schuyler File, P. L. Prattis Papers, Moorland-Spingarn Collection, Howard University, Washington, D.C.

3. Hill and Rasmussen, *Black Empire*, 280.

4. "The Rise of the Black Internationale," *Crisis* 45 (August 1938): 255–57, 274, 277.

5. Heinrichs, "Role of the United States Navy," 212, and *American Ambassador*, 314.

6. *Pittsburgh Courier*, 2 September 1939, quoted in Dalfiume, "'Forgotten Years,'" 301.

7. Lindbergh, "Aviation, Geography, and Race."

8. "Lindbergh's Claptrap," *Chicago Defender*, 6 January 1940, 14. The *Defender* approvingly reprinted the *New York Amsterdam News*'s editorial reply to Lindbergh's article.

9. "The Truth about Slavery," *Chicago Defender*, 30 December 1939, 11.

10. Ibid.

11. Smith, *To Save a Nation*, 112–13, 121, 125–26.

12. McNutt to Du Bois, 13 February 1939, in Aptheker, *Correspondence of W. E. B. Du Bois*, 2:184–85.

13. Du Bois to McNutt, 25 February 1939, ibid., 185.

14. Hikida to Du Bois, [14 March], 15, 24 April, 20 May, 15 October 1936, and Du Bois to Hikida, 1, 21 April 1936, all in Du Bois, *Papers*, reel 45, frames 1041–59; Kearney, "Afro-American Views," 137. Hikida Yasuichi provided Du Bois with a list of Japanese officials to contact in Manchuria, northern China, and Japan. Hikida also volunteered to schedule meetings and lecture dates for Du Bois.

15. White, *A Man Called White*, 68–69; Kearney, "Afro-American Views," 137.

16. Elsbree, *Southeast Asian Nationalist Movements*, 3–18.

17. Christopher Thorne, "Racial Aspects of the Far Eastern War," 338.

18. Ernest Allen, "When Japan Was the 'Champion of the Darker Races.'"

19. "Detroit Field Division Report" and "Japanese Influence among Negroes," both ca. August 1943, in Hill, *RACON*, 111–12, 514–17.

20. Benyon, "Voodoo Cult," 894; Turner, *Islam in the African-American Experience*, 102–5; Clegg, *An Original Man*, 297–98 n. 36.

21. E. P. Eldridge to Director of Naval Intelligence, 12 September 1933, reel 20, frame 547, *FSAA*.

22. Moore to MID, War Department, "Special Report on Pacific Movement," 25 October 1933, reel 20, frame 550, *FSAA*.

23. In September the communist *Daily Worker* also reported on Japanese propaganda activities in Kansas City. See the chronology in Hill, *RACON*, 665, and [E. P. Eldridge to Director Naval Intelligence] quoting *Kansas City Post Journal* of 23 November 1933, reel 20, frame 555, *FSAA*.

24. Moore to MID, War Department, "Summary of Intelligence," VII Corps Area, November 1933, reel 32, frame 326, *MIRSR*.

25. O. A. Dickinson to Acting Chief of Staff, G-2 [Intelligence], War Department, 21 December 1933, reel 20, frame 563, *FSAA*.

26. E. M. Landis to Assistant Chief of Staff, G-2, 21 February 1934, reel 30, frame 3, and J. Edgar Hoover to Lieutenant Colonel C. K. Knulsen, MID, 10 April 1934, reel 30, frame 30, *MIRSR*.

27. BC Report, 16 April 1934, Surveillance of Afro-Americans, reel 20, frame 605, *FSAA*.

28. "Statement obtained from POLICARPIO MANANSALA, alias ASHIMA NICOME-

SIKI PACIFICAE, alias ASHIMA TAKIS KINNOUSUKI, alias ADACI KINNOUSUKI, alias DR. TAKIS, alias DR. KOO," 17 April 1934, reel 20, frames 595–601, *FSAA.*

29. "Japanese Imperialism and the Negro People," [April 1934], reel 20, frames 602–4, *FSAA.*

30. Harry Jung to General Staff, War College, 15 November 1935; Nulsen to Jung, 21 November 1935, reel 20, frames 613–15, *FSAA.*

31. *Pittsburgh Courier* article in Lieutenant Colonel C. L. Clark to Assistant Chief of Staff, G-2, War Department, 16 June 1939, reel 20, frames 616–17, *FSAA.*

32. Clark to Assistant Chief of Staff, G-2, ibid.

33. Ernest Allen, "When Japan Was the 'Champion of the Darker Races,'" 27–28.

Chapter 5

1. Johnson, *Along This Way*, 399; Hill, *RACON*, 510; Kearney, "Afro-American Views," 129–33. In 1929 Johnson attended a conference sponsored by the Institute of Pacific Relations in Kyoto. He expressed "boundless admiration for the energy, the enterprise, the genius for organization" of the Japanese, but he found the intellectual qualities of the Chinese more to his liking and preferred them as companions to the Japanese, who left him "rather cold."

2. Kearney, "Afro-American Views," 123–25.

3. Report of Hikida *shokutaku* on "The War and Black Persons," October 1942, File I 460-1-3, Documents Related to Racial Problems (*Minzoku Mōndai*) and Problems of Black Persons (*Kokujin Mōndai*), Foreign Ministry Record Office (Gaikoshiryokan), Tokyo.

4. "Autobiography of Rayford Logan," manuscript, box 166-32, Logan Papers.

5. Borg, *The United States and the Far Eastern Crisis*, 74–76; Graebner, "Hoover, Roosevelt, and the Japanese," 33; Thomson, "Role of the Department of State," 94–97; Iriye, "Role of the United States Embassy in Tokyo," 108–10.

6. Kamikawa Hikomatsu, "The American and Japanese Monroe Doctrines," *Contemporary Japan* (August 1939), translated and condensed in Lebra, *Japan's Greater East Asia Co-Prosperity Sphere*, 25–30.

7. Finkle, *Forum for Protest*, 199–200.

8. Price to Anderson, 17 April 1939, Marian Anderson Benefit, American Committee for Non-Participation in Japanese Aggression Files, Littauer Center of Public Administration, Harvard University, Cambridge; Cohen, "Role of Private Groups," 438. Price also wanted to sign black actor-singer and social activist Paul Robeson for the event. The committee received funds from the Nationalist government.

9. Hoover to Brigadier General Edwin M. Watson, 30 November 1939, transmitting "Report on Japanese Propaganda in the United States," Official File 10 B, folder 12, box 11, Justice Department, FBI Reports, FDR Papers. FBI director

Hoover forwarded a copy of this report to the White House with a note explaining that he had been informed that the original was prepared for Madame Chiang Kai-shek for use by the Chinese government.

10. Dikotter, *Discourse of Race* and "Racial Identities in China," 404–12; Snow, *Star Raft*; Ch'en, *China and the West*, 79–80.

11. Dikotter, *Discourse of Race*, 114. On Lin Shu, see Arkush and Lee, *Land without Ghosts*, 77–80.

12. Document no. 115, New York to Tokyo, 11 December 1940, message no. 762, in U.S. Department of Defense, *"MAGIC" Background*, 1:A-74.

13. Document no. 174, Los Angeles to Tokyo, 9 May 1941, message no. 067, ibid., 1:A-99.

14. Intercept from Tokyo, 11 June 1941, cited in Hill, *RACON*, 511.

15. Washburn, *Question of Sedition*, 32–33.

16. Hill, *RACON*, 6.

17. Louis Allen, "Japanese Intelligence Systems"; Barnhart, "Japanese Intelligence before the Second World War"; Kumamoto, "The Search for Spies," 56. Before the attacks on Pearl Harbor Japanese intelligence activities focused on areas of immediate operational concern to the army and navy, namely Hawaii and Southeast Asia.

18. Hill, *RACON*, 523–25.

19. Washburn, *Question of Sedition*, 33–40.

20. See the statement to this effect made shortly after Pearl Harbor by the NAACP's Roy Wilkins in Dalfiume, "'Forgotten Years,'" 308.

21. Matthews, "Our Stake in the Far Eastern Crisis," *Baltimore Afro-American*, 6 December 1941, 4.

22. *Baltimore Afro-American*, 6 December 1941, 7.

23. Prattis, *Pittsburgh Courier*, 6 December 1941.

24. "Rogers Says," *Pittsburgh Courier*, 6 December 1941, 7.

25. *Baltimore Afro-American*, 20 December 1941, 1.

26. *Pittsburgh Courier*, 20 December 1941, 12.

27. *Pittsburgh Courier*, 27 December 1941, 9.

28. "Underestimating Japan," *Pittsburgh Courier*, 20 December 1941, 6.

29. *Baltimore Afro-American*, 3 January 1942, 1.

30. "The World Today," *Pittsburgh Courier*, 10 January 1942, 1.

31. "Views and Reviews," *Pittsburgh Courier*, 31 January 1942, 6.

32. Christopher Thorne, "Racial Aspects of the Far Eastern War," 344.

33. Kearney, "Afro-American Views," 141.

34. Logan to Harold Isaacs, 17 July 1961, Isaacs Folder, box 166-14, Logan Papers.

35. Washburn, *Question of Sedition*, 63.

36. Ibid., 62.

37. Letters, *Baltimore Afro-American*, 3 January 1942, 4.

38. Ibid., 28 February 1942, 4.

39. Ibid., 28 March 1942, 4.

40. Dower, *War without Mercy*, 37–39; "U.S. Bans Reference to 'Racial War' on Air," *Baltimore Afro-American*, 20 December 1941, 5.

41. "White Man's War," *Crisis* 49 (April 1942): 2.

42. Hill, *RACON*, 8–13; Washburn, *Question of Sedition*.

43. Letters, *Baltimore Afro-American*, 28 February 1942, 4.

44. Big Parade, *Baltimore Afro-American*, 14 February 1942, 4.

45. This was the banner headline in the *Baltimore Afro-American*, 13 December 1941.

Chapter 6

1. Author's interview with McCloy, 2 August 1984.

2. Hill, *RACON*, 5–7.

3. Ibid., 6–7.

4. Ibid., 7.

5. "Japanese Influence and Activity among the American Negroes," in Hill, *RACON*, 510.

6. Document no. 115, New York to Tokyo, 11 December 1940, message no. 762, U.S. Department of Defense, *"MAGIC" Background*, 1:A-74.

7. "Dustin Off the News," *Chicago Defender*, 27 December 1941, 1.

8. Buck, *American Unity and Asia*, 17, 22. Buck's letter to the *New York Times* and "Tinder for Tomorrow" speech were published along with several other essays in book form during the first year of the war.

9. "The Negro and the War," *PM*, 25 February 1942, in Negro Troops: Chronology, 1942–43, *SCCF*.

10. "Why Singapore Fell to the Japs," *Baltimore Afro-American*, 28 February 1942, 1.

11. "Nazis Worry about Japanese Victories," *Baltimore Afro-American*, 28 February 1942, 5.

12. "Plea to Colored Americans," *Baltimore Afro-American*, 7 March 1942, 9.

13. "Wisdom of Pearl Buck" and "Chiang Kai-shek's Warnings," *Baltimore Afro-American*, 7 March 1942, 4.

14. "Race and Color," *Baltimore Afro-American*, 21 March 1941, 1.

15. Washburn, *Question of Sedition*, 62.

16. "Violation of Alien Act Jails Harlem Nazi," *Baltimore Afro-American*, 14 March 1942, 2. On Hoover's problems with Biddle, see Hill, *RACON*, 10–11. In the meantime Jordan was arrested and fined $300 for violating the Alien Registration Act of 1940. Jordan, a West Indian, had moved three times without notifying authorities of his change of address.

17. Capeci, "Lynching of Cleo Wright."

18. Hill, *RACON*, 9, 53-54 n. 39.

19. "Jap Fifth Columnists among Colored Stir Missouri Leaders," *Baltimore Afro-American*, 21 March 1942, 9.

20. Louis Allen, *Singapore*, 261. This was out of a total of sixty-five thousand Indian troops. As Allen has noted, some of these joined the INA with the hope of facilitating a later escape to India.

21. "Japanese Racial Agitation among American Negroes," 15 April 1942, case 14, Operations and Plans Division (OPD) 291.21, WDGS.

22. Fredrickson, *Black Liberation*, 218.

23. Dallek, *Roosevelt*, 225–26. The term "fifth column" came into popular use in 1936, when fascist sympathizers rose up against the Republican government in Madrid as four fascist columns closed in on the city.

24. Jensen, *Army Surveillance*, 215–22.

25. "Japanese Racial Agitation among American Negroes," OPD 291.21, WDGS.

26. Averell Harriman to Secretary of State, 26 February 1942, *FRUS, 1942*, 1:608. CIG's identification of Indian Muslims as under Japanese influence would have surprised the British, who were counting on predominantly Muslim northern India to provide the main force for the defense of the subcontinent. More than 75 percent of the soldiers in the colonial army were Muslims.

27. On CIG's role in plant security, see Jensen, *Army Surveillance*, 219–23.

28. Entry for 26 March 1942, in Nicholas, *Washington Dispatches*, 27.

29. "Guest Columnist," *Pittsburgh Courier*, 28 March, 1942, 1.

30. *New York World Telegram*, 28 April 1942; Finkle, *Forum for Protest*, 64–67.

31. "NAACP Challenges Pegler to Prove Press Disloyal," *Baltimore Afro-American*, 9 May 1942, 8; Washburn, *Question of Sedition*, 84–85. The *Pittsburgh Courier* predicted that Pegler's blast was the opening round in an administration crackdown on the black press. The *Chicago Defender* accused Pegler of writing at the behest of the Navy Department, which sought to keep black Americans in the service only as mess men.

32. For readers' responses to Pegler's column, see "Many Groups Join in Condemnation of White Writer," *Pittsburgh Courier*, 16 May 1942, 5.

33. "Japanese Are Wasting Time," *Pittsburgh Courier*, 16 May 1942, 13.

34. "Our Editors Speak," *Baltimore Afro-American*, 30 May 1942, 6.

35. Diary of Henry L. Stimson, 12 May 1942, Stimson Papers, Yale University, New Haven.

36. Hill, *RACON*, 27.

37. Division of Research, Office no. 6 (Hikida report), "The War and Black Persons," October 1942; Minister Marishima (Lisbon) to Foreign Ministry, Reports on Black Rioting, 1943; Hikida Yasuichi, translation of Emmett Scott, *American Negroes in World War I*—all in Problems of Black Persons (*Kokujin Mōndai*), Documents Related to Racial Problems (*Minzoku Mōndai*), File I 460-1-3, Foreign Ministry Record Office (Gaikoshiryokan), Tokyo.

38. Stimson to White, 22 May 1942, in Hastie, *Papers*, Part II, Civil Rights, reel 34.

39. On Stimson's racial views, see Hodgson, *The Colonel*.

40. Diary of Harold Ickes, 24 May 1942, Ickes Papers, reel 5, Manuscript Division, Library of Congress, Washington, D.C.

41. Entry for 20 June 1942, in Nicholas, *Washington Dispatches*, 47.

Chapter 7

1. "What Are We Fighting For?," *PM*, 10 April 1942, in Negro Troops: Chronology, 1942–43, *SCCF*.

2. The *Philadelphia Inquirer* and *New York Times* are quoted in "Nation Is Ready for a Second Emancipation," *Baltimore Afro-American*, 11 April 1942, 12.

3. Embree to Marvin McIntyre (Secretary to the President), 3 February 1942, with enclosure, and FDR to Embree, 13 March 1942, File on Colored Matters (Negroes), Official File 93, FDR Papers. FDR told Embree that he thought the various commissions on employment and social security met current needs and that postwar planning would have to be deferred until after the present crisis passed.

4. The president declined to send a message of greeting to the conference. Harry Laidler to FDR, 5 May 1942, with enclosure, and Stephen Early (Secretary to the President), to Laidler, 7 May 1942, ibid.

5. "The Necessity of War," *Baltimore Afro-American*, 11 April 1942, 4.

6. "Nation Is Ready," *Baltimore Afro-American*, 11 April 1942, 12.

7. "Chiang Kai-shek's Warnings" (7 March 1942, 4) and "China Is Astonished by Our Weakness" (14 March 1942, 4), *Baltimore Afro-American*. Chiang also expressed his grave concern to FDR privately in T. V. Soong to Roosevelt, 25 February 1942, transmitting Chiang to Roosevelt, 24 February 1942, *FRUS, 1942*, 1:604–6.

8. Washburn, *Question of Sedition*, 104–5.

9. "Survey of Intelligence Materials," 27 May 1942, Office of Facts and Figures, Bureau of Intelligence, in Hastie, *Papers*, Part II, Civil Rights, reel 36.

10. Breckinridge Long to Sumner Welles, 25 February 1942, *FRUS, 1942*, 1:606–7.

11. Hill, *RACON*, 10–11; *New York Times*, 15 September 1942, 1, 16. Much to their consternation, FBI officials learned of the actual indictment from press reports.

12. "12 Negro Chiefs Seized by FBI in Sedition Raids" (22 September 1942) and "Another Negro Fanatic Seized as Plot Leader" (23 September 1942), *Chicago Daily Tribune*; "Seize 84 Negroes in Sedition Raids," *New York Times*, 22 September 1942, 22.

13. "Seize 84 Negroes in Sedition Raids," *New York Times*.

14. Richard Rovere, "To Nowhere and Japan," *Nation*, 19 September 1942, 234–35.

15. Ibid.

16. Ottley, *New World A-Coming*, 340–41.

17. Ibid., 338–39.

18. Wynn, *Afro-American*, 104–5; Ottley, *New World A-Coming*, 335.

19. Emphasis in the original. "Japanese Influence," in Hill, *RACON*, 512–13.

20. "Filipino Witness Accuses Jordan," *New York Times*, 18 December 1942, 20; Hill, *RACON*, 507–34 (Nakane, Manansala, and Jordan). According to the *New York Times*, when he testified against Jordan, Manansala explained his use of the aliases Dr. A. Takis and Mimo De Guzman by saying, "when I see a name that appeals to me, I just use it." For reasons that remain unclear, the FBI preferred to use the name De Guzman in its report, although they acknowledged that his actual name was Manansala.

21. Hill, *RACON*, 507–34.

22. "Willkie Speech at Los Angeles," *Crisis* 49 (September 1942): 296.

23. For Willkie's relationship with the NAACP and his stand against racism, see Neal, *Dark Horse*, 273–76.

24. Cayton, "Fighting for White Folks," *Nation*, 26 September 1942, 267–70. A 1942 poll of readers of Chicago newspapers found that black Americans were among the groups, another being persons under 45 years old, that were "least favorable toward aiding Britain." When prewar isolationist sentiment was taken into account, African Americans were "slightly less favorable toward Britain than whites and somewhat more favorable toward Russia." "A Chicago Study of Attitudes," August 1942, box 1715, RG 44, Records of Office of General Research, Bureau of Special Services, OWI, National Archives, II, College Park.

25. Cayton, "Fighting for White Folks," 267–70.

26. Locke, "The Unfinished Business of Democracy," *Survey Graphic* 31 (November 1942): 479.

27. Berle, "The Challenge of Color," *Survey Graphic* 31 (November 1942): 506–8.

28. "The Savior of the Darker Races," *Survey Graphic* 31 (November 1942): 546.

29. Walter White to Berle, 13 July 1942, and Berle to White, 15 July 1942, (Wh) File, Berle Papers. In his letter to White, Berle mentioned his having been asked to write an article for *Survey*. He seemed surprised that the editors wanted him to consider "the 'colored' as a 'world-wide problem' " and admitted that he found that "the problems raised with respect to existing empires are enough to make any serious thinker prematurely bald."

30. Lauren, *Power and Prejudice*, 146.

31. Ibid., 147.

32. Dabney, "Nearer and Nearer the Precipice," *Atlantic* 171 (January 1943): 94–100.

33. Finkle, *Forum for Protest*, 72.

34. Williams, "Harlem at War," *Nation*, 16 January 1943, in Negro Troops: Chronology, 1942–43, *SCCF*.

Chapter 8

1. Conn, *Buck*, 151, 154–55, 248–50; Libscomb et al., *Worlds of Pearl S. Buck*, 22 (quotation); Langston Hughes, "My America," in Logan, *What the Negro Wants*, 305. When Hughes suggested sending representatives of the black cultural elite into the South to counter the stereotypes perpetuated by the film industry, he recommended that they be accompanied by liberal white southerners like Erskine Caldwell, Paul Green, or Pearl Buck.

2. "Plea to Colored Americans," *Baltimore Afro-American*, 7 March 1942, 9.

3. "More Pearl Bucks" (10 January 1942, 4) and "Thanks to Pearl Buck" (21 March 1942, 4), *Baltimore Afro-American*.

4. *Baltimore Afro-American*, 7 March 1942, 4. The editors of the *Pittsburgh Courier* (6 December 1941, 6) called Buck an "outstanding friend."

5. "Rankin Scores Pearl Buck for Equality Views," *Baltimore Afro-American*, 27 June 1942, 6. Buck's letter and the Red Cross story appeared on the first page of the *Afro-American*, 29 November 1941.

6. "Pearl Buck's 10 Points," *Baltimore Afro-American*, 13 June 1942, 1, 4.

7. Bibb, "Darker Races of Earth May Gain Parity by the Awakening of China," *Pittsburgh Courier*, 27 December 1941, 13.

8. "Free Us Now, Not after the War—White" (27 June 1942, 1), "China Is Astonished by Our Weakness" (14 March 1942, 4), and "The Necessity of War" (11 April 1942, 4), *Baltimore Afro-American*.

9. Memorandum for the Files, 25 May 1942, Colored Matters File (Negroes), Official Files 93, FDR Papers. White also recommended sending a delegation of Americans, including Wendell Willkie, Justice Felix Frankfurter, and a distinguished African American.

10. "Telling Oriental Types Apart Great Mental Game on Coast," *Baltimore Afro-American*, 3 January 1942, 4.

11. "Chinese Welcome U.S. Entry into Struggle against Japan," *Baltimore Afro-American*, 24 January 1942, 5. T. C. Duncan, a dancer who witnessed the attack on Singapore, told reporters that the Japanese had murdered civilians and were "the cruelest people on earth." "Dancer Survivor of Singapore," ibid., 16 May 1942, 3.

12. Biographical material on Liu, including an abridged article in *Asia* magazine by Lin Yutang, can be found in Liu Liang-Mo, folder 17, box 83, USC. Liu's appearance at Lincoln University is probably another example of how Pearl Buck introduced the "new" China to black Americans. Buck was on the board of directors at United China Relief.

13. "Conference at L.U. Urges Mixed Army," *Baltimore Afro-American*, 16 May 1942, 1. Prattis is listed as attending the meeting.

14. "China Speaks," *Pittsburgh Courier*, 11 September 1942, 7.

15. Buck's address at Lincoln was reprinted in full in the *Baltimore Afro-American*, 16 May 1942, 8. The second quotation is from "The Chinese Mind and India," in Buck, *American Unity*, 85.

16. Conn, *Buck*, 93–100.

17. Lee, *Employment of Negro Troops*, 436. The army did think that the Chinese would protest the deployment of black combat troops in the theater because they would feel that the United States was not sending its best-trained troops.

18. *Baltimore Afro-American*, 30 May 1942, 6.

19. Lin, "East and West Must Meet," *Survey Graphic* 11 (November 1942): 560. For another work that spoke of China's ancient respect for all men, see Soper, *Racism*, 107–9. Soper's book, written with the aid of two Chinese authors, was based on a series of conferences on racism held during 1942–43.

20. "Minnie the Moocher," the signature Cab Calloway song, included the following lyrics: "He took her down to Chinatown / He showed her how to kick the gong around." "Minnie the Moocher," Transcribed from Calloway and His Orchestra, recorded 23 December 1930, From Calloway and His Orchestra, 1930–31, The Chronological Classics 516, The Works of Cab Calloway, ⟨http://www2.crosswinds. net/micronesia/meglorenz/mfiles/minnieth.html⟩ (7 May 1999).

21. Ottley, *New World A-Coming*, 53–56.

22. On Madame Chiang's visit, see Jesperson, *American Images of China*, 82–107.

23. White to Clare Booth Luce, 1 December 1942; White to Eleanor Roosevelt, 5 December 1942; White to Wendell Willkie, 16 December 1942; Eleanor Roosevelt to White, 11 February 1943; White to Madame Chiang Kai-shek, 16 February 1943—all in Madame Chiang File, box A 168, Group II, NAACP Papers.

24. "China Speaks" (20 March 1943, 6) and "Race Active in Honoring China's First Lady" (20 March 1943, 12), *Pittsburgh Courier*; Jesperson, *American Images of China*, 99.

25. Press release, 5 March 1943, Madame Chiang File, box A 168, Group II, NAACP Papers.

26. "Aid to China Not What It Should Be," *Pittsburgh Courier*, 13 March 1943, 4 (quotation); "Wanted: Clarification of Issues," *New York Amsterdam News*, 10 April 1943, 6; "Chinese Realism and Nordic Hypocrisy," *Chicago Defender*, 17 April 1943, 14; "The Negro Press," in Hill, *RACON*, 441. The *Amsterdam News* and the *Defender* also expressed concern about Allied prejudice toward China. FBI agents monitoring the black press considered the question itself as deliberately provocative.

27. "Race Active in Honoring China's First Lady," *Pittsburgh Courier*, 20 March 1943, 12.

28. *Pittsburgh Courier*, 27 March 1943, 1.

29. "Madame Chiang a Southerner" (6 March 1943, 4) and "Mme. Chiang Recognizes No 'Race'" (27 March 1943, 1), *Baltimore Afro-American*.

30. Libscomb et al., *Worlds of Pearl S. Buck*, 8.

31. For examples of the mixed reaction to Madame Chiang's visit, see "People and Places" (favorable) and "National Grapevine" (critical), *Chicago Defender*, 13 March 1943, 15; "Labor" (critical), *Baltimore Afro-American*, 13 March 1943,

7; "Madame Chiang Sees Race Vital in U.S. Democracy" (favorable), *Chicago Defender*, 27 March 1943, 1; and "Hear China's First Lady" (favorable), *Baltimore Afro-American*, 27 March 1943, 13. Walter White, who wrote the "People and Places" column for the *Defender*, remained enamored of the "terrifyingly calm and beautiful woman" and enthused about her speech at Madison Square Garden.

32. "Madame Chiang," *Pittsburgh Courier*, 17 April 1943, 13; "China's First Lady Too Busy for Afro Talk," *Baltimore Afro-American*, 6 March 1943, 16. The *Afro-American* complained that Madame Chiang snubbed a group of African American children who saved their pennies to support three Chinese orphans.

33. "Race, Colonies, and Imperialism," 15 June 1943, Speeches, box 166-26, Logan Papers; "We Discriminate against Each Other, Mrs. Pearl Buck Avers," 20 March 1943, *Baltimore Afro-American*, 5. Buck's speech was a general call for racial understanding. Among other things, she spoke of the prejudice "light skinned colored people practice" against "their darker brothers." Logan referred to Serb exploitation of Croats, Indian exploitation of Africans in South Africa and Kenya, and Chinese exploitation of natives in Java and Burma.

34. Minutes of the Council of Executives, 20 July 1943, Board of Directors Correspondence, box 5, USC; Helen K. Stevens to Walter White, 22 July 1943, China Blood Bank File, box A 170, Group II-A, General Office File, NAACP Papers. During a meeting of the board of directors of United China Relief, the parent organization for the China Blood bank, Stevens explained that because most of the inhabitants of Chinatown were male and eligible for the draft, there were few Chinese donors available in New York. She then reported that the board had voted to ask for donations from black citizens "as an experiment in race relations."

35. For a sampling of the black response to the Red Cross and segregated blood, see Logan, *What the Negro Wants*, 311; Marguerite L. Martin, "The Negro and the War," *PM*, 25 February 1942, in Negro Troops: Chronology, 1942–43, *SCCF*; "The Bunk," *Baltimore Afro-American*, 13 March 1943, 15; "Pupils Assail Blood Policy," *New York Amsterdam News*, 1 May 1943, 6; "Flay Red Cross Blood Segregation," *Chicago Defender*, 4 December 1943, 14; Dower, *War without Mercy*, 348 n. 40.

36. White to New York Branches, NAACP, 3 August 1943, and Stevens to White, 4 August 1943, China Blood Bank File, box A 170, Group II-A, NAACP Papers.

37. Divine, *American Immigration Policy*, 149. During the hearings on the bill Representative Ed Gossett of Texas stated that he "and the rest of the boys down below the Mason Dixon line do not like the idea of trying to tie this thing up with social equality and racial equality."

38. "China Speaks," *Pittsburgh Courier*, 2 October 1943, 6.

39. Koshiro, "Trans-Pacific Racism," 62.

40. Ibid., 63; Divine, *American Immigration Policy*, 148–49.

41. "Jim Crow against the Chinese," *New York Amsterdam News*, 23 October 1943, 14 (quotation); "Labor," *Baltimore Afro-American*, 21 August 1943, 4; "America Race Prejudice Is Winning for Japan," *Chicago Defender*, 4 September 1943, 1.

42. "President Roosevelt Speaks Out" (23 October 1943, 6), "The World" (16 October 1943, 4); and Milton R. Konvitz, "Problem of Racial Equality Must Be Met at Peace Table" (20 November 1943, 13, reprinted from *The New Leader*), *Pittsburgh Courier*.

43. "Chinese Anti-Negro Discrimination Hit," *Pittsburgh Courier*, 11 December 1943, 1. The paper referred to the "alleged bias practiced by Chinese."

44. "Non-Whites," *Pittsburgh Courier*, 11 December 1943, 11.

45. "China Speaks," *Pittsburgh Courier*, 25 December 1943, 6.

46. Ibid.

47. "Chinese Consul to Act on Bias Reports," *Pittsburgh Courier*, 25 December 1943, 1.

48. "China Speaks," *Pittsburgh Courier*, 29 January 1944, 6.

Chapter 9

1. Dallek, *Roosevelt*, 498–500, 535–36; Schaller, *U.S. Crusade in China*, 155–63, 172–73; Kimball, *The Juggler*, 131.

2. "Colored Take Over Jap Hotel" (15 May 1943, 14) and "Race May Lose Little Tokyo If Japs Return" (26 August 1944, 4), *Baltimore Afro-American*; "A Contagious Disease" (25 December 1943, 14) and "The Japanese in Our Midst" (5 August 1944, 14), *Chicago Defender*; Plummer, *Rising Wind*, 75; Leonard, "Years of Hope," 69–73; Taylor, *Seattle's Central District*, 127, 173–74.

3. "Sergeant Fetches Japs' Gold Teeth" (1 May 1943, 1) and "No Jap Bones as Souvenirs" (1 July 1944, 4), *Baltimore Afro-American*.

4. *Chicago Defender*, 16 January 1943, 14 (insect powder); "A Nation Divided," *Baltimore Afro-American*, 26 January 1943, 4.

5. *Baltimore Afro-American*, 25 September 1943, 2, and 11 December 1943, 1.

6. Sullivan (*Days of Hope*, 169–91) analyzes the importance of the 1944 campaign for black and white progressives in the South.

7. "Dark Races to Rule the World, Says Rosenwald Fund Head," *Baltimore Afro-American*, 10 June 1944, 10; Embree to Marvin McIntyre (Secretary to the President), 3 February 1942, with enclosure, and FDR to Embree, 13 March 1942, Colored Matters File (Negroes), Official File 93, FDR Papers.

8. "A Message," *Baltimore Afro-American*, 24 June 1944, 10; "The Negro and the Peace," in Resolutions Adopted at the War-Time Conference of the NAACP, Chicago, 12–16 July 1944, reel 11, part 1, NAACP Papers.

9. "World View," *Chicago Defender*, 26 August 1944.

10. "Invitation to China" (2 September 1944, 4) and "What about China?" (23 September 1944, 4), *Baltimore Afro-American*.

11. "Mr. Chan's Grave," *Pittsburgh Courier*, 16 September 1944, 7.

12. "Treatment Accorded to Chinese Clue to Fate of Colored Peoples," *Philadelphia Tribune*, 14 October 1944, 4.

13. "Policing of World Proposed by China," *New York Times*, 29 August 1944, 1; Reston, *Deadline*, 134–35. The series won Reston his first Pulitzer Prize.

14. "Russians to Support Race Parity" (23 September 1944, 1) and "Pearl Buck Recalls" (30 September 1944, 2), *Pittsburgh Courier*. Buck's letter appeared in the *New York Times* on 19 September. Russia was rumored (incorrectly) to favor the proposal as well.

15. "Race Equality in the Peace," *Crisis* 51 (October 1944): 312.

16. White to Du Bois, 3 October 1944, in Du Bois, *Papers*, reel 56, frame 426. Above his name Du Bois wrote "good idea" but below his signature he added the postscript, "I do not find this specific idea in the *[New York] Times*." It is unclear if he simply missed the 29 August issue of the *Times* that reported on China's proposal or if he meant that he did not see anything pertaining to racial equality in the final draft submitted to the conference by the Chinese. The latter seems more likely, in which case Du Bois correctly sensed that the racial equality clause was already a dead issue at Dumbarton Oaks.

17. Permanent International Organization, Tentative Draft, 21 August 1943, Subject File: International Organization, box 3, Pasvolsky Papers.

18. Ruth Russell, *United Nations Charter*, 328–29.

19. Main Points in the Chinese Tentative Proposals, 31 August 1944, International Organizations, box 6, Pasvolsky Papers; "Tentative Chinese Proposals for a General International Organization," 23 August 1944, *FRUS, 1944*, 1:718–28.

20. "Notes on the Principle of the Equality of Races," n.d., Dumbarton Oaks Miscellany, box 1, Koo Papers.

21. Diary entries for 30 August, 27 September 1944, Koo Papers.

22. Diary entry for 27 September 1944, Koo Papers.

23. Schaller, *U.S. Crusade in China*, 168–75.

24. Diary entry for 28 September 1944, Koo Papers. The Americans, however, had taken no chances. As Dr. Hoo and Ambassador Koo later discovered, Kung's reversal had resulted from a private conversation with a U.S. official. Speaking to the ambassador, Hoo observed that Kung's reasons for retracting the racial equality proposal were "word for word" the same as those used by the American representative in a separate conversation several days earlier.

25. Lauren, *Power and Prejudice*, 148–50; Plummer, *Rising Wind*, 118–19. Lauren sees Koo as genuinely concerned with establishing the principle of racial equality. Plummer concludes that the ambassador's readiness to retract the Chinese proposal and his interpretation of racial equality as being concerned mainly with immigration betrayed his lukewarm support for the idea.

26. "Chinese Drop Oaks Fight for Racial Equality," *Chicago Defender*, 14 October 1944.

27. "National Grapevine" and "Negroes at the Peace Table," *Chicago Defender*, 2 December 1944.

28. Du Bois, *Color and Democracy*, 9, 58–59.

29. "People, Politics, and Places," *Chicago Defender*, 13 January 1945, 11.

30. "World View," *Chicago Defender*, 25 November 1944, 24 February 1945.

31. Ibid., 16 December 1944.

32. "People, Politics, and Places," *Chicago Defender*, 3 March 1945, 11. This statement also appears in White, *Rising Wind*, 154–55.

33. Janken, *Logan*, 145–66.

34. Logan, *What the Negro Wants*, 258.

35. Ibid., 84–86.

36. Ibid, 343.

37. Ibid, 131.

38. Ibid., 306.

39. Ibid., 161–62.

40. Ibid., 298.

41. "Chinese Author Discusses Negro," *Chicago Defender*, 24 February 1945, 18.

42. "Tan GI'S Open Burma Road" (27 January 1945, 2) and "Brooks Tells of Entry into China" (10 February 1945, 2), *Chicago Defender*; Lieutenant Colonel George Hibbert to Cheves, 4 May 1945, Afro-American Soldiers File, 3-G, Wedemeyer Papers.

43. "Conference with Newspaper Correspondent—Harold Isaacs," 5 February 1945, and "Conference with Newspaper Correspondents—Brooks and Bolden," 6, 8 February 1945, Afro-American Soldiers File, 3-G, Wedemeyer Papers.

44. "War Scribe Returns from Far East," *Chicago Defender* 15 September 1945, 8. When Frank Bolden returned to the United States in September, he declared that he was going to "rewrite all dispatches the censors held up and refused to transmit."

45. "Brooks Tells of Entry into China," *Chicago Defender*, 10 February 1945, 2.

46. "China Denies Bar on Negro Troops," *Chicago Defender*, 17 February 1945, 1.

47. Minutes of Meeting No. 25 with Generalissimo, 31 December 1944, in Generalissimo Minutes, Book 1, Commanding General Files—Wedemeyer, RACC.

48. Lieutenant Colonel Edwin O. Shaw to Brigadier General Lewis Pick, 19 January 1945, Decimal File 291.2, box 57, Adjutant General Correspondence, India-Burma Theater, RACC.

49. Lieutenant Colonel W. E. Bennett to Wedemeyer, 17 January 1945, ibid.

50. Lieutenant Colonel C. A. Davis to Cheves, 23 January 1945, forwarding Chien Ta-chun, Chief First Department, to Wedemeyer, 14 January 1945, ibid.

51. Mark M. Gebhart to Commanding General, Rear Echelon, China Theater, 31 January 1945, ibid.

52. Minutes of Meeting No. 38 with Generalissimo, 7 February 1945, Generalissimo Minutes, Book 1, Commanding General Files—Wedemeyer, RACC.

53. Major Kenneth A. Smith to Brigadier General Lewis Pick, 14 February 1945, Decimal File 291.2, Adjutant General Correspondence, India-Burma Theater, RACC.

54. "Chinese Commander Praises Road Builders," *Pittsburgh Courier*, 10 March 1945, 1.

55. "Chinese Are Question Mark in Common Struggle [of] Colored Peoples of the World," *Pittsburgh Courier*, 21 April 1945, 7.

56. Ibid.

57. Lieutenant Colonel George W. Hibbert to Cheves, 4 May 1945, Wedemeyer to Hurley, 15 May 1945, Transmitting Files, and Hurley to Wedemeyer, 11 June 1945, all in Afro-American Soldiers File, 3-G, Wedemeyer Papers.

58. Wedemeyer to Hurley, 15 May 1945, ibid.

59. "History of the 858th Engineer Aviation Battalion," 1 January 1943–December 1945, ENBN—858.01, RG 407, Records of the Adjutant General, Federal Records Center, Suitland, Md.; "China Gets Its First American Negro Troops," *Chicago Defender*, 2 June 1945, 3.

60. Carol Anderson, "From Hope to Disillusion," 535. Mary McLeod Bethune, W. E. B. Du Bois, and Walter White represented the NAACP as consultants to the U.S. delegation.

61. "The San Francisco Conference," ca. 25 April 1945, Writings by Logan, Autobiography, box 166-33, Logan Papers; Carol Anderson, "From Hope to Disillusion," 538. Logan called the provision prohibiting interference in the domestic affairs of member nations "the joker" that trumped the racial equality clause.

62. Carol Anderson, "From Hope to Disillusion," 539–42; Plummer, *Rising Wind*, 149–50.

63. "The San Francisco Conference," ca. 25 April 1945, Writings by Logan, Autobiography, box 166-33, Logan Papers; Carol Anderson, "From Hope to Disillusion," 538. Logan reports that he found Prattis outside "crying like a baby" and complaining that although "our boys" were dying to save China from Japan, they could not even get seated at a Chinese restaurant.

64. "The San Francisco Conference," ca. 25 April 1945.

65. White to Roy Wilkins, 14 May 1945, quoted in Carol Anderson, "From Hope to Disillusion," 540; "San Francisco," *Crisis* 52 (June 1945): 161; "U.S. and Colonialism," *Defender*, 26 May 1945, 13.

66. John Robert Badger, "China Refuses to Take Stand for Racial Equality" (12 May 1945, 4), and "Full Independence Opposed by Parley" (26 May 1945, 1), *Chicago Defender*.

67. "Chinese Leader Invites Negroes to China, Hits American Jim Crow" (26 May 1945, 4), and John Robert Badger, "Crisis in China" (30 June 1945, 13), *Chicago Defender*.

68. Logan, *The Negro and the Post-War World*, 79.

Epilogue

1. "Tan Sailors in Guam" (16 June 1945, 2) and "Bomber Pilots Headed for Pacific" (30 June 1945, 1), *Chicago Defender*.

2. "Watching the Big Parade," *Baltimore Afro-American*, 9 June 1945, 4.

3. "Tokio, Here We Come Again" (18 September 1943, 19) and "Fighting a Racial War" (28 July 1945, 4), *Baltimore Afro-American*.

4. "Simple and the Atom Bomb," *Chicago Defender*, 18 August 1945, 12; Kearney, "Afro-American Views," 188–89; Cayton, *Long Old Road*, 276.

5. "Hirohito Must Go," *Baltimore Afro-American*, 18 August 1945, 1.

6. "All Over" (18 August 1945, 1) and Langston Hughes, "V. J. Night in Harlem" (25 August 1945, 12), *Chicago Defender*; Boyer, *By the Bomb's Early Light*, 198–99.

7. "Winds of Time," *Chicago Defender*, 25 August 1945, 13.

8. Wilkinson, "Shanghai Perspective."

9. Emphasis in the original. Helen Fletcher Anderson, "Through Chinese Eyes," 144.

10. Christopher Thorne, *Allies of a Kind*, 730.

11. Wright, *Color Curtain*; Pinkney, *Red, Black, and Green*, 118–50; Interview with Huey Newton, in Meier, Rudwick, and Broderick, *Black Protest Thought*, 495–515; Snow, *Star Raft*.

12. Sitkoff, *New Deal for Blacks*, 160–61; "World View" (30 January 1943), "Here to Yonder" (18 December 1943), "Soviets Demand Race Equality at Peace Table" (20 January 1945, 1), and "World View" (28 July 1945, 12), *Chicago Defender*; "It Is Not Russia That Threatens Democracy," *Pittsburgh Courier*, 14 October 1944, 7; "G.I. Tells of Lack of Bias in Russia," *Baltimore Afro-American*, 28 October 1944, 9. Before World War II, black American visitors to the Soviet Union had given similar accounts of life there.

13. "San Francisco Not All," *Baltimore Afro-American*, 19 May 1945, 4.

14. Gerald Horne, *Black and Red* and *Communist Front?*.

15. Statements Regarding Troops of the 591st Ordnance Ammunition Company, 49th Ordnance Battalion, 47th Quartermaster Battalion, 591st Ordnance Company, 3509th Quartermaster Truck Company, 4383rd Quartermaster Truck Company, 540th Port Company, 541st Port Company, and 561st Composite Service Company, all in File 291.2, India-Burma Theater, RACC.

16. Gerald Horne, "Race for the Planet," 161. Horne has suggested that "One simple, albeit crude, way to look at what happened intellectually, politically, and ideologically to African-Americans over the past forty-five years is to posit that the 'New Delhi Negroes' (Martin Luther King, Bayard Rustin, and others) triumphed over the 'Moscow Negroes' (Du Bois, Robeson, and company) and the 'Tokyo Negroes' (the Nation of Islam)." Horne's delineation of various factions in the African American community is illustrative of the range of causes and the variety of political remedies embraced by civil rights activists during the 1930s and 1940s, before the Cold War, but only if one allows for a degree of fluidity in the membership of these different groups. Before the Japanese attack on Pearl Harbor, those who saw race as the defining feature of domestic politics and international affairs found it possible to support Indian independence and defend Japa-

nese imperialism or, alternatively, to oppose British colonialism while endorsing the Soviet Union's anti-imperialism. Du Bois proved somewhat exceptional in his ability to do all of the above.

17. "Madame Pandit Wins over Maryland Theatre Barrier," *Pittsburgh Courier*, 14 April 1945, 1; "Portrait of Mme. Pandit," *Chicago Defender*, 30 June 1945, 14.

18. Fredrickson, *Black Liberation*, 252–65; Peffer, *Randolph*, 156–58, 161; Meier and Rudwick, "Origins of Nonviolent Direct Action," 833–930.

19. Brands, *Specter of Neutralism*, 133–38; Cohen, *Dean Rusk*, 206–7; McMahon, "Choosing Sides in South Asia," 198–222. The shift in U.S. policy toward India began in the last years of the Eisenhower administration and continued in the early 1960s.

20. Gerald Horne, *Communist Front?*, 167 (Acheson); Isaacs, *New World of Negro Americans*, 9 (Rusk).

21. Plummer, *Rising Wind*, 67.

22. For a brief summary, see Blum, *V Was for Victory*, 207–20.

23. William Phillips to Roosevelt, [14 May 1943], *FRUS, 1943*, 4:220–22.

24. "Annual Report of Church Contributions," 1 May 1945, box 34, USC. It will be recalled that early in the war Horace Cayton, Walter White, and Roi Ottley all spoke of African American fund-raising on behalf of China. In 1944 and 1945, the years for which records are available, major black churches (AME, AME Zion, and National Baptist) contributed a total of $1,425 to United China Relief, with all but $100 provided by the Baptists. The $50 contributions from AME and AME Zion were the smallest amounts given and appear to have been only token offerings. It is impossible to determine if these meager contributions reflected a lack of support for Nationalist China among black Americans or a decision on the part of United China Relief to give a lower priority to soliciting funds from black churches.

25. It is noteworthy that Walter White, the most ardent supporter of China during the war, chose not to mention his own efforts on behalf of China when he wrote his memoir. See White, *A Man Called White*.

26. Emphasis in the original. Isaacs, *New World of Negro Americans*, 22.

Bibliography

Primary Sources

Manuscript Collections

Cambridge, Massachusetts

Littauer Center of Public Administration, Harvard University
  American Committee for Non-Participation in Japanese Aggression Files

College Park, Maryland

National Archives, II
  Record Group 44, Bureau of Special Services, Records of the Office of General
    Research, Office of War Information

Hyde Park, New York

Franklin D. Roosevelt Library
  Adolf Berle Papers
  Francis Biddle Papers
  Franklin D. Roosevelt Papers

New Haven, Connecticut

Yale University Library
  Henry L. Stimson Papers (microfilm)

New York, New York

Butler Memorial Library, Columbia University
  H. V. Wellington Koo Papers

Princeton, New Jersey

Seeley G. Mudd Manuscript Library, Princeton University
  United Services to China Papers

Stanford, California

Hoover Institution on War, Revolution, and Peace
  Albert C. Wedemeyer Papers

Suitland, Maryland

Federal Records Center
  Record Group 407, Records of the Adjutant General
  Record Group 493, Records of the Allied and Combined Commands, China-
    Burma-India Theater of Operations

Tokyo, Japan

Foreign Ministry Record Office (Gaikoshiryokan)
  I 460-1-3 Documents Related to Racial Problems (Mînzoku Mōndai), Problems
    of Black Persons (Kokujin Mōndai)

Washington, D.C

Library of Congress
  Harold Ickes Papers
  National Association for the Advancement of Colored People Papers
  Leo Pasvolsky Papers
Moorland-Spingarn Research Center, Howard University
  Rayford Logan Papers
  P. L. Prattis Papers
  Mary Church Terrell Papers
National Archives
  Record Group 165, Records of the War Department, Army General and Special
    Staffs

Interview

John J. McCloy, 2 August 1984, New York, N.Y.

Published Works

Aptheker, Herbert, ed. *A Documentary History of the Negro People in the United
  States, 1910–1932.* Secaucus, N.J.: Citadel Press, 1973.
———, ed. *The Correspondence of W. E. B. Du Bois.* Amherst: University of Mas-
  sachusetts Press, 1976.
Chambers, John Whiteclay, II, ed. *The Eagle and the Dove: The American Peace
  Movement and United States Foreign Policy, 1900–1922.* New York: Garland
  Publishers, 1976.
Du Bois, W. E. B. *Papers of W. E. B. Du Bois.* Ann Arbor, Mich.: University Micro-
  films, 1986.

Federal Surveillance of Afro-Americans, 1917–1925 . Frederick, Md.: University Publications of America, 1986. Microfilm.

Foner, Philip S. *American Communism and Black Americans: A Documentary History, 1919–1929.* Philadelphia: Temple University Press, 1987.

Foner, Philip S., and Daniel Rosenberg, eds. *Racism, Dissent, and Asian Americans from 1850 to the Present: A Documentary History.* Westport, Conn.: Greenwood Press, 1993.

Harlan, Louis R., and Raymond W. Smock, eds. *The Booker T. Washington Papers.* 14 vols. Urbana: University of Illinois Press, 1972–89.

Hastie, William H. *The William H. Hastie Papers.* Frederick, Md.: University Publications of America, 1986.

Hill, Robert A., ed. *The Crusader.* 6 vols. New York: Garland, 1987.

———, ed. *The FBI's RACON: Racial Conditions in the United States during World War II.* Boston: Northeastern University Press, 1995.

———, ed. *The Marcus Garvey and Universal Negro Improvement Association Papers.* 9 vols. Berkeley: University of California press, 1983–85.

Lebra, Joyce C. *Japan's Greater East Asia Co-Prosperity Sphere in World War II: Selected Readings and Documents.* New York: Oxford University Press, 1975.

Link, Arthur S., et al., eds. *The Papers of Woodrow Wilson.* 69 vols. Princeton: Princeton University Press, 1966–94.

Marks, George P., III. *The Black Press Views American Imperialism.* New York: Arno Press, 1971.

Meier, August, Elliot Rudwick, and Francis L. Broderick, eds. *Black Protest Thought in the Twentieth Century.* 2d ed. Indianapolis: Bobbs-Merrill, 1971.

National Association for the Advancement of Colored People. *Papers of the NAACP, Part 1: Meetings of the Board of Directors, Records of the Annual Conferences, Major Speeches, and Special Reports.* Frederick, Md.: University Publications of America, 1982. Microfilm.

Schomburg Center for Research in Black Culture. *Schomburg Center Clipping File, 1925–1974.* Alexandria, Va.: Chadwyck-Healey, 1986. Microfiche.

U.S. Department of Defense. *The "MAGIC" Background of Pearl Harbor.* 8 vols. Washington, D.C.: GPO, 1978.

U.S. Department of State, *Foreign Relations of the United States.* Washington, D.C.: GPO, 1942–44.

U.S. Military Intelligence Reports: Surveillance of Radicals in the United States, 1917–1941. Frederick, Md.: University Publications of America, 1984. Microfilm.

Periodicals

Asian Review (Tokyo)
Atlantic
Baltimore Afro-American

Chicago Defender
Chicago Tribune
Cleveland Advocate
Colored American Magazine (Boston)
The Crisis: A Record of the Darker Races
Crusader (Harlem)
Messenger
Nation
New Republic
New York Age
New York Amsterdam News
New York Times
Philadelphia Tribune
Pittsburgh Courier
Survey Graphic
Voice of the Negro

Secondary Sources

Aarim, Najia. "Chinese Immigrants, African Americans, and the Problem of Race in the United States, 1848–1882." Ph.D. diss., Temple University, 1996.

Allen, Ernest, Jr. "When Japan Was the 'Champion of the Darker Races': Satokata Takahashi and the Flowering of Black Messianic Nationalism." *Black Scholar* 24 (1994): 23–46.

Allen, Louis. "Japanese Intelligence Systems." *Journal of Contemporary History* 22 (October 1987): 547–62.

———. *Singapore, 1941–1942*. London: Davis Poynter, 1977.

Anderson, Carol. "From Hope to Disillusion: African Americans, the United Nations, and the Struggle for Human Rights, 1944–1947." *Diplomatic History* 20 (Fall 1996): 531–64.

Anderson, Helen Fletcher. "Through Chinese Eyes: American China Policy, 1945–1947." Ph.D. diss., University of Virginia, 1980.

Anderson, Jervis. *A. Philip Randolph: A Biographical Portrait*. New York: Harcourt, Brace, Jovanovich, 1972.

Arkush, R. David, and Leo O. Lee, trans., eds., *Land without Ghosts: Chinese Impressions of America from the Mid-Nineteenth Century to the Present*. Berkeley: University of California Press, 1989.

Asada, Sadao. "Japan and the United States, 1915–1925." Ph.D. diss., Yale University, 1963.

Bailey, Thomas A. *Woodrow Wilson and the Great Betrayal*. New York: Macmillan, 1945.

Barnhart, Michael A. "Driven by Domestics: American Relations with Japan and Korea, 1900–1945." In *Pacific Passages: The Study of American-East Asian Re-*

lations on the Eve of the Twenty-first Century, edited by Warren I. Cohen, 190–212. New York: Columbia University Press, 1996.

———. "Japanese Intelligence before the Second World War: 'Best Case' Analysis." In *Knowing One's Enemies: Intelligence Assessment before the Two World Wars*, edited by Ernest R. May, 424–55. Princeton: Princeton University Press, 1984.

Beasley, W. G. *Japanese Imperialism, 1894–1945*. Oxford: Clarendon Press, 1987.

———. *The Modern History of Japan*. London: Weidenfeld and Nicholson, 1963.

Benyon, Erdmann Doane. "The Voodoo Cult among Negro Migrants in Detroit," *American Journal of Sociology* (May 1938): 894–907.

Blum, John Morton. *V Was for Victory: Politics and Culture during World War II*. New York: Harcourt Brace Jovanovich, 1976.

Borg, Dorothy. *American Policy and the Chinese Revolution, 1925–1928*. New York: Octagon, 1968.

———. *The United States and the Far Eastern Crisis of 1933–1938: From the Manchurian Incident through the Initial Stages of the Undeclared Sino-Japanese War*. Cambridge: Harvard University Press, 1964.

Borg, Dorothy, and Shumpei Okamoto, eds. *Pearl Harbor as History: Japanese-American Relations, 1931–1941*. New York: Columbia University Press, 1973.

Boyer, Paul. *By the Bomb's Early Light: American Thought and Culture at the Dawn of the Atomic Age*. New Preface by the Author. Chapel Hill: University of North Carolina Press, 1994.

Boyle, John Hunter. *Japan: The American Nexus*. New York: Harcourt Brace Jovanovich, 1993.

Brands, H. W. *The Specter of Neutralism: The United States and the Emergence of the Third World, 1947–1960*. New York: Columbia University Press, 1989.

Broussard, Albert S. *Black San Francisco: The Struggle for Racial Equality in the West, 1900–1954*. Lawrence: University Press of Kansas, 1993.

Bruni, Andrew. *Robert L. Vann of the Pittsburgh Courier: Politics and Black Journalism*. Pittsburgh: University of Pittsburgh Press, 1974.

Buck, Pearl. *American Unity in Asia*. New York: John Day, 1942.

Bunche, Ralph J. *A World View of Race*. Port Washington: Kennikat Press, 1938.

Capeci, Dominic J., Jr., "The Lynching of Cleo Wright: Federal Protection and Constitutional Rights during World War II." *Journal of American History* 74 (March 1986): 859–87.

Carrier, Fred. *Ideas That Shaped the West and the World*. 2d ed. Dubuque, Iowa: Kendall Hunt, 1996.

Cayton, Horace. *Long Old Road*. Seattle: University of Washington Press, 1964.

Chambers, John Whiteclay, II, ed. *The Eagle and the Dove: The American Peace Movement and United States Foreign Policy, 1900–1922*. New York: Garland, 1976.

Ch'en, Jerome. *China and the West: Society and Culture, 1815–1937*. Bloomington: Indiana University Press, 1979.

Chung, Sue Fawn. "From Fu Manchu, Evil Genius, to James Lee Wong, Popular Hero: A Study of the Chinese-American in Popular Periodical Fiction from 1920–1940." *Journal of Popular Culture* 1 (Winter 1976): 534–47.

Clarke, J. Calvitt, III. "Periphery and Crossroads: Ethiopia and World Diplomacy, 1934–1936." Paper presented at the 13th International Conference of Ethiopian Studies, Kyoto, Japan, December 1997.

Clegg, Claude Andrew, III. *An Original Man: The Life and Times of Elijah Muhammad*. New York: St. Martin's Press, 1997.

Cohen, Warren I. *America's Response to China*. 3d ed. New York: Columbia University Press, 1990.

———. *The Chinese Connection: Roger S. Greene, Thomas W. Lamont, George E. Sokolsky, and American–East Asian Relations*. New York: Columbia University Press, 1978.

———. *Dean Rusk*. Totowa, N.J.: Cooper Square Publishers, 1980.

———. The Role of Private Groups in the United States." In *Pearl Harbor as History: Japanese-American Relations, 1931–1941*, edited by Dorothy Borg and Shumpei Okamoto, 421–58. New York: Columbia University Press, 1973.

Conn, Peter. *Pearl S. Buck: A Cultural Biography*. Cambridge: Cambridge University Press, 1996.

Connaughton, R. M. *The War of the Rising Sun and the Tumbling Bear: A Military History of the Russo-Japanese War, 1904–5*. London: Routledge, 1988.

Dalfiume, Richard. "The 'Forgotten Years' of the Negro Revolution." In *The Negro in Depression and War: Prelude to Revolution, 1930–1945*, edited by Bernard Sternsher, 301–17. Chicago: Quadrangle Books, 1969.

Dallek, Robert. *Franklin D. Roosevelt and American Foreign Policy, 1932–1945*. New York: Oxford University Press, 1995.

Daniels, Roger, and Harry H. L. Kitano. *American Racism: Exploration of the Nature of Prejudice*. Englewood Cliffs, N.J.: Prentice-Hall, 1970.

DeConde, Alexander. *Ethnicity, Race, and American Foreign Policy: A History*. Boston: Northeastern University Press, 1992.

Dikotter, Frank. *The Discourse of Race in Modern China*. Stanford: Stanford University Press, 1992.

———. "Racial Identities in China: Context and Meaning." *China Quarterly* 138 (June 1994): 404–12.

Dingman, Roger. *Power in the Pacific: The Origins of Naval Limitation, 1914–1922*. Chicago: University of Chicago Press, 1976.

Divine, Robert A. *American Immigration Policy, 1924–1952*. New Haven: Yale University Press, 1957.

———. *Second Chance: The Triumph of Internationalism in America during World War II*. New York: Atheneum, 1971.

Doenecke, Justus D. *When the Wicked Rise: American Opinion Makers and the Manchurian Crisis of 1931–1933*. Lewisburg, Pa.: Bucknell University Press, 1984.

Dower, John W. *War without Mercy: Race and Power in the Pacific War*. New York: Pantheon Books, 1986.

Draper, Theodore. *The Roots of American Communism*. New York: Viking Press, 1957.

Du Bois, W. E. B. *Color and Democracy: Colonies and Peace*. New York: Harcourt, Brace, 1945.

———. *Dark Princess: A Romance*. Millwood, N.Y.: Kraus-Thomson Organization Ltd., 1974.

———. "Inter-Racial Implications of the Ethiopian Crisis: A Negro View." *Foreign Affairs* 14 (October 1935): 82–92.

Dudden, Arthur Power. *The American Pacific from the Old China Trade to the Present*. New York: Oxford University Press, 1992.

Elsbree, Willard H. *Japan's Role in Southeast Asian Nationalist Movements, 1940–1945*. Cambridge: Harvard University Press, 1953.

Esthus, Raymond A. *Theodore Roosevelt and the International Rivalries*. Claremont, Calif.: Regina Press, 1970.

Finkle, Lee. *Forum for Protest: The Black Press during World War II*. Rutherford, N.J.: Farleigh Dickinson University Press, 1975.

Foner, Philip S., and Herbert Shapiro. *American Socialism and Black Americans: From the Age of Jackson to World War II*. Westport, Conn.: Greenwood Press, 1977.

Franklin, John Hope, and Alfred A. Moss Jr. *From Slavery to Freedom: A History of Negro Americans*. 6th ed. New York: McGraw-Hill, 1988.

Fredrickson, George M. *Black Liberation: A Comparative History of Black Ideologies in the United States and South Africa*. New York: Oxford University Press, 1995.

Gaddis, John Lewis. *Russia, the Soviet Union, and the United States: An Interpretive History*. 2d ed. New York: McGraw-Hill, 1990.

Gaines, Kevin. "Black Americans' Racial Uplift Ideology as 'Civilizing Mission': Pauline Hopkins on Race Imperialism." In *Cultures of United States Imperialism*, edited by Amy Kaplan and Donald Pease, 433–55. Durham, N.C.: Duke University Press, 1993.

Gallicchio, Marc. "Colouring the Nationalists: The African-American Construction of China in the Second World War." *International History Review* 20 (September 1998): 571–96.

Gatewood, Willard B., Jr. *Black Americans and the White Man's Burden*. Urbana: University of Illinois Press, 1975.

Gibbons, Floyd. *The Red Napoleon*. 1929. Reprint, Carbondale: Southern Illinois University Press, 1976.

Gilbert, Peter, ed. *The Selected Writings of John Edward Bruce: Militant Black Journalist*. New York: Arno Press, 1971.

Gossett, Thomas F. *Race: The History of an Idea in America*. New Edition. New York: Oxford University Press, 1997.

Graebner, Norman A. "Hoover, Roosevelt, and the Japanese." In *Pearl Harbor as History: Japanese-American Relations, 1931–1941,* edited by Dorothy Borg and Shumpei Okamoto, 25–52. New York: Columbia University Press, 1973.

Gulick, Sidney. *The American Japanese Problem: A Study of Racial Relations of the East and the West.* New York: Charles Scribner's Sons, 1914.

Hardie, Frank. *The Abyssinian Crisis.* Hamden, Conn.: Archon Books, 1974.

Harding, Vincent. *The Other American Revolution.* Atlanta: Center for Afro-American Studies, 1980.

Harris, Joseph E. *African-American Reactions to War in Ethiopia, 1936–1941.* Baton Rouge: Louisiana State University Press, 1994.

Heinrichs, Waldo H., Jr. *American Ambassador: Joseph Grew and the Development of the United States Diplomatic Tradition.* New York: Oxford University Press, 1986.

———. The Role of the United States Navy," in *Pearl Harbor as History: Japanese-American Relations, 1931–1941,* edited by Dorothy Borg and Shumpei Okamoto, 197–224. New York: Columbia University Press, 1973.

Hellwig, David Johns. "The Afro-American and the Immigrant, 1880–1930: A Study of Black Social Thought." Ph.D diss., Syracuse University, 1973.

———. "Afro-American Reactions to the Japanese and the Anti-Japanese Movement, 1906–1924." *Phylon* 38 (Winter 1977): 93–104.

Hess, Gary R. *America Encounters India, 1941–1947.* Baltimore: Johns Hopkins University Press, 1971.

Higham, John. *Strangers in the Land: Patterns of American Nativism, 1860–1925.* New York: Atheneum, 1963.

Hill, Robert A., and R. Kent Rasmussen, eds. *Black Empire: George S. Schuyler Writing as Samuel I. Brooks.* Boston: Northeastern University Press, 1991.

Hodgson, Godfrey. *The Colonel: The Life and Wars of Henry Stimson, 1867–1950.* New York: Knopf, 1990.

Holt, Thomas C. "African-American History." In *The New American History,* edited by Eric Foner, 311–32. Philadelphia: Temple University Press, 1997.

Horne, Gerald. *Black and Red: W. E. B Du Bois and the Afro-American Response to the Cold War, 1944–1963.* Albany: State University of New York Press, 1986.

———. *Communist Front? The Civil Rights Congress, 1946–1956.* Rutherford, N.J.: Farleigh Dickinson University Press, 1988.

———. "Race for the Planet: African-Americans and U.S. Foreign Policy Reconsidered." *Diplomatic History* 19 (Winter 1995): 159–65.

———. "Who Lost the Cold War?" *Diplomatic History* 20 (Fall 1996): 613–26.

Howell, David L. "Ethnicity and Culture in Contemporary Japan." *Journal of Contemporary History* 31 (January 1996): 171–90.

Hunt, Michael H. *Ideology and U.S. Foreign Policy.* New Haven: Yale University Press, 1987.

Ienaga, Saburo. *The Pacific War: World War II and the Japanese, 1931–1945.* New York: Pantheon, 1978.

Iriye, Akira. *Across the Pacific: An Inner History of American-East Asian Relations.* New York: Harcourt, Brace, 1967.

———. *After Imperialism: The Search for a New Order in the Far East.* Cambridge: Harvard University Press, 1965.

———. *Pacific Estrangement: Japanese and American Expansion, 1897–1911.* Cambridge: Harvard University Press, 1972.

———. *Power and Culture: The Japanese-American War, 1941–1945.* Cambridge: Harvard University Press, 1981.

———. "The Role of the United States Embassy in Tokyo." In *Pearl Harbor as History: Japanese-American Relations, 1931–1941,* edited by Dorothy Borg and Shumpei Okamoto, 107–26. New York: Columbia University Press, 1973.

Isaacs, Harold. *Images of Asia: American Views of China and India.* New York: Harper and Row, 1972.

———. *The New World of Negro Americans.* New York: John Day, 1963.

———. *No Peace for Asia.* 1947. Reprint, Cambridge: MIT Press, 1967.

Janken, Kenneth. *R. Rayford Logan and the Dilemma of the African-American Intellectual.* Amherst: University of Massachusetts Press, 1993.

Jansen, Marius B. *The Japanese and Sun Yat-Sen.* Cambridge: Harvard University Press, 1954.

Jensen, Joan M. *Army Surveillance in America, 1775–1980.* New Haven: Yale University Press, 1991.

Jesperson, T. Christopher. *American Images of China, 1931–1949.* Stanford: Stanford University Press, 1996.

Johnson, James Weldon. *Along This Way: The Autobiography of James Weldon Johnson.* New York: Viking, 1968.

Jung, Moon-Ho. "The Influence of 'Black Peril' on 'Yellow Peril' in Nineteenth-Century America." In *Privileging Positions: The Sites of Asian American Studies,* edited by Gary Y. Okihiro, Marilyn Alquizola, Dorothy Fujita Rony, and K. Scott Wong, 349–63. Pullman: Washington State University Press, 1995.

Kapur, Sudarshan. *Raising Up a Prophet: The African-American Encounter with Gandhi.* Boston: Beacon, 1992.

Kawamura, Noriko. "Wilsonian Idealism and Japanese Claims at the Paris Peace Conference." *Pacific Historical Review* 66 (November 1997): 503–26.

Kearney, Reginald. "Afro-American Views of Japanese, 1900–1945." Ph.D. diss., Kent State University, 1991.

Kimball, Warren F. *The Juggler: Franklin Roosevelt as Wartime Statesman.* Princeton: Princeton University Press, 1991.

Knock, Thomas J. *To End All Wars: Woodrow Wilson and the Quest for a New World Order.* Princeton: Princeton University Press, 1992.

Koshiro, Yukiko. "Trans-Pacific Racism: The U.S. Occupation of Japan." Ph.D. diss., Columbia University, 1992.

Krenn, Michael L. "'Unfinished Business': Segregation and U.S. Diplomacy at the 1958 World's Fair." *Diplomatic History* 20 (Fall 1996): 591–612.

Kumamoto, Bob. "The Search for Spies: American Counterintelligence and the Japanese American Community, 1931–1942." *Amerasia Journal* 6 (Fall 1979): 45–74.

Kusmer, Kenneth L. "Toward a Comparative History of Racism and Xenophobia in the United States and Germany, 1865–1933." In *Bridging the Atlantic: Europe and the United States in Modern Times,* edited by Hermann Wellenreuther and Elisabeth Glaser. New York: Cambridge University Press. Forthcoming.

LaFeber, Walter. *The Clash: A History of U.S.-Japan Relations.* New York: W. W. Norton, 1997.

Lauren, Paul Gordon. *Power and Prejudice: The Politics and Diplomacy of Racial Discrimination.* Boulder, Colo.: Westview Press, 1988.

Lee, Ulysses S. *The Employment of Negro Troops: The U.S. Army in World War II: Special Studies.* Washington, D.C.: GPO, 1966.

Leonard, Kevin Allen. "Years of Hope, Days of Fear: The Impact of World War II on Race Relations in Los Angeles." Ph.D. diss., University of California, Davis, 1992.

Lester, Julius, ed. *The Seventh Son: The Thought and Writings of W. E. B. Du Bois.* New York: Random House, 1971.

Lewis, David Levering. *W. E. B. Du Bois: Biography of a Race, 1868–1919.* New York: Henry Holt, 1993.

———. *W. E. B. Du Bois: A Reader.* New York: Henry Holt, 1995.

Libscomb, Elizabeth J., Frances E. Webb, and Peter Conn, eds. *The Several Worlds of Pearl S. Buck.* Westport, Conn.: Greenwood, 1994.

Lindbergh, Charles A. "Aviation, Geography, and Race." *Reader's Digest* (November 1939): 64–67.

Little, Lawrence S. "A Quest for Self-Determination: The African Methodist Episcopal Church during the Age of Imperialism, 1884–1916." Ph.D. diss., Ohio State University, 1993.

Locke, Alain. *The New Negro: An Interpretation.* New York: Arno Press, 1968.

Logan, Rayford. *The Betrayal of the Negro from Rutherford B. Hayes to Woodrow Wilson.* New York: De Capo Press, 1997.

———. *The Negro and the Post-War World: A Primer.* Washington, D.C.: Minorities Publishers, 1945.

———, ed. *What the Negro Wants.* Chapel Hill: University of North Carolina Press, 1944.

McMahon, Robert J. "Choosing Sides in South Asia." In *Kennedy's Quest for Victory: American Foreign Policy, 1961–1963,* edited by Thomas G. Paterson, 198–222. New York: Oxford University Press, 1989.

McWilliams, Carey. *Prejudice: Japanese-Americans: Symbol of Racial Intolerance.* Hamden, Conn.: Archon Books, 1971.

Marable, Manning. *W. E. B. Du Bois: Black Radical Democrat.* Boston: Twayne, 1986.

Meier, August, and Elliott Rudwick. "The Origins of Nonviolent Direct Action in

Afro-American Protest: A Note on Historical Discontinuities." In *We Shall Overcome: The Civil Rights Movement in the United States in the 1950's and 1960's*, edited by David J. Garrow, 833–930. Brooklyn: Carlson Publishing, 1989.

Miller, Kelly. *Race Adjustment and the Everlasting Stain*. New York: Arno Press, 1968.

Mockler, Anthony. *Haile Selassie's War: The Italian-Ethiopian Campaign, 1935–1941*. New York: Random House, 1984.

Morikawa, Jun. *Japan and Africa: Big Business and Diplomacy*. Trenton, N.J.: Africa World Press, 1997.

Morris, I. I. *Nationalism and the Right Wing in Japan: A Study of Post-war Trends*. London, 1960.

Myrdal, Gunnar. *An American Dilemma: The Negro Problem and Modern Democracy*. New York: Harper Torchbooks, 1944.

Naisson, Mark. *Communists in Harlem during the Depression*. Urbana: University of Illinois Press, 1983.

Neal, Steve. *Dark Horse: A Biography of Wendell Willkie*. Garden City: Doubleday, 1984.

Neu, Charles E. *Troubled Encounter: The United States and Japan*. New York: John Wiley and Sons, 1975.

Nicholas, H. G., ed. *Washington Dispatches*. Chicago: University of Chicago Press, 1981.

Oehling, Richard A. "The Yellow Menace: Asian Images in American Film." In *The Kaleidoscopic Lens: How Hollywood Views Ethnic Groups*, edited by Randall M. Miller, 182–206. Englewood, N.J.: Jerome S. Ozer Publisher, 1980.

Ottley, Roi. *New World A-Coming*. New York: Arno Press, 1968.

Padmore, George, ed. *Colonial and Colored Unity: A Programme of Action*. London: Hammersmith Bookshop, Ltd., n.d.

———. *Pan-Africanism or Communism*. New York: Anchor Books, 1972.

Park, Robert Ezra. *Race and Culture*. New York: Free Press, 1950.

Peattie, Mark R. "Forecasting a Pacific War, 1912–1933: The Idea of Conditional Japanese Victory." In *The Ambivalence of Nationalism: Modern Japan between East and West*, edited by James W. White, Michio Umegaki, and Thomas R. H. Havens, 115–31. Lanham: University Press of America, 1990.

———. "Japanese Attitudes toward Colonialism, 1895–1945." In *The Japanese Colonial Empire, 1895–1945*, edited by Raymon Myers and Mark R. Peattie, 80–127. Princeton: Princeton University Press, 1984.

Perry, John Curtis. *Beneath the Eagle's Wings: Americans in Occupied Japan*. New York: Dodd, Mead, 1980.

Pfeffer, Paula F. *A. Philip Randolph: Pioneer of the Civil Rights Movement*. Baton Rouge: Louisiana State University Press, 1990.

Pinkney, Alphonso. *Red, Black, and Green: Black Nationalism in the United States*. Cambridge: Cambridge University Press, 1976.

Plummer, Brenda Gayle. *Rising Wind: Black Americans and U.S. Foreign Affairs, 1935–1960.* Chapel Hill: University of North Carolina Press, 1996.

Polenberg, Richard. *War and Society: The United States, 1941–1945.* Philadelphia: J. B. Lippincott, 1972.

Powers, Richard Gid. *Not without Honor: The History of American Anticommunism.* New York: Free Press, 1995.

Reston, James. *Deadline: A Memoir.* New York: Times Books, 1991.

Robertson, Esmonde M. *Mussolini as Empire-Builder: Europe and Africa, 1932–1936.* New York: St. Martin's Press, 1977.

Rosenberg, Emily S. *Spreading the American Dream: American Economic and Cultural Expansion, 1898–1945.* New York: Hill and Wang, 1982.

———. "Walking the Borders." *Diplomatic History* 14 (Fall 1990): 565–73.

Rosenberg, Jonathan. "'The Morning Cometh': The First World War and the Struggle for Racial Justice in America." Paper presented to the Society for Historians of American Foreign Relations, Annapolis, Md., June 1995.

Rotter, Andrew J. "In Retrospect: Harold R. Isaacs's *Scratches on Our Minds.*" *Reviews in American History* 24 (September 1996): 177–88.

Rudwick, Elliot M. *W. E. B. Du Bois: Propagandist of the Negro Protest.* New York: Atheneum, 1978.

Russell, Ruth. *A History of the United Nations Charter.* Washington, D.C.: Brookings Institution, 1958.

Schaller, Michael. *The U.S. Crusade in China, 1938–1945.* New York: Columbia University Press, 1979.

Schmidt, Hans. "Democracy for China: American Propaganda and the May Fourth Movement." *Diplomatic History* 22 (Winter 1998): 1–28.

Scott, William R. *The Sons of Sheba's Race: African-Americans and the Italo-Ethiopian War, 1935–1941.* Bloomington: Indiana University Press, 1993.

Shankman, Arnold. *Ambivalent Friends: Afro-Americans View the Immigrant.* Westport, Conn.: Greenwood Press, 1982.

Sitkoff, Harvard. *A New Deal for Blacks: The Emergence of Civil Rights as a National Issue.* New York: Oxford University Press, 1978.

Skinner, Elliot P. *African-Americans and U.S. Policy toward Africa, 1850–1924.* Washington, D.C.: Howard University Press, 1992.

Smith, Geoffrey S. *To Save a Nation: American Countersubversives, the New Deal, and the Coming of World War II.* New York: Basic Books, 1973.

Snow, Philip. *The Star Raft: China's Encounter with Africa.* New York: Weidenfeld and Nicolson, 1988.

Soper, O. Edmund Davison. *Racism: A World Issue.* New York: Negro Universities Press, 1947.

Spickard, Paul R. *Japanese Americans: The Formation and Transformation of an Ethnic Group.* New York: Twayne, 1996.

Stavrianos, L. S. *Global Rift: The Third World Comes of Age.* New York: William Morrow, 1981.

Steel, Ronald. *Walter Lippmann and the American Century*. Boston: Little, Brown, 1980.

Stein, Judith. *The World of Marcus Garvey: Race and Class in Modern Society*. Baton Rouge: Louisiana State University Press, 1986.

Stephan, John J. *Hawaii under the Rising Sun: Japan's Plans for Conquest after Pearl Harbor*. Honolulu: University of Hawaii Press, 1984.

Stephens, Michelle A. "Black Transnationalism and the Politics of National Identity: West Indian Intellectuals in Harlem in the Age of War and Revolution." *American Quarterly* 50 (September 1998): 592–607.

Stoddard, Lothrop. *The Rising Tide of Color against White World Supremacy*. New York: Charles Scribner's Sons, 1920.

Storry, Richard. *The Double Patriots: A Study of Japanese Nationalism*. Westport, Conn.: Greenwood Press, 1973.

Sullivan, Patricia. *Days of Hope: Race and Democracy in the New Deal Era*. Chapel Hill: University of North Carolina Press, 1996.

Takaki, Ronald. *Strangers from a Distant Shore: A History of Asian Americans*. Boston: Little, Brown, 1989.

Takemoto, Yuko. "W. E. B. Du Bois and Japan." *Shien* (March 1994): 79–96.

Taylor, Quintard. *The Forging of a Black Community: Seattle's Central District from 1870 through the Civil Rights Era*. Seattle: University of Washington Press, 1994.

Thomson, James C., Jr. "The Role of the Department of State." In *Pearl Harbor as History: Japanese-American Relations, 1931–1941*, edited by Dorothy Borg and Shumpei Okamoto, 81–106. New York: Columbia University Press, 1973.

Thorne, Christopher. *Allies of a Kind: The United States, Britain, and the War against Japan, 1941–1945*. New York: Oxford University Press, 1978.

———. "Racial Aspects of the Far Eastern War of 1941–1945." *Proceedings of the British Academy* 68 (1992): 329–77.

Tinker, Hugh. *Race, Conflict, and the International Order*. New York: St. Martin's Press, 1977.

Toll, William. *The Resurgence of Race: Black Social Theory from Reconstruction to the Pan-African Conferences*. Philadelphia: Temple University Press, 1979.

Turner, Richard Brent. *Islam in the African-American Experience*. Bloomington: Indiana University Press, 1997.

Urquhart, Brian. *Ralph Bunche: An American Life*. New York: W. W. Norton, 1993.

Von Eschen, Penny M. "Challenging Old Cold War Habits: African Americans, Race, and Foreign Policy." *Diplomatic History* 20 (Fall 1996): 627–38.

———. *Race against Empire: Black Americans and Anticolonialism, 1937–1957*. Ithaca: Cornell University Press, 1997.

Wagatsuma, Hiroshi. "The Social Perception of Skin Color in Japan." In *Modern Japan: An Interpretive Anthology*, edited by Irwin Scheiner, 51–76. New York: Macmillan, 1974.

Washburn, Patrick S. *A Question of Sedition: The Federal Government's Investiga-*

tion of the Black Press during World War II. New York: Oxford University Press, 1986.

Weinberg, Meyer, ed. *W. E. B. Du Bois: A Reader*. New York: Harper and Row, 1970.

Weinstein, Jay. "Fu Manchu and the Third World." *Society* 21 (January–February 1984): 77–82.

White, Walter. *A Man Called White*. New York: Arno Press, 1969.

———. *Rising Wind*. Westport, Conn.: Negro Universities Press, 1971.

Wilkinson, Mark F. "A Shanghai Perspective on the Marshall Mission." In *George C. Marshall's Mediation Mission to China, December 1945–January 1947*, edited by Larry I. Bland, 327–55. Lexington, Va.: George C. Marshall Foundation, 1998.

Williams, Henry. *Black Response to the American Left, 1917–1929*. Princeton: Undergraduate Studies in History, 1973.

Wright, Richard. *The Color Curtain: A Report on the Bandung Conference*. Cleveland: World Publishers, 1956.

Wynn, Neil A. *The Afro-American and the Second World War*. New York: Holmes and Meier, 1975.

Index

Couch, William T., 191
Council on African Affairs, 73, 165, 184
The Crisis, 18, 69, 120
Crusader, 42
Cuba, 9, 11

Dabney, Virginius, 155–56
Daniels, Roger, 55
Dark Princess (Du Bois), 39
Debs, Eugene V., 40
Democratic Party, 10, 184
Development of Our Own, 94–95, 100–101, 147–48
Dewey, Thomas, 184
Double V campaign, 116, 118, 125, 130, 172, 182, 198
Du Bois, W. E. B., 10, 18, 27, 39, 44, 49, 65, 168, 175, 184, 186, 217 (n. 70); on Japan, 7, 19, 71, 92, 204–5; on China, 16, 74, 189; and World War I, 18, 26, 33–34, 39; and Ethiopian crisis, 71–72; Asian trip of, 74, 104; and Sino-Japanese War (1937–41), 74–75
Dumbarton Oaks conference, 184–87

East, Edward M., 72
East St. Louis, Mo., 19, 33, 147
858th Engineer Aviation Battalion, 200
Embree, Edwin, 140, 183–84
Ethiopian crisis, 68–71
Ethiopian Pacific movement, 70–71, 123, 131
Ethiopian prophecy, 8
The Everlasting Stain (Miller), 40
Executive Order 8802, 106, 133

Fair Employment Practices Commission, 1, 203
Federal Bureau of Investigation (FBI), 45, 128, 130, 137, 144; investigation of Japanese influence among African Americans, 103, 107, 122–24, 147
Fifth-column movements, 123, 130–31, 229 (n. 23)
"Fighting for White Folks?" (Cayton), 149–50
Finkle, Lee, 116, 157
Fire in the Flint (White), 92, 103
Fitzgerald, F. Scott, 37
Fortune, Thomas T., 8, 55
Franklin, John Hope, 18, 71
Fukushima Shintaro, 145–46
Fu Manchu, 37

Gaimushō. *See* Japan: Foreign Ministry of
Gandhi, Mohandas, 43–44, 66, 69, 208
Garvey, Marcus, 20, 44, 47–48, 50–51, 60
Gibbons, Floyd, 31–32
Gordon, Mittie Maud Lena, 111, 145
Grant, Madison, 35–36
Greater East Asia Co-Prosperity Sphere, 93, 111
Guardian, 20
Gulick, Reverend Sydney, 62

Haiti, 18, 104, 151–53
Hannigan, Commandant J. J., 47–48
Harding, Vincent, 34
Harlem, 34, 39, 69, 71, 110, 119, 123, 144, 157–58, 167, 204
Harper, Lucius C., 124, 134–36, 166
Harrison, Hubert H., 34, 39
Hastie, William, 161, 168
Haynes, George Edmund, 150
Hellwig, David, 54–55
Hikida Yasuichi, 103–5, 108, 123
Hill, Leslie Pinckney, 191
Hill, Robert, 110, 120
Hobson, J. A., 18

Hoo, Victor, 187–88
Hoover, Herbert, 64, 184
Hoover, J. Edgar, 45, 110, 123, 127
Hoover-Stimson doctrine, 65
Horne, Gerald, 239 (n. 16)
House, Colonel Edward, 23, 29
Hughes, Charles Evans, 48, 52
Hughes, Langston, 192, 204, 232 (n. 1)
Hughes, William, 24
Hurley, Patrick J., 199

Ickes, Harold, 137
Immigration, 3, 14; National Origins
    Act and, 35, 52. *See also* Chinese
    exclusion
India, 32, 113, 129; Pacific war and,
    139, 142, 181; rally for, 165; racial
    views of, 199, 207–8
India-Burma theater, 194, 198, 207
Indian National Army (INA), 12, 229
    (n. 20)
International Congress against Colo-
    nial Oppression and Imperialism,
    38, 218 (n. 23)
International Council of the Women
    of the Darker Races, 40–41, 219
    (n. 40)
International League of the Darker
    Races, 20
International Liberal Club, 80
Iriye, Akira, 15
Isaacs, Harold, 1, 193–97, 199–200,
    212
Ishii Kikujirō, Viscount, 23, 60

Japan, 3–4, 32, 42, 59, 62, 64, 73–
    74, 115, 130, 204, 206; African
    American views of, 1, 3, 15, 16, 23,
    25, 61, 65, 102; racial equality pro-
    posals and, 3, 21–24, 43, 55, 123,
    186; as champion of darker races,
    15, 17, 25, 28, 31, 40, 63, 80–82,

93–94, 100, 152, 209; Ethiopian
    crisis and, 70–72; Foreign Ministry
    (Gaimushō), 103–4, 109–10, 136
Japanese, 15, 53–54, 59; racial views
    of, 49, 61–62, 113–14, 124, 135
Japanese relocation, 182
"A Japanese Sees the Negro" (Hikida),
    103
Japan Institute, 123, 148
Jim Crow, 33, 164, 192, 199, 201
Johnson, Albert, 144
Johnson, Hiram, 26
Johnson, James Weldon, 23, 25–26, 35,
    49, 102, 226 (n. 1)
Jones, Stanley E., 141
Jordan, Leonard Robert (Robert O.
    Jordan), 70, 123, 131, 144, 146, 157

Kansas City, Mo., 95–96
Kapur, Sudarshan, 43
Karakhan of Kazan, 30–31
Katsura Taro, 17
Kawakami, K. K., 49, 55, 62, 221 (n. 6)
Kearney, Reginald, 14, 91
Keene, Donald, 61
Kitano, Harry, 55
Kokuryūkai (Black Dragon Society),
    59–60, 70, 145, 147
Koo, Dr. Itake. *See* Manansala, Poli-
    carpio
Koo, V. K. Wellington, 22, 24, 187
Korea, 6, 13, 62
Kountze, Mabe, 89
Krock, Arthur, 186
Kung, H. H., 187–88
Kunming, 193, 196–97, 200

Lansing, Robert, 33
League for Industrial Democracy, 140
League of Nations, 21, 68, 70, 183
Lenin, V. I., 18
Lewis, Ira F., 133

Liberals, 142–43, 157, 208

Liberty, 31

Lincoln University, 161

Lindbergh, Charles, 87–89, 112

Lin Shu, 108

Lin Yutang, 150, 164, 167, 193

Lippmann, Walter, 26

Little, Lawrence, 8

Litvinov, Maxim, 68–69

Liu Liang-Mo, 161, 164–65, 175, 178–79, 199

Living Age, 145–46

Locke, Alain, 38, 150–51, 167

Lodge, Henry Cabot, 25

Logan, Rayford, 1, 3, 104–6, 173, 184, 191, 201–2

Long, Breckinridge, 143

Los Angeles, Calif., 176, 182

McCloy, John J., 122, 136

McClure, Major General Robert, 196

McKinley, William, 9–10, 12

Madison Square Garden, 168–69

MAGIC, 109, 122, 136

Makino Nobuaki, Baron, 21–23, 60

Manansala, Policarpio (Dr. Itake Koo, Ashima Takis), 97–100, 111, 131–32, 144, 147–48, 231 (n. 20)

Manchukuo, 72, 74, 118, 123

Manchuria, 6, 13, 62, 104, 207. *See also* Manchukuo

March on Washington movement, 106

Marshall, General George C., 136

Marshall, Thurgood, 184

Matthews, Ralph, 112, 114, 121, 163–64, 203

May Fourth Movement, 27

Mays, Benjamin, 102

Merrill, Major General Frank, 194

Messenger, 42

Mexico, 32, 37

Miles, Brigadier General Sherman, 131

Military Intelligence Division (MID), 45, 95, 99, 110; Counter Intelligence Group (CIG), 129–33

Miller, Kelly, 40

Mississippi, USS, 204

Mohammed, Elijah, 145

Monroe Doctrine, 104, 111, 114. *See also* Asian Monroe Doctrine

Moore, Major J. M., 95–96

Moton, Robert Russa, 102

Mukden incident, 6, 64

Mussolini, Benito, 68, 70, 80

Naisson, Mark, 67

Nakane Naka (Major Takahashi Satakata), 94–95, 100, 131–32, 145, 147–48

Nation, 25–26, 31, 149, 157

National Association for the Advancement of Colored People (NAACP), 16, 18, 20, 27, 34, 60, 69, 77, 103, 148, 168, 184, 208; Pegler and, 133; China Blood Bank and, 173–74; membership of, 223 (n. 56)

National Association of Colored Graduate Nurses, 184

National Conference of Social Workers, 183

National Equal Rights League, 20

National Negro Associations conference, 121, 129

National Negro Business League, 128

National Negro Publishers' Association, 193

National Origins Act (1924), 85–87

Nation of Islam, 131. *See also* Temple of Islam

Negro News Syndicate, 124, 146

Negro World, 44, 49

The New Negro (Locke), 38

Newspapers. *See* Black press *and specific newspapers*